Praise for *The Pursuing God*

I commend this book front, left, and center because it thinks deeply and cares immensely for the moral vision of the Christian faith. Challenges to the Christian faith by the current generation are not your father's or grandfather's pushbacks. This generation questions, probes, and walks away from the Bible and the Christian faith for moral reasons, and the challenges to the faith are profoundly moral. Joshua Ryan Butler is in tune with both this generation and with deep Christian thinking, and offers to those who question the faith not "answers to your questions," but deeper questions about those questions.

—Scot McKnight, Julius R. Mantey Professor of
New Testament, Northern Seminary

Every now and again someone writes a book that breaks your heart in all the right ways. Among those books, once in a blue moon, there is birthed a volume that gently gathers the scattered shards of your heart and patiently, artfully puts it back together anew, piece by piece. This is one of those volumes. In *The Pursuing God*, Joshua Ryan Butler holds up a king-sized mirror to the heart of God and invites everyone to look inside. It's beautiful in there. Breathtakingly beautiful.

—Evan Wickham, Worship Pastor of A Jesus
Church: Westside

The Pursuing God is a fiery prophetic word—a flaming arrow shot across the dark landscape of dead religion; piercing our moral codes and feeble attempts to find our way to God. Our work is not to find him, but to stop and be found.

—John Sowers, P
Project

I just can't do it. I can't slug my way through yet another Christian book talking about the same old stuff in the same old predictable verbiage. This is why Joshua Ryan Butler is quickly becoming one of my favorite Christian writers. His lively prose nurtures thick theological reflection, creating a profound and profoundly accessible book. Joshua's first gem, *The Skeletons in God's Closet*, messed with my mind—in a good way. *The Pursuing God* messed with my heart—in a redemptive way—by reintroducing me to a scandalous God who aggressively pursues us with stubborn delight. Hands down: this is THE book to read for 2016! For everything that's good and holy, please read this book—Chapters 7 and 8 alone are worth its price in gold.

—Preston Sprinkle, Professor, Speaker, and Author of
*People to Be Loved: Why Homosexuality Is Not Just
an Issue* and *Charis: God's Scandalous Grace for Us*

Joshua Ryan Butler may well be the most spiritually perceptive writer of his generation. In spite of centuries of misunderstandings, clichés, distortions, and false caricatures that surround the story of Jesus, Butler sees the gospel clearly for what it has always been—what it was always meant to be. With singing prose and profound perception, Butler helps readers see and encounter the God who so generously gives, who so desperately pursues, who so dearly loves the world.

—Sarah Thebarge, Author of *The Invisible Girls*

Joshua Ryan Butler heralds a God of extraordinary love who takes us by surprise in the incarnation, crucifixion, and resurrection of Jesus Christ. In vibrant prose, *The Pursuing God* paints a dramatic, textured, and beautiful portrait of the God who we constantly underestimate. Butler presents Christian doctrine in color and in motion, testifying to a good news that is so much greater than we could have invented ourselves.

—J. Todd Billings, Girod Research Professor
of Theology, Western Theological Seminary,
Holland, MI

Artfully, beautifully, and emotionally written. Joshua deconstructs some of the most powerfully embedded caricatures we have around God and replaces them with gospel truth. The more I read this book, the more magnificent God became to me, and it left me feeling more free to be human, mess and all.

—David Lomas, Pastor of Reality San Francisco,
Author of *The Truest Thing About You*

It takes a brilliant mind to understand the most difficult questions about God and the gospel. But it takes a prophetic voice to communicate those truths to the masses. Joshua Ryan Butler is that mind and voice. In his book, *The Pursuing God*, Butler tells us the truth about God—that he absolutely, recklessly loves us to death—while not shying away from the difficult passages of Scripture that, at first glance, can seem to tell us otherwise. His work here is deeply theological, but so uniquely accessible, I'd recommend it to anyone. It's a monumental book and an instant favorite.

—Nish Weiseth, Author of *Speak: How Your Story
Can Change the World*

Joshua Ryan Butler is enthralled by the vision of a beautiful God whose goodness goes down deep into his bones and he wants us to share it. Unlike so many today, though, his way of inviting us into that vision is not to paper over the dark stains that mar our popular pictures of God, but to face them head-on. In *The Pursuing God*, Butler sets out to restore a portrait of the biblical gospel of God's incarnate, crucified, and risen Son, correcting our worst caricatures of sacrifice and atonement, and revealing the glory of the triune God who has been relentlessly seeking to restore us to himself.

—Derek Rishmawy, Theologian and Blogger at
derekzrishmawy.com

How in this broken world are we to live out a pure, gospel-driven compassion, taking Jesus' love into the darkest places of the world, without a wise, gentle shepherd's hand? Joshua Ryan Butler is a twenty-first century thinker who straddles opposing worlds: those of the artist, the dreamer, the skeptic, the academic, the clinician, the idealist and the theologian—as a sure-footed guide he walks with us; turning old, worn-out theological concepts on their head, startling the reader with unforgettable paradigms of God's goodness and generosity and love. It's only upon this foundation that one can effectively "enter into the happiness of God" and thus, being transformed by God's pursuing love, love.

—Celestia G. Tracy, Cofounder and Director of
Mending the Soul Ministries

Joshua has an uncanny ability to take deep theological concepts and not only make them accessible, but beautiful. In a day and age when it is normal for orthodox Christian views to be caricatured in the most unflattering of terms, *The Pursuing God* recovers the grace of orthodoxy by flipping those caricatures on their heads so that we might see just how astounding God's love is for us.

—Nate Pyle, Pastor of Christ's Community
Church, Indiana; Author of *Man Enough: How
Jesus Redefines Manhood*

The Pursuing God bridges the gap between pastoral concerns and rich theological study, asking the right questions and offering excellent and accessible answers. Joshua Ryan Butler digests a mountain of research and thought into a warm and approachable book, speaking clearly to the questions we find welling up within ourselves as members of Christ's church.

—Adam J. Johnson, Assistant Professor
of Theology, Biola University; Author
of *Atonement: A Guide for the Perplexed*

I found myself smiling and thinking my way through *The Pursuing God*. Joshua's captivating gift of storytelling makes potentially thorny spiritual concepts wonderfully accessible. His newest offering invites readers to take another look at God and risk comparing our culture-crafted caricatures to the Original.

—Dr. Alicia Britt Chole, Author of *40 Days of Decrease* and *Anonymous: Jesus' Hidden Years and Yours*

Every generation needs new theologians standing on the shoulders of those who have preceded them. We need these "new" theologians to exemplify the humility that traverses across traditions, cultures, and generations so that they may speak winsomely and wisely to our present times. Joshua Ryan Butler is this kind of theologian. He embodies what he writes and passes on the faith with soulful prose. This book is astounding and will spur you on to greater love. I highly recommend a slow and applied read of *The Pursuing God*.

—Tyler Johnson, Lead Pastor of Redemption Church, Arizona

The God that Joshua Ryan Butler proposes in his book is the God my soul recognizes, the God I want to know and know and know. It is the God I wish the world could see through the human-made haze of askew impression.

—Erika Morrison, Author of *Bandersnatch*

THE PURSUING GOD

A Reckless, Irrational, Obsessed Love
That's Dying to Bring Us Home

JOSHUA RYAN BUTLER

W PUBLISHING GROUP

AN IMPRINT OF THOMAS NELSON

Published in Nashville, Tennessee, by W Publishing Group, an imprint of Thomas Nelson. W Publishing and Thomas Nelson are registered trademarks of HarperCollins Christian Publishing, Inc.

Published in association with literary agent Blair Jacobson of D. C. Jacobson & Associates, LLC, an Author Management Company, www.dcjacobson.com.

Thomas Nelson titles may be purchased in bulk for educational, business, fund-raising, or sales promotional use. For information, please e-mail SpecialMarkets@ThomasNelson.com.

Unless otherwise noted, Scripture quotations are taken from the Holy Bible, New International Version®, NIV®. Copyright © 1973, 1978, 1984, 2011 by Biblica, Inc.™ Used by permission of Zondervan. All rights reserved worldwide. www.zondervan.com.

Scripture quotations marked ESV are taken from the ESV® Bible (The Holy Bible, English Standard Version®). Copyright © 2001 by Crossway, a publishing ministry of Good News Publishers. Used by permission. All rights reserved. Scripture quotations marked JUB are taken from the Jubilee Bible © 2000. 2000, 2001, 2010 by LIFE SENTENCE Publishing. Scripture quotations marked KJV are taken from the Holy Bible, King James Version (public domain). Scripture quotations marked THE MESSAGE are taken from *The Message* by Eugene H. Peterson. © 1993, 1994, 1995, 1996, 2000, 2001, 2002. Used by permission of Tyndale House Publishers, Inc. Scripture quotations marked NASB are taken from the NEW AMERICAN STANDARD BIBLE®, © The Lockman Foundation 1960, 1962, 1963, 1968, 1971, 1972, 1973, 1975, 1977, 1995. Used by permission. (www.Lockman.org) Scripture quotations marked NKJV are taken from the NEW KING JAMES VERSION®. © 1982 by Thomas Nelson. Used by permission. All rights reserved. Scripture quotations marked NLT are taken from the *Holy Bible*, New Living Translation. © 1996, 2004, 2007, 2013 by Tyndale House Foundation. Used by permission of Tyndale House Publishers, Inc., Carol Stream, Illinois 60188. All rights reserved. Scripture quotations marked TNIV are taken from the Holy Bible, Today's New International® Version TNIV® Copyright © 2001, 2005 by International Bible Society®. All rights reserved worldwide. "TNIV" and "Today's New International Version" are trademarks registered in the United States Patent and Trademark Office by International Bible Society®.

Certain names and details have been changed to protect privacy. Permission has been granted for use of real names, stories, and correspondence with some individuals.

Library of Congress Cataloging-in-Publication Data is on file with the publisher and the Library of Congress.

ISBN 978-0-7180-2160-3 (trade paper)

Printed in the United States of America

1 2 3 4 5 6 RRD 15 16 17 18 19

To
my sweetest, darling daughter
Aiden Ivey Butler
Pull your ear up close and let me tell you a secret:
I love you

MILEPOSTS

III. RISING UP FROM THE WATERS
resurrection

The Pursuing God

*T*his is not a book about our pursuit of God; it's about God's pursuit of us.

We often act as if God's lost, treating the Almighty as if he's gone missing, our Creator crouching in the cosmos behind a couch somewhere, playing hide-and-seek and waiting for us to follow any trail of breadcrumbs we can find to pick up the hunt and discover the divine. We emphasize "searching for God," "exploring spirituality," and "finding faith." We send satellites and smoke signals into the sky . . .

And hope the heavens respond.

But what if we have it backward? What if God's the one pursuing us, and our job is not to discover the light but to simply step out of the shadows? Not to hit the trailhead on the hunt, but to give up our hiding spot in the bushes? Not to ramp up our search for God, but to receive God's search for us?

Jesus reveals a God who relentlessly comes after our restless hearts. If you hear the phrase "the pursuit of God" and the first thing that comes to mind is *your* pursuit of God, rather than God's pursuit of you, the aim of this book is to turn that around.

A. W. Tozer once said, "What comes into our minds when we think about God is the most important thing about us."[1] It shapes, forms, and defines us. Unfortunately, many of us are burdened by some toxic thoughts about God. While the word *theology* can be intimidating, it basically means "what we think about God." We'll get into some theology in the pages ahead, but we'll keep it down-to-earth and relevant to life today.

Along the way we'll tackle some tough topics people struggle with, like sacrifice, wrath, and atonement, confronting popular caricatures and offering paradigm shifts to help clear away some poisonous misconceptions. Our goal is to replace duty with desire, to exchange obligation for affection, to give up striving to make ourselves worthy of God's love and start receiving God's love that makes us worthy.

In the nineteenth century, English poet Francis Thompson wrote a famous poem about God titled "The Hound of Heaven." I like to think Thompson chose this title because, like a hound closing in on a rabbit, God's reckless love is on the prowl, willing to crash through our distance and crush down our idols to get to our heart. God's divine grace bears down upon us, calling us to turn and receive his love. As his footsteps draw closer, the sound of his voice breaks through the silence, and the light of his encroaching presence begins to pierce the darkness. The question we're then faced with is not whether we've been good enough, jumped high enough, or sought hard enough. . . .

The question is, do we want to be found?

PART I

The Artist in the Painting

INCARNATION

CHAPTER 1

Into the Canvas

I once had a vision of an artist painting a masterpiece. With lavish brushstrokes and bold strikes, he threw splashes of rich, beautiful color, pouring himself into his painting with passion on a large, wall-sized canvas bordered by an ornate gold frame. When the masterpiece was complete, he stood back and gazed with joy upon the wonder his hands had made.

As if to say, "It's good."

Something strange, however, happened next: a small, dark spot appeared in the center of the painting. I thought, *What is that?* The artist watched as the mold-like decay began to spread, like a crack in the windshield that starts at a point but gradually expands its fissures and fractures into the whole. The invasive intruder began to stretch its thin, straggly arms, creeping its corruption throughout the canvas. The masterpiece was threatened with destruction.

What will the artist do? I wondered.

What happened next was the strangest, most bizarre thing I would ever have expected: the artist lifted his leg, extended it

3

forward, and . . . *stepped into* the painting. First his leg entered the canvas, then his torso, and finally his head. Then, with a *whoosh!* the integration was complete: the artist stood *within* the work his hands had made, at the center of the masterpiece.

That's weird, I thought.

But even stranger was what happened next: the moldy rot began to *attack the artist!* The great painter had positioned himself in such a way that the central point of invasion was right over his heart. As the tentacles retreated from the cornered edges, they sank into the artist himself, blow by blow. The creator received the corruption at the core of his masterpiece.

Until finally, with a *whoomph!* it was gone.

The masterpiece was restored. The artist had absorbed the destructive power until it was extinguished.

To my surprise, however, the great painter didn't step back out of the painting. Having united his life with the canvas, he remained permanently at the center of his restored masterpiece.

In a way, however, *restored* doesn't seem like the right word, because the work was now even more glorious with his presence inside. He brought radiance and beauty such that the painting seemed to glow with his life. There was a sense that this was always the way it was intended to be: the artist at the center of his painting.

This was the true masterpiece.

A PICTURE OF THE GOSPEL

This is a picture of the gospel. In the coming chapters, we'll use this "artist in the painting" image to guide us through some tough topics, like sacrifice, wrath, and atonement—I think it will help us see how these arise *from* the goodness of God, rather than in spite of or in contradiction to it. But first, let's unpack the parable.

Jesus is the Great Artist, the one "through [whom] all things were made," the "image of the invisible God . . . in [whom] all things were created," the "heir of all things . . . through whom also [God] made the universe."[1] Jesus pours himself into creation as a great painter pours himself into his masterpiece, with passion, creativity, and imagination. The heavens and earth display the glory of Christ, the Master Craftsman.

When sin enters, however, it defaces and destroys. Its dark tentacles stretch and spread through God's good world, unleashing dissolution and decay. The Great Painter's masterpiece is threatened with destruction. Rather than discard this world and start a new one, Jesus' solution is to step *into* his painting. At his birth, the Artist steps into his masterpiece. Through his incarnation, the Creator enters his creation, merging his eternal life with the canvas of his world, becoming part of the work his hands have made.

Jesus *is* God in the painting.

In his earthly walk and ministry, Jesus lives the life we couldn't live—embodying the kingdom for which we were made and bringing restoration to his creation. In his death on the cross, he dies the death we should have died—absorbing the sin, decay, and destruction we have unleashed into his masterpiece and carrying it with him into the grave. And in his resurrection and ascension, he is exalted at the center of creation as its Lord, to restore the masterpiece of his world in the power of his Spirit to the glory of God the Father.

Jesus at the center is, in an important sense, the way it was always destined to be. "Before the foundation of the world,"[2] Peter tells us, Jesus was destined to accomplish this. Jesus is not only our origin but our destination, both the "once upon a time" and "happily ever after" of our world. "There is but one Lord, Jesus Christ," Paul reminds us, "through whom all things came and through whom we live."[3] As early church father Athanasius observed, it is right that

> the renewal of creation has been wrought by the Self-same Word Who made it in the beginning . . . for the One Father has [effected] the salvation of the world through the same Word who made it in the beginning.[4]

Jesus is both kickoff and closure, start and finish, A to Z—beginning and end.

Jesus *wants* to be with us. He doesn't just fix the painting then leave his body behind; he doesn't step back out of the painting. Rather, he remains permanently embedded in the canvas of creation through his resurrected body. God makes his home with us in Christ. And when his kingdom comes in glory, his restoring work will permeate the world through his presence at the center of the new creation.[5]

The Creator creates us for communion with him. The Deliverer desires to dwell with us forever. The Resurrector reaches out to us for relationship. We're invited to participate in the restoring life of Jesus, the Artist at the center of the painting.

GETTING DIRTY

So is God afraid of getting dirty? Some people fear God is a clean freak, backing away, frightened, at the first sight of our mess so as to not get tainted. In light of the great painter entering the painting: Is the Artist scared of our mess? Does the Creator back away from the corruption? Is God willing to get dirty?

It depends what we mean by *dirty*. If we mean *physical* dirt, God has no problem with that. In the beginning, the Creator reaches deep into the soil with divine hands to plant a garden, forms humanity from the dust of the earth, places his lips upon us to blow the breath of life into our lungs, then walks in the garden with us, kicking up dust with bare feet.[6]

The Creator is distinct from his creation, in holy power and awesome majesty, yet he is intimate with the work of his hands, like an artist who pours himself passionately into his masterpiece. The Craftsman crafts dirt and sky, bone and bark, roots and rivers— then steps back upon completion to declare it *good*.[7] And when we jumble things up, God pursues us. Our heavenly Father comes after us. Jesus breaks into the painting—the Word through whom the world was made becomes flesh—taking on dirt and blood and bone to pursue us in the muck and the mess we make.

Divinity gets dusty as the Father, through the Son, in the Spirit, comes after our world. God isn't afraid of getting dirty.

CHAPTER 2

Pulling Back the Rib Cage

God has no problem getting *physically* dirty, as we saw in the last chapter. But there is a second sense in which *God getting dirty* can be taken. What if we mean *spiritual* dirt, as in "Can God sin?" Can the Artist participate in unleashing the dark, destructive decay into his masterpiece? Historically, the question has been asked, "Could Jesus have sinned?"

This sounds like a simple question. "No, of course not," we quickly answer. But if we say *no*, we must ask, "Why?" Was Jesus forced to obey by something outside himself? A victim of fate controlled by marionette strings from above? If we say *yes*, did we simply get lucky, with salvation hanging on the line of his whim? Would all have been lost if Jesus had joined our rebellion? There's more to this question than first meets the eye: Can Jesus get *spiritually* dirty?

Jesus' wilderness temptation is a good place to explore this question. Right before Jesus launches his ministry, he "was led by the Spirit into the wilderness" to be tested,[1] where he fasts forty days and forty nights before the devil comes to tempt him. Wait a second: Does that sound familiar? *Forty in the wilderness? Temptation?* Ring any bells? Can you think of any Old Testament stories with *forty in the wilderness* and *temptation*?

That's right: Israel's temptation in the wilderness.

Jesus' temptation mirrors Israel's forty years in the wilderness in a whole bunch of ways. God led Israel into the wilderness after freeing her from Egypt's clutches, similar to the Spirit leading Jesus into the wilderness. What was God's purpose? "God led you . . . in the wilderness," Moses tells her, ". . . to humble and test you in order to know what was in your heart, whether or not you would keep his commands."[2]

Like Israel, Jesus is now led into the desert to be tested—we're about to see what's in his heart. Israel did not do too well on the test. In fact, she flunked.

Now Jesus is here; let's see how he does.

TAKE US BACK TO EGYPT

Jesus' first test involves food. "After fasting forty days and forty nights," we're told, "he was hungry."[3] Uh, no duh. That's like saying, "After swimming for an hour, he was wet." Anyone fasting forty days would be starving, quite literally. Talk about stating the obvious.

But Jesus' hunger emphasizes something important: his humanity. The Artist feels the weight of his painting. The Son of God knows the hunger pangs, bears the burden, and doesn't pull out his Creator of the World ID card to use his status and opt out of suffering.

So Satan tempts him: *Turn these stones to bread.*

Use your privilege to avoid pain. Turn from your Father's provision and look to yourself for food. But even after forty days of fasting, Jesus' eyes are not curved inward upon his aching belly, but outward upon his loving Father. Jesus responds, "Man shall not live on bread alone, but on every word that comes from the mouth of God."[4]

Now, this is where it gets *really* interesting: Jesus is quoting the Old Testament here, and not just any verse, but Moses' words to Israel in the wilderness, when she cried out in hunger against God. Israel was hungry in the desert (as Jesus is now), so she turned against God and complained:

> If only we had died by the LORD's hand in Egypt! There we
> sat around pots of meat and ate all the food we wanted, but
> you have brought us out into this desert to starve this entire
> assembly to death.[5]

Israel failed the test; she revealed in her heart that she did not trust God.

At the first sign of trouble, she cried: *Take us back to Egypt. Back to bondage. Back to the empire of the serpent.* God provided anyway, as he planned to, with manna in the wilderness. But Israel's outstretched fist showed she was ready to jump ship at the first sign of trouble. She was called to bring restoration to God's masterpiece, but simply doubled down on the distrust that distanced our world from God in the first place.

Jesus, in contrast, displays trust in the wilderness, looking to his Father for provision. When he quotes Moses, saying, *We don't live on bread alone*, he's tugging Israel's temptation back into the picture. Jesus succeeds where Israel failed. The Savior gets an A on the test she flunked. The Artist refuses to participate in the destruction that afflicts his masterpiece.

One exam down; two to go.

SUICIDE OR SALVATION

Satan next tempts Jesus, "Throw yourself from the temple! God will send his angels to rescue you."[6] Here the idea is: Walk through the crowded capital of Jerusalem, up to the heights of the Most Holy Place on Mount Zion, and jump—if your Father truly loves you, he'll rescue you in front of all the people, with a miraculous display of supernatural fireworks. *Force God's hand! Show everyone who you really are!*

It's either suicide or salvation.

Jesus again quotes Moses: "Do not put the Lord your God to the test."[7] This comes from Israel's second temptation: the wilderness was dry; the people were thirsty; Israel needed water. They were ready to stone Moses, saying, "Why did you bring us up out of Egypt to make us and our children and livestock die of thirst?"[8] They turned against God again.

God provided, as he planned to, and quenched their thirst with water from a rock. But their grouchy grumbling revealed what was in their hearts: they did not trust God. So Moses calls the place *Massah* (which means "testing") and *Meribah* (which means "quarreling") "because the Israelites quarreled and because they tested the LORD saying, 'Is the LORD [really] among us?'"[9]

Israel was *spiritually* dirty, with broken trust and a lack of faith.

Jesus, in contrast, trusts the Father. He does not *need* to ask whether God is really with him, really for him, really ready to deliver. Jesus doesn't put God to the test, because he trusts the Father for his ultimate deliverance—and will ultimately trust him all the way to the cross. When the people mock Jesus at his crucifixion—*If you are truly the Son of God, come down from there!*—it echoes this temptation to call on God's angels for rescue and bring himself down for all around Mount Zion to see.[10]

Israel failed its test at a rock, from which God gave life-giving water. Jesus passed his test at a rock—both here at Mount Zion and ultimately at Golgotha (both of which are rocky)—to bring the water of life gushing forth to a thirsty, rebellious world.

Because Jesus is spiritually clean.

RIGHT THING, WRONG TIME

Satan takes one last crack at it: "*Bow down to me, and I will give you the kingdoms of the world.*"[11] Turn from your Father, and you can have it all. This is a test of worship. The irony is this: Jesus already has it all; the kingdoms of the world are destined for his inheritance. He will be exalted by his Father as Lord of the world—but he will do this through sacrificial love, giving his life for us. The problem is not *what* Satan offers, but *how* he offers it.

Satan offers the kingdom without the cross.

So Jesus again quotes Moses: "Worship the Lord your God, and serve him only." Once more, this also comes from Israel in the wilderness. She bowed down to the golden calf, to goat idols, worshipping other gods and finding herself under the death-dealing power of the Law. And it didn't stop when she came out of the wilderness. Throughout her history, Israel looked to Baal and Molech, the starry hosts and the gods of the nations, to provide when she feared God would forsake her.

Jesus, in contrast, worships God alone.

Jesus passes all three tests, succeeding where Israel failed. But he also succeeds here where Adam and Eve failed. They, too, were tempted with food by a twisting of God's words, and they bowed to the tempter when offered the kingdoms of the world. And Jesus is succeeding here where *we* fail: we don't trust God; we bail at the first sign of trouble; we want to rule the earth on our own and live without God. We are not the solution; we are the problem.

Jesus, however, refuses to participate in the corruption we unleash. The Artist will not contribute to the decay that afflicts his world. These tests are like exploratory surgery: they open Jesus' chest, pull back his rib cage, and reveal what's in his heart.

He's spiritually clean.

CHAPTER 3

The New Captain

In light of Jesus' temptation, let's return to the question: "Could Jesus have sinned?" It depends on what we mean by *could have*. The phrase can be taken two different ways. If we're referring to his external circumstances, as in, *Did Jesus truly have the opportunity to sin?* then the obvious answer is yes. Jesus was surrounded by a situation that pressed the option upon him with force.

Jesus was hungry, thirsty, and tired—he experienced the horrible heaviness of our humanity—and the option to give in was open. If Jesus had never entered our world, or had simply come as a ghost, or had kept himself at some safe distance from the full-freighted frailty of our flesh, it would not have been a true temptation. But Jesus carried our infirmities, bore our weakness, and as Hebrews puts it, was "tempted in all things as we are, yet without sin."[1]

The Artist felt the full brunt of affliction in his painting—and didn't bail.

15

TRULY HUMAN

If we're referring, however, to his *internal affections*, as in, *Would Jesus have sinned?* then the answer is no. Jesus trusts the Father. He loves God with all his heart, mind, soul, and strength. He is in perfect submission to the goodness of God. Jesus is not coerced into obeying by something *outside of* himself; Jesus' obedience flows from who he is *inside of* himself, because of his *very* self—his perfect affection for the Father.

Jesus' incorruptible will is compelled by love.

So Jesus *could have* sinned (the opportunity was presented to him on the outside), but he *would not* have sinned (because of who he is on the inside). Jesus faced the external fork in the road, but his internal compass would never walk down that dark path. Jesus' temptation in the desert, and his trial on the cross, reveal who he is on the inside: clean.

The security of our salvation is bound up in *who Jesus is*.

This is why the church has historically taught that Jesus *cannot* sin. (The fancy name for this doctrine is *impeccability*.) Some people get confused by this, as if it means Jesus has an unfair advantage, like a baseball player on steroids: *Of course he'll knock it out of the park!* Or an Olympic athlete who steps down to play with the kindergarten team: *Of course she'll win!*

Is winning really fair if the chips are stacked before the game? Is Jesus' victory legitimate if he's *unable* to sin? There's an unhelpful assumption here, though: that sin is an essential part of being human. This is backward: sin attacks and degrades our humanity. It makes us less human, not more.[2] By not sinning, Jesus is *more human* than we are. He's less like an athlete using steroids, and more like an athlete who never ate Twinkies. Less like an adult competing against kindergartners, and more like an adult who actually trained because she enjoys the sport—while we sat around all year, watching TV, eating potato chips, and didn't even bother to show up to the race.

Jesus doesn't use a *superhuman* advantage to win; he refuses the *inhumanity* we all participate in. The Artist is unwilling to unleash corruption into his painting, and thus is *more* a part of his masterpiece than we are. His incorruptible will makes him not less human, but more.

Jesus is true humanity.

UNLEASHING LOVE

After Jesus' wilderness temptation, he launches his ministry—and he ministers in power. We see Jesus everywhere setting things right, back the way they're supposed to be. The sick are healed, captives are released, demons are cast out, and the blind can see. Jesus refuses to participate in the corruption we unleash, and unleashes instead the power of God's kingdom.

Patches of redemption are breaking into the corrupted painting.

Jesus goes everywhere, "proclaiming the good news of the kingdom and healing every disease and sickness."[3] Jesus brings God's life-giving, vibrant power—like spots of green grass growing afresh on a dead and dried-up summer lawn—into a dry and thirsty land. It's like the tale of King Midas, where everything he touches turns to gold—only with King Midas it became a curse that hardened those he loves, whereas everything Jesus touches comes back to valuable life through love.

The Artist is restoring his masterpiece.

Jesus is a conduit for the kingdom, doing all *kinds* of miracles. And John reminds us of their *scope*: "If every one of them were written down, I suppose that even the whole world would not have room for the books that would be written."[4] Take all the libraries in the world, pull out all the books, and open them up: they wouldn't have room to describe the full-ness of life-giving power Jesus unleashes into his world. This reminds me of the classic hymn "The Love of God," which boldly proclaims:

> *Could we with ink the ocean fill, and were the skies*
> *of parchment made,*
> *Were every stalk on earth a quill, and every man a*
> *scribe by trade;*
> *To write the love of God above would drain the ocean*
> *dry;*
> *Nor could the scroll contain the whole, though*
> *stretched from sky to sky.*[5]

Jesus pours out the love of God, intending to fill the world with it.

Jesus is true humanity, and he can't get *spiritually* dirty. Not because he's backing away from our mess, but because as he dives into it, it cannot corrupt him. Not because he's unwilling to step into our pain and brokenness, but because as he jumps in, he brings healing and restoration with him. Jesus' movement is *toward* the muck of the world, willing to fully enter our filth and grime, but our sin can't taint his soul.

Because you can't get Jesus dirty; he can only make you clean.

O CAPTAIN, MY CAPTAIN

What is Jesus' obedience accomplishing? He is becoming the "new head" of humanity. The early church had a fancy Latin word for this: *recapitulation*, which comes from *re-*("new") and *-capito* ("head"). Our English word *captain* comes from this same root *capito*—a captain is the "head," or authority, of a ship. Jesus is being established as the captain of creation.

And his goal is to right the ship.

Think of earth as a sinking ship. God placed Adam at the helm, and he steered it into the rocks. So God made Israel the new captain to set the ship aright, and they kept ramming it into the rubble as well. And this isn't only Adam and Israel; this is us. We've torn the ship of creation asunder: holes have burst through the sides; water's flooding in; we're heading toward the rocks and a watery grave.

We've sought to rule the earth without God, to live our lives independent of our Maker, to sever creation from Creator, and in so doing we've dragged creation back down into the watery abyss from which it came.

So God finally says, *All right! I'll take care of this myself.* The Father sends his Son to take the helm and, in the power of their Spirit, they're out together to set creation straight. In Jesus, God is righting the ship: filling the holes, emptying the water, and steering it clear from the rocks. Through Christ's righteousness, God is rebuilding what our rebellion has destroyed.

The Captain is setting the vessel back on course. And Jesus steers us toward a destination greater than the port from which we embarked. Rather than simply return things to their original state, creation will be glorified through the indwelling presence of its Creator; humanity will be healed in union with our God. The ship of life, with our great Captain at the helm, is headed toward paradise—with us on deck. Captain and crew.

God with us.

DIRTY JOB

Jesus is more than an example to be followed; he's a Savior to be trusted. This is why we miss the point if we see Jesus' wilderness temptation as only how to overcome temptation, with advice like "Jesus used Scripture, so you should too." This focuses on a flea and misses the elephant in the room. The point is not, "He did it; you can too!" The point is, "You *don't* do it; so Jesus did it for you."

Jesus is not teaching a Beating Temptation 101 seminar, he's saving the world. He's not showing us how to pass the test; he's passing it for us. Jesus is succeeding where we failed, living the life we haven't in order to set the world right and bring us back to God.

If we're united to Jesus, he's going to gradually make us more like himself. We'll get better at resisting temptation over time, as we're formed into his image and shaped by the beauty of his holiness. But this isn't our starting point; it starts with Jesus.

Jesus is reversing the curse, cleaning up the mess we made, trusting the Father in those places where we've turned away. The gospel doesn't say, *We need to do better.* It says, *We need the power of God.* A moralist looks at Jesus in the desert and immediately jumps to, *We need to pony up, try harder, and be faithful under temptation!* A worshipper observes the wilderness around her and responds more simply: *We need Jesus!*

Jesus is faithful under temptation, even to the point of a cruel and unwarranted death, so that we might live again in him. Jesus finds us in the distant land where we got lost, and lifts us on his back to carry us home.

GARDENS IN THE WILDERNESS

So can Jesus get dirty? Physically, well, yes! God takes the dust, clay, and soil of the earth unto himself in Christ. Jesus' divinity is bound together with our humanity in inseparable union. The Father, through the Son, and in the Spirit, embraces the earth back to himself. The Creator is not afraid of his creation.

But can he get dirty spiritually? After all, he is sinless, incorruptible, pure. And not only that, but surprisingly, his own purity spreads. Everywhere Jesus goes, he unleashes the power of God's kingdom like a river of fresh water washing through the land. As Jesus walks through wastelands, gardens spring up beneath his feet.

I love the story of the hemorrhaging woman who reaches out to touch Jesus. She's been bleeding for twelve years with a nasty disease and has been seen as dirty by her community. She has spent all her money seeing various doctors, while her condition has only gotten worse. So she presses in through the large crowd gathered around Jesus and goes for broke, thinking, *If I just touch his clothes, I will be healed.*[6]

As she reaches out and touches the edge of his jacket, her bleeding immediately stops. Feeling the "power . . . gone out" from him, Jesus turns around to ask, "Who touched my clothes?"[7] The disciples laugh: *Dude, you've got people pressing in on all sides— everybody's touching you!*

But this touch was different; she was reaching out in faith.

Discovered, she trembles and confesses: *It was I!* Why was she afraid? In those days, her condition would have made her "unclean."[8] This didn't mean she had done anything sinful or morally wrong, but health and hygiene rules would have kept her from fully participating in public life. And if she touched someone (like the crowd she's been pressing up against trying to get to Jesus), they'd be considered unclean too, until they purified themselves.

Everyone's about to realize they need to go home and take a bath.

She's probably seen herself as a messy inconvenience for a long time. And she just touched Jesus: Will this holy, respected, busy figure be annoyed that she just made him "unclean"? No. In fact, her encounter with Jesus has the opposite effect. He tells her, "Daughter, your faith has healed you. Go in peace and be freed from your suffering."[9]

Rather than transferring her impurity to him, he transfers his purity to her. And instead of inflicting him with her uncleanness, he delivered to her his power. Before Jesus she is not an inconvenience to be dismissed, but a work of glory to be displayed.

Because you can't get Jesus dirty; he can only make you clean.

BECOMING SIN

There is, however, an important sense in which Jesus *does* get spiritually dirty. Paul declares about Jesus on the cross, "God made him who had no sin to be sin for us."[10] What does this mean? How did Jesus, who was spiritually clean, *become* sin? How did the great Painter become identified with the corruption in his painting?

We'll look at this more in the coming chapters, for it gets us into the language of sacrifice, a mysterious topic in its own right. But for now, we can say this: the Artist absorbs the dark, deadly destruction in his masterpiece, soaking it into the dregs, until it destroys him—in order to restore his masterpiece. Jesus is willing to go to the greatest of lengths to make his home with us.

KEY IDEA

Caricature: Jesus stays at a distance and tells us how to get clean.

Gospel: Jesus gets dirty, in order to make us clean.

CHAPTER 4

God on the Prowl

When I hear people say, "God can't stand the presence of sin!" (and I've heard this a lot over the years), I imagine God as a '60s housewife, shrieking and pulling up his checkered skirt to clamber atop the kitchen table when sin enters like a spider. Or maybe household pests are not the problem, but safety is, and God is like a banker avoiding the dark alley after work, afraid of the muggers who might lurk therein. Or perhaps he's bashful—like my grandma at an R-rated movie, cheeks red and flushed in the presence of naughtiness.

"God can't stand the presence of sin" is usually followed by the advice, "so you better stay away from sin, or he will stay away from you." I get the logic: God is holy, sin is ugly, and the holiness of God must be protected from the horror of sin. But can our sin taint God? When sin steps into the room, does he bolt for the door? When we mess up, does he run away?

Is God afraid to get dirty?

BOOTING MR. CLEAN

I think some of us picture God as being like Mr. Clean: large, bald, and clothed in white—with bulging muscles, a tough-guy earring, and a penchant for cleanliness. He likes to keep things neat and tidy, so he uses bleach and disinfectant with latex gloves to scrub the walls of his heavenly home throughout the day. He's got Tupperware for the leftovers, shoe organizers for the closet, and a spick-and-span garage with everything in its proper place.

Gotta keep the muck away.

Unfortunately, we've been playing outside . . . sin is like dirt, and we've been building tree forts, bouncing in mud puddles, and wrestling with the neighborhood dog. So as the sun's going down, and we decide to head home, covered in greasy grime as we clamber onto the front patio, God backs away and shouts, "You are a mess! I do not want that filth in my house. *Stay out!*"

Mr. Clean gives us the boot, retreats into his heavenly home . . . and slams the door behind him. Then he posts a guard angel as sentry with broom in hand at the front door, to keep watch and whisk away any unwelcome intrusion of our greasy, grimy, grubby paws.

Because God can't stand the presence of sin.

In this picture, we *want* inside: the warmth of the fire, the comfort food, the fatherly embrace. Perhaps we could break in? Tear down the door with a final show of determination? Force our way through to show Dad we're dying to be with him? But he's strong. All it takes is a quick, intimidating glance from beneath that furrowed brow and a bulge of his biceps to know he's got the muscle power to enforce his cleanly ways.

We want God, but God's pulling away.

Perhaps we could clean up our act? Leave the adventurous

life behind and play it safe? We could shower off with the neighbor's hose, throw on a tie, and try to keep up with our valedictorian sister and straight-A brother—they seem to regularly get his famous wink and nod of approval to know they're on his good side.

So we jump through the hoops, climb the corporate ladder, and contentment starts to set in . . . but not for long. We can play the religious game for a while, but the competition starts to tear at our souls. We begin to resent the rock stars who perform better, and look down at the ragamuffins who won't play along. We feel pressure to please others, and pretend we don't long for life beyond the pristine walls of our protected home. We toss a blanket over our true desires and mask how we really feel.

But we can never seem to get *all* that dirt out from under our fingernails. So we put on the latex gloves to cover our grubby fingerprints beneath. Because God can't stand the presence of sin . . .

Or can he?

Here's the good news: God's not afraid of our germs, scared for his safety, or backing away from the messes we make. He is not the one running; we are. The gospel proclaims our core problem is not that God can't stand to be in the presence of sin; it's the opposite.

Sin can't stand the presence of God.

Let's look at three pivotal scenes from the biblical story: the first takes place in a garden, the second on a mountain, and the third in the presence of the sun. All three set the stage for seeing the reckless, irrational, obsessed extent God's willing to go to bring us home.

RUSTLING IN THE BUSHES

The garden of Eden. This is the scene where sin first steps onstage, so it's a good place to start. When Adam and Eve devour the flesh of that forbidden fruit, God doesn't respond as you might expect. He doesn't recoil in disgust, shouting, *"OH NO! AWAY FROM ME YOU DIRTY FRUIT EATERS!"* Instead, it's the rebels who make a break for it, bolting behind the bushes.

God, in contrast, is on the prowl. Like a parent searching high and low, banging on all the neighborhood doors, looking for his lost and wandering children, God bustles through the brambles and briars, rustling through the wild and shaking up the jungle, calling, *Where are you!?!*[1]

The Father goes looking for his runaway kids.

"Where are you?"

When Adam and Eve sin, they find themselves naked as the day they were born, shivering in the easterly wind that begins to encroach on the garden. So they put on camouflage and duck for cover: they sew some leaves into makeshift clothes and stake out a place to hide. As they hear God's voice approaching, ringing clearer in their ears, drawing ever closer, they only crouch further in.

Eventually, they're discovered.

The leaves overhead recede like curtains as the Father's hand pulls back the branches and the face of love peers in. Adam sheepishly responds, "I heard you in the garden, and I was afraid because I was naked; so I hid."[2] Wait. Fear? For being *naked*? Up until now, nakedness was not a problem. Adam's and Eve's eyes weren't even on themselves; they lived in the love of God. With their gaze turned outward toward God and each other, they lived in the confident freedom of the One who named and called them.

But with their headfirst dive from grace, their gaze has now turned inward, curled in upon themselves as they crash into the chaotic waters below. Intimacy is replaced by insecurity, freedom by fear, trust by terror. More than simply teeth breaking flesh on forbidden fruit, this rebellion shakes the very foundations of the world. This is a root that goes much deeper, into the place of trust, into the heart.

See, the serpent's seduction has attacked the character of God, striking at his very heart: *He knows that when you eat of it, you will be like God.*[3] *Your Father pretends to care for you, but he's holding out on you, covering his back, protecting himself. That generous smile is a surface facade. Your Creator's ultimately just protecting his power, keeping you down, making sure you march in step and stay in line.*

Adam and Eve have taken the bait.

Trust is broken.

TO BE LIKE GOD

You will be like God. This is a tempting affair: we want to be *like* God rather than *with* God, to determine good and evil for ourselves, to rule the earth on our own. Adam and Eve's story is our story. As theologian Thomas K. Johnson has observed, we "can take the account of Adam and Eve hiding from God behind a bush or tree as a metaphor for the history of the human race."[4] Much of the Christian tradition has seen *pride* at the root of our fall: our desire to exalt ourselves and live independently from God is the soaring platform that catapults us headlong into the Great Descent.

Ego, beware.

Our Creator becomes competition. Rather than receive life from his generous hand, we allow our broken trust to distort our perception. Our heavenly Father starts to look like the Wizard of Oz: we assume that lurking behind the powerful drapery and majestic veneer must lie the fragile ego of a small-minded manipulator looking out for his own. His power, his reputation, his glory.

God's protecting himself.

And we take the bait. Like fish on a hook, we devour the lie and find ourselves snared. The damage is done well before our teeth have torn the apple's skin. The outer bite marks are simply the signpost of our inner torn will. Our broken trust is intimacy severed, communion torn asunder. A rupture is introduced, a rebel force unleashed, that will seek to tear heaven and earth apart.

We have created something new in the world: distance from the Father. Only, this distance is not truly a *created thing*. It is an un-thing, an anti-creation, a not-the-way-things-are-supposed-to-be thing. This crack in the foundation will fissure its way through creation, with the stark new reality of this distance characterized by one thing: destruction.

When this distance is introduced, however, when sin first enters the world, notice one thing: who flees and who pursues. God goes searching in the garden. He responds to our distance by crossing the divide. He sets sail to find us, invades our shores, and ambushes our defenses, pulling back our facades and crying out:

"Where are you?"

God still comes for us today, calling, "Where are you?" God wants to be with us. The question is: Do we want to be with God?

BOOTED FOR THEIR OWN PROTECTION

"Okay," we might say skeptically, "but doesn't God *boot them* from the garden?" Yes, but notice why: "lest he put out his hand and take also of the tree of life, and eat, and live forever."[5] In other words, God protects us from being stuck in this messed-up state forever. This isn't Mr. Clean saying, "Yikes! You're gonna get my garden dirty." This is our heavenly Father calling things as they really are and caring for us in our corrupted condition. It is a punishment, but it is not mean-spirited or vindictive. It is congruent with our desire to live apart from God.

Eviction from Eden is for our benefit and protection, not God's. Yet once outside the garden, the Great Gardener continues the search into the thorny chaos and wilderness wasteland of our wandering world. This brings us to our next scene.

CHAPTER 5

Coming Down the Mountain

Mount Sinai. God has rescued Israel from Egypt's oppression, carried her through the desert upon the strength of his shoulders, and brought her to a mountain for a wedding. She is the bride, he is the groom, and they are entering into *covenant* together. Israel comes to the mountain to be wedded with God.

In a telling scene, Moses comes down the mountain shining brightly with the glory of God. He's been in God's presence, and now, like the moon reflecting the sun, God's glory is entering into the presence of his people. How do the people respond? They run. Like Adam and Eve, they make a break for it. They sprint toward the shadows to hide from the glory of the King.

Adam and Eve covered themselves with leaves; the people here asked Moses to cover his face with a veil, to keep their distance from the incoming presence of God. Hebrew scholars have observed how the language and imagery at Mount Sinai draws from the story of Adam and Eve in the garden. Let's take a look at how.

RUNAWAY BRIDE

When Israel first comes to Sinai, God proposes—asking the people whether they want this covenant, this marriage, this union—and "all the people answered together": *Yes!*[1] They put the engagement ring on their finger and declare that they want to marry their Creator.

So in preparation for the ceremony, God tells them to take three days preparing for his arrival. On the third day, he will descend upon the mountain to meet with them as they arise to join him and enter into covenant with him in the ceremony. They are not to approach the mountain until they hear the blast of the ram's horn. Then, when the trumpet blasts, the wedding ceremony begins and they are to come up the mountain to join into union with their God and King.[2]

So for those first three days, like a bride doing her hair and nails and putting on that shiny dress, they get themselves ready for the big event. When the third day arrives, God comes down to the mountain. As his feet touch the rocky surface, Sinai is shaken by the incoming presence of God: "the whole mountain trembled violently" with thunder, lightning, smoke, and the sounding of a trumpet.[3] The mountain becomes a place where heaven and earth meet, where Creator and creation connect, where God descends into the presence of his people, and the wedding ceremony begins.

Things don't go quite as planned, however. Rather than ascend the mountain as expected, the bride "trembled with fear" and "stayed at a distance."[4] She doesn't trust that God is for her and, rather than approach the mountain in faith to meet with her Creator, she tells Moses, "Speak to us yourself and we will listen. But do not have God speak to us or we will die."[5] Moses encourages the bride to not be afraid, to walk into the presence of their

Creator—but the people "remained at a distance" and Moses goes forth alone to encounter and meet with God.[6]

> *The wedding day comes, and Israel runs.*
> *The Creator arrives; his beloved hides.*
> *God's people are a runaway bride.*

Like Adam and Eve in the garden, God offers Israel *life*, in union with him, but she rejects it and receives instead *the knowledge of good and evil*, the Law. Now, the Law is good, and God gives it to his people, but God's primary purpose in bringing Israel to the mountain is not to give her the Law; it's to give her himself. We tend to think of the Ten Commandments as legalistic rules and regulations to keep a distant, uptight God happy. But Israel understood them as wedding vows, commitments of fidelity and devotion, aimed at the flourishing of their life together.

And they're pretty simple vows:

> *Don't cheat on me with other gods.*
> *Remember to rest so we can celebrate life together.*
> *Don't lie, cheat, murder, or steal.*
> *Let's live together forever![7]*

The Ten Commandments are not "how to get God to like you"; they're "how to live together *because* God likes you." The Creator wants to undo what was done at Eden, to restore a people into union with him, who will turn around and offer that restoration to the world. God's purpose for Israel is to become "a kingdom of priests and a holy nation," set apart to display his glory and offer his life-giving presence to the surrounding empires.[8]

But she runs.

CHEATING ON THE HONEYMOON

So God proposes a second time, again asking the people whether they want this covenant. And once more, "all the people answered with one voice and said, 'All the words that the LORD has spoken we will do.'"[9] In an encore, the bride says, "Yes!" They want to get married.

So God starts making plans for a home. He brings Moses up the mountain and gives him blueprints for a *tabernacle*, basically a place where he can move in with his people. God's not only going to meet them halfway down the mountain; he's going to move into the neighborhood. God's committed to being with them, but because of the hardened condition of their hearts, his presence will be graciously veiled by a tent. Can you imagine constructing a house for the Builder of the universe? Moses gets the architectural design and is ready to head down the mountain.

Only, back at the foot of Sinai, things have quickly taken a turn for the worse: Israel is having an affair. The people wanted another god, one they can control, because once again they don't trust that God is with or for them.[10] So Aaron the priest gathers the gold and burns it down to build a big, shiny cow. Moses comes down the mountain to find Israel running wild, worshipping their golden calf with all the debauchery and destruction associated with ancient idol worship.[11]

Israel is caught cheating *on her wedding night*.

God steps out of the room for a minute to plan their home together, and returns to the hotel to find his blushing bride in bed with another man. The irony is thick. This is not one year, five years, ten years into the marriage—after the flame of love has grown cold and temptation struck hard—it's at the very moment she just devoted herself to God. In the words of Old Testament scholar John Sailhamer:

> Just at the moment when God was giving Moses the law on Mount Sinai, Israel was breaking it at the foot of the mountain. Israel had just heard the Ten Commandments. God had commanded that they not bow down to idols or have "other gods." Yet, just then, Israel had fashioned a golden idol and was bowing down to it.[12]

Israel has an affair on the honeymoon, and God is rightly livid. She's already run back into the arms of the cruel, abusive gods she was just delivered from in Egypt. The bride is still in front of the altar, at the foot of the mountain where she just made her vows, and she's already broken the opening ones: to put God first, with no other gods or idols.

Moses smashes the Ten Commandments at the foot of the mountain, a dramatic display of how the people have just crushed the covenant to which they've committed. Then Moses destroys the golden calf, crushes it to powder, sprinkles it on the water—and makes the people drink it. There's a humorous image implied here: later that day, the people would have been urinating the golden calf all over the desert.

The affair is over, but the sting of broken trust remains.

So Moses goes back up the mountain to meet with God, who, surprisingly, remains faithful even when his bride is unfaithful. God reveals his glory to Moses, replaces the stone tablets Moses broke, and renews the covenant with his bride. This is the moment when Moses comes back down the mountain, his face shining brightly, "because he had been talking with God."[13]

But once again, for a third time, the people run.

THE KNOWLEDGE OF GOOD AND EVIL

Just as he did in the garden of Eden, God offers *life* with him, but his people reject it and receive instead *the knowledge of good and evil*—the Law. God wants relationship; we settle for rules. The Law is good, but God's deeper desire is not to give us a bunch of regulations, it's to give us himself.

Have you ever wondered why there are so many pages on the Law in the Old Testament? Some people think God just wants to create a bunch of hoops for us to jump through before he'll be with us, but most of the Law arises in response to Israel's *rejection* of life with God—the Creator who wants to be with them. For example, the *high priest* leads the way in the golden calf incident, so right after this event come the laws for the priests: *twenty-two chapters* known as the Priestly Code![14]

Immediately after this, there's a short little story where the people worship goat idols; this time it's not the priests who are emphasized, but *the people* as a whole. So right after this comes *nine more chapters* of laws for *everyone*, known as the Holiness Code.[15]

Do you see the pattern? God offers marital bliss, and the farther the runaway bride dashes into the distance, the deeper she finds herself drowning under a spiraling system of laws, spinning out into crazy proportions. As Sailhamer has observed, when we look at the overall structure of the story, it appears that "God's original plan for Israel at Sinai did not include the vast collections of law found [there]. Rather . . . the Mosaic law was added to the Sinai covenant because of Israel's many transgressions in the wilderness. . . . There is an ever-increasing cycle of disobedience and the addition of more laws."[16]

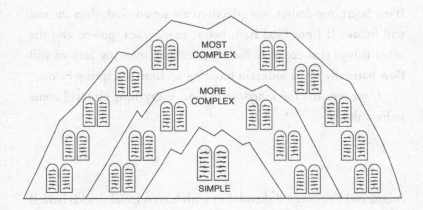

God brings his people to the mountain for a wedding, and they settle for an instruction manual instead. As Paul put it, the Law "was added because of transgressions."[17] The Creator offers *light* and *life* with him; we reject it and run toward *darkness* and *death* in separation from him.

There is a good purpose behind the Law—it tries to restrain the destructive power of our sin. When crime and injustice run rampant, law and order are important for the community to flourish. A world without murder, adultery, and greed would be a better place to live. And the Law's boundaries point us toward what God is like and wants for his world. If I worship idols or kill my neighbor, I'm probably not doing a good job loving God and others. This reveals our need for grace.

But if there were no sin, the law would be unnecessary. If we were immersed in life with God, we wouldn't need a rule book. Augustine famously said, "Love God and do what you please."[18] This sounds strange at first glance. "If I do whatever I want, won't I do things God doesn't like?" But the premise is that I first *love* God.

If my heart, my desires, my affections are set on God, then the rest will follow. If I put God first, before money, sex, power, and the other things that compete for my affection, then my actions will flow naturally like a fountain bursting up from the spring below.

If we put first the kingdom of God, everything else will come in its wake.

Adam and Eve covered themselves with leaves; Israel shields herself from the presence with a veil. It's an ironic image: the bride throws a veil over the glory of the groom. In both these stories, the creatures reject their Creator; the kingdom secedes from the King; we want our distance. Because sin can't stand the presence of God.

But God keeps coming after us.

And all this points to Jesus.

CHAPTER 6

Romance in the War Zone

I ncarnation. Jesus *is* God searching in the garden of his world, calling out for his lost and wandering children: *"Where are you?"* He is the glory of God coming down the mountain—from heaven to earth—to dwell in the presence of his people. Jesus is God's presence crashing into the neighborhood, as the Creator breaks into our world, divinity takes on flesh, and the king is born.

Jesus is the Pursuing God.

LIGHT OF THE WORLD

What's the most famous verse in the Bible? Most folks would probably say John 3:16. Fans hold it up on signs at football games, restaurants put it on their Dixie cups, and it's scrawled in graffiti on subway walls. But sometimes familiarity breeds contempt. We get so used to something that we miss the shock value it holds. So let's revisit it for a second:

For God so loved the world that he gave his one and only Son . . .

Observe that God's love, his head-over-heels affection and desire for the world, is at the center of this story. God gives generously of that which is most precious to him, his Son. The greatness of the gift is a signpost to the extravagance of the love. When God romances us, he doesn't just send flowers, give chocolates, or mail a Hallmark card from a distant heaven.

He gives us himself, in love.

And we're not all that lovable. Jesus doesn't enter a holiday resort but a raging war zone. "The world" has negative connotations in John: it's a place of corruption and rebellion, distance and death, the far-off country and land of exile. This isn't a Bahama cruise; it's a dangerous slum. We're not Disneyland; we're Gotham.

Surprisingly, however, Jesus doesn't come to wag a pointing finger, give us a lecture, and point out all the ways we've made a royal mess of things. No, John continues, "God did not send his Son into the world to condemn the world, but to save the world through him."[1] God's mission isn't to tell us how dirty we are; it's to wash us clean. It isn't to shout at us to get our act together; it's to invite us to drop the act and be together—with him. It isn't to point out our distance; it's to throw us over his shoulders and bring us home.

If God wants us, what's the problem then? Our problem, John goes on to tell us, is not that we didn't try hard enough, jump high enough, or perform well enough to earn God's affection. Rather, our real problem is that we "loved darkness rather than light."[2] We *love* the darkness: want it, crave it, need it. Eugene Peterson translates it this way:

God-light streamed into the world, but men and women everywhere ran for the darkness.[3]

Like Adam and Eve ducking in the bushes, we run for cover from the presence. Like Israel throwing a mask over Moses, we try and shield ourselves from the glory. Sunrise dawns, and we jet for the shadows. Glory arises, and we crawl for the shade. Our problem is not that we're reaching out for God and he's refusing to be found. It's the opposite: God's reaching out for us, and we're scattering in other directions.

God loves us, but we love darkness. God moves toward us. But sin can't stand the presence of God.

CAN'T STAND

So let's return to that phrase: *God can't stand the presence of sin.* Is it true? I think it all depends on what we mean. The phrase can be taken two ways. First, it could mean, "God can't stand *to be in* the presence of sin." This is what many people seem to mean, that God backs away in disgust as soon as we mess up, and it's on us to get our act together and go find him again. As we've seen, this is false.

The gospel moves in the other direction.

Second, however, it could be taken to mean, "God can't stand *what* the presence of sin *does* to his world." And this, I believe, is undoubtedly true. God *hates* sin. He hates it not because it gets him dirty, but because it alienates us from him and tears apart his creation. Like a rising landfill trashing up God's beautiful garden, sin is a stench in his nostrils. As an affair with cruel, abusive lovers betrays the affectionate husband, sin offends him, the One we were made for.

Because the Creator loves his creation, he gets *angry* at the destructive power that attacks the object of his affection and strikes at him as the Lover. In the words of pastor and professor Hans Boersma, "God's love requires that he become angry when his love is violated. For God not to get angry . . . would demonstrate indifference, not love."[4] God is not indifferent. God is dead set against sin—literally, on the cross—*because* of his outrageous love for the world, not in spite of it.

The question here is one of movement: Who's running from whom? As we've seen, God searches in the garden; we duck in the bushes. God comes down the mountain; we back into the desert. God shines like the sun; we crawl into the shadows. God wants intimacy; we prefer to be left alone. God loves us; we love darkness.

God doesn't run from sin; sin runs from God.

RECEIVING THE PURSUIT

So what does it mean to welcome the pursuit of God? We'll get more into this in the chapters that follow, but for now we can say this: God comes for us, and he can take whatever we've got to bring. There's no one too distant, no person too far. The Father's not afraid of being tainted, scared for his safety, concerned for his reputation. God's goodness and mercy are on the hunt, tracking down our world to captivate us by love, encroaching closer and closer, with us locked in their sights.

God's on the prowl; we are the prey.

Will we get transparent, honest, and vulnerable with where

we're at before him? Will we lay our cards on the table and allow ourselves to be transformed by his redemptive Spirit? Will we lay down our guns and have the faith, courage, and trust to step into life with our Creator? God wants to be with us; the question is whether we want to be with God.

Like Adam, we're invited to take off the fig leaves. Like Israel, we're beckoned to let the veil be pushed aside. In Jesus, we're invited to receive the King of the universe, whose arms are outstretched on the cross to embrace and make us whole. We don't need to discover the light, but simply to step out of the shadows. We don't have to make ourselves lovable, but only to let him place the wedding ring on our finger.

Before the Pursuing God the question we're faced with is not whether we've searched hard enough, explored long enough, or jumped high enough. Our question is a much simpler one:

Do we want to be found?

KEY IDEA

Caricature: God can't stand to be in the presence of sin.
Gospel: Sin can't stand to be in the presence of God.

CHAPTER 7

Reckless Love

The word *lost* has fallen on hard times. It can sound arrogant and condescending, as if we have it all together while *the lost* need to get their act together. As if we're the brilliant insiders with all the answers, they the bumbling outsiders with only questions. As if we're the oasis of perfection that they, the thirsty travelers in the desert, must journey to in order to drink deeply from our waters and all would be well.

As if.

The problem is, when Jesus uses the term, it actually has the *opposite* connotation. Jesus flips the direction of movement. Being lost doesn't mean you must go out to find God; it means God is coming to find you. Let's take a look at Luke 15, where Jesus shares three famous stories of a lost sheep, a lost coin, and a lost son. We'll see that in each, *lost* doesn't mean "idiot," "fool," or "outsider."

Lost means loved.

LOST MEANS LOVED

Jesus opens with a story of a shepherd—we'll call him Billy. Billy's hanging out in the fields one day with his hundred sheep, when he suddenly realizes: *One's gone missing!* So Jesus asks his audience the obvious question: *Wouldn't you leave the ninety-nine out in the open country and go after that one lost sheep until you find it?* Our twenty-first-century Western heads bob up and down (with our total lack of shepherding experience), and say, "Yes, of course! You love that lost sheep. Definitely, you drop everything and run out to find it."

Dumb Westerners.

The safe bet is the ninety-nine. Why leave them open to wolf attacks, wandering bears, and robbers? They're easy prey for predators. You might wind up walking home with ninety-nine problems and a sheep, just one—it's bad economics. So when Jesus asks his question, know-it-all-Joe in the back probably raises his hand and answers, "You count your ninety-nine blessings, chalk up your loss, and protect what you have." Stick with the safe bet: stay with the ninety-nine.

But God missed Economics 101.

Like God, Billy sets out on the hunt, leaving the safe bet to go find the one. Billy tracks the open plains, bumbles through the brambles, climbs the rocky crags, and finally comes upon her. When Billy's shadow falls across that naughty little lamb, I'd expect a livid lecture: "What were you doing running off like that? Do you know how worried I've been? You could've gotten yourself killed. *Why can't you be like your ninety-nine responsible brothers and sisters?*"

But Jesus tells us there's no finger-wagging, no "I told you so," no "If you ever again . . ." Instead, this shepherd, joyfully puts it on his shoulders and goes home. Then he calls his friends and neighbors together and says, "Rejoice with me; I have found my lost sheep."[1]

Okay, that's a *crazy* reaction—for two reasons. First, Billy's *joyful*: grinning ear to ear and pumping his fist in the air that he's found her. The divine Shepherd greets us not with a stern reprimand but with joy; God delights in discovering us, his lost and wandering lamblet. And rather than give us a road map with directions to find our way back home, God's thrilled to throw us over his shoulders and carry us there himself.

So, *lost* here does not mean you must go find God and his crew. It means the opposite: God's left his crew to come find you.

Jesus tells us God is a reckless shepherd.

BILLY'S BLOCK PARTY

The second crazy thing is this: Billy throws a party—the last thing I'd want to do. I'd be too tired, exhausted, wiped out. I'd simply crash onto the couch, put my feet up on the coffee table, flip on Hulu, and call it a day. But not God; God says it's time for a neighborhood bash.

Who celebrates their pet with a party? We lost our cat, Iggy, once. The clumsy thing lost her balance on the bathroom window, slipped a story and a half down into the bushes, then ran off confused and scared. To be fully honest, I wasn't too attached—but my wife loved that cat. So I canceled all my afternoon appointments and scoured the neighborhood, searching high and low for hours.

Eventually, we found her and were glad. But I was "let's get takeout and watch Netflix" glad, not "let's spend hundreds of dollars on a block party to tell all our friends our cat's back!" glad. I can hear our neighbors now: "You want us to come over and celebrate *what*?" God celebrates people we wouldn't expect. He leaves the safe bet and searches harder and farther than you'd imagine—for us. And when he finds us, he throws the biggest party the town's ever seen.

Jesus starts with Billy the shepherd, but he's only setting the stage for the next two stories and the bigger point he wants to make.

A CRAZY WOMAN

Jesus moves seamlessly into a story about a woman—we'll call her Annie. Annie loses one of her ten coins, so she goes on the hunt. Unfortunately, this is before the day of metal detectors—so she flips the couch cushions, sweeps through the house, and scours every nook and cranny. The sun eventually goes down, so we'd expect her to retire for the evening. But not Annie. Rather than give up, Jesus tells us, she lights a lamp and continues the search into the night.

This is one determined woman.

Once again, Jesus asks the obvious question: *Wouldn't you . . . ?* I'm not so sure. I love my sleep. I've got nine other perfectly good coins. Work comes bright and early in the morning. Now I'm going to be up all night? Besides, I'll probably tire myself out and sleep through my alarm, which will further exacerbate the tensions with my boss and cause me to lose my job . . . where I earn my coins.

I'd chalk up the loss, count my nine blessings, and go to bed.

But God slept through math class.

Our Creator is not an accountant calmly counting the cost, Jesus tells us, not a levelheaded lady demurely discerning the decision. No, our Maker is Crazy Annie, up all night turning over couches and looking for that one missing Roosevelt. God is a frantic woman tearing the house apart in search of lost change.

Again, as before, *lost* does not mean we must go find God. No one expects the coin to pick itself up and search for the woman—the object in question is a sedentary hunk of metal. On the contrary, the movement is from the opposite direction: Jesus emphasizes not our pursuit of God, but God's pursuit of us.

We *are* the coin; it's a picture of us. We're sitting under the dresser, stuffed under the couch pillow, satisfied in the musty corner. We're content where we are: the shadows are comforting; the cushion's warm; we've grown accustomed to the smell. But hear the revolutionary ruckus approaching: the couch just got flung over; the lamp went crashing to the ground; the whirlwind's getting closer.

God's reckless love is tearing the house apart to find us.

Both Billy the Shepherd and Crazy Annie reveal that *lost* means not worthless, but wanted. Not villain, but valued. It does not mean lazy; *lost* means loved. God's pursuit is reckless, like a bull in a china closet, willing to crash through our social circumstances and crush down our idols to get to our heart.

And Jesus raises the stakes. He moves from Billy's one-sheep-out-of-a-hundred to Annie's one-coin-out-of-ten, upping the percentage from 1 percent to 10 percent, raising the object of affection from a lamb to cold, hard cash. Now the stage is set: in the final story, he's about to double down and raise the stakes to 50 percent, going all in with an infinitely greater object of affection . . .

CHAPTER 8

Olympic Father

Jesus' climactic story opens with a father and two sons. The younger son—we'll call him Joe—asks dad for his inheritance, packs his bags, and sets off for a distant land. This sounds normal today. We tell our kids: *Stop living in your parents' basement! Get out into the world and make a name for yourself.* But in Jesus' day, this was sacrilege: it was the equivalent of flipping your dad the bird and telling him to take a long walk off a short pier.

Joe is abandoning his family, his community, and their God. He's not asking to go care for a sick grandma or find a job in the city to help pay the family bills; his purposes aren't noble. He's not being commissioned to explore uncharted territory or make peace with national enemies.

Rather, he sets sail to squander dad's hard-earned cash in "wild living."[1] He's off to the big city for sex, drugs, and rock 'n' roll. His motives are selfish, out to feed his gluttony, follow his lust, and fuel his pride. He declares his independence and buys a one-way ticket to Babylon.

LIFE AFTER GOD

Back then, a son asking for the inheritance was a slap in the face. The money would be his when his father passed away, but this son wants it *now*, on his own terms, essentially saying, *"Drop dead, Dad!* I don't want life with you. I just want what I can get out of you." So he stands over the casket, snatches all the cash he can, and sets out for a far-off land.

In ancient cultures, the inheritance was a great responsibility: a call to honor your ancestors' legacy, to steward the land for your community, to care for the generations to come. The blessing of the inheritance was for the well-being of the community, to be used in self-giving service, not self-centered greed. It was a call to *love*.

So Joe's committing an act of treason, betraying the blessing and harming the neighborhood—leaving not only a grieving father in his wake, but a fractured community, with anticipated family fallout for generations to come. In many ancient societies, rebellion like this was a serious enough offense for the community to warrant the death penalty.[2]

The father, however, generously obliges. Like a genie summoned from the lamp, he accomodates his son, granting his dangerous wish. He unloads the bank account, waves good-bye, and watches his child ride off into the sunset.

This is our story. We want to rule the world without God. We want to live our lives in independence rather than communion. We snatched the billions and bolted for the distant land, grabbing what we could to live without him. Beyond the horizon lies destruction. We have squandered Dad's generosity on ourselves, and endure our exile far from the face of the Father.

The One for whom we were made.

But when the party lights fade, the keg tap stops dripping, and the cash flow runs dry, the younger son finds himself isolated and alone. The good-time friends walk away, the ladies who loved him don't come around anymore, and feast turns to famine in a foreign land. The daydream turns into a nightmare as Joe smashes into rock bottom and his fall comes to a crashing halt. Rudely awakened, Jesus tells us, Joe takes a job for a local farmer:

> He went and hired himself out to a citizen of that country, who sent him to his fields to feed pigs. He longed to fill his stomach with the pods that the pigs were eating, but no one gave him anything.[3]

Tending pigs doesn't sound like a great job to me, but it was even worse for Joe. Pork was off-limits for the Jews. Pigs were associated with the Gentiles: seen as dirty and unholy.[4] And he's not just seeing people scarf down bacon; he's in the mud raising it for them: pig dung under his fingernails, dirt caked on his overalls, and hungry enough to wrestle the pigs for their scraps of food.

With this little detail, Jesus simply hammers home the bigger message: Joe's at his lowest point. His status as "pig boy" drives the final nail into the coffin: he is distant, dirty, and disgraced. He is unholy.

THE FINISH LINE

So Joe listens to the voices in his head and has a conversation with himself: *Why not go home? Even Dad's hired hands have food to spare, and here I am starving to death! I know what I'll do: I'll go home, tell him what a mess I've made of things, and beg for forgiveness. I know there's no chance of being a son again, but maybe, just maybe, if I'm lucky, I could get hired on with the staff at the family farm.*[5]

It's easy for us to think, *Of course his dad will hire him back on.* But remember: in the ancient Middle East, this wasn't a sure bet. He's offended not just his family, but the community. Worst-case scenario, the neighborhood could give him the death penalty.[6] We miss the tension here, that going home is an intimidating prospect. But it's better than starving, so he heads for home.

I wonder what emotion he experienced along the way. Was it fear of how his father would respond? Shame at how he'd ruined the family name? Embarrassment at the prospect of locking eyes with his goody-two-shoes older brother, who stayed on the honor roll and made the family proud? Was it simply self-interest, hoping he would survive the situation?

Whatever the boy's thoughts, the father has something entirely different in mind. Dad spots him from a mile away, on the same distant horizon he fled to so long ago. It's as if the father's been looking, longing, waiting with eager expectation for any sign of his runaway child.

And when he spots him, he runs.

Like an Olympic athlete, he bolts from the starting line: feet flying, legs swinging, kicking up dust. This would have been a great disgrace in Jesus' day: the great patriarch letting himself go, the lord of the land's robe blowing in the wind, underwear peeking out above those bony, bare knees for the whole community to see. But the father doesn't care. He's running full throttle, going the distance, as a sweat breaks from his brow and steam pumps like a locomotive from the side of his labored mouth.

God is a gold-medal runner, and the finish line is his child.

DISCO PARTY

As the father draws close, I picture the son's head averted, bowed in shame, missing the penetrating gaze of love that's locked on, zeroed in, crashing down upon him like a missile. Dad closes the distance, and Joe starts in on the little speech he's prepared: "Father, I have sinned against heaven and against you. I am no longer worthy to be called your son—"[7] But he can't even get to the next sentence. The father interrupts him mid-speech, Jesus tells us, and "threw his arms around him and kissed him."[8]

Wait, Dad! You need to hear the rest . . . I hear the son trying to interrupt. But the father's having none of it. He's too busy shouting out with joy:

> Quick! Bring the best robe and put it on him. Put a ring on his finger and sandals on his feet. Bring the fattened calf and kill it. Let's have a feast and celebrate. For this son of mine was dead and is alive again; he was lost and is found.[9]

Watch this: God greets the lost with joy, not guilt. *Throw the crown back on. Treat him like royalty. Let's get this party started. My child is home.* The Father is not an academic waiting to give us a lecture, but a disco owner waiting to throw us a celebration.

Of course, if the son had come home with the booze and prostitutes and a sense of entitlement, simply wanting to trash his father's home for the next rager, the reception would have been different. The posture of confession and humility is significant. But God's not setting unnecessary obstacles in the way. He's on the lookout for repentance, waiting to receive us into his kingdom.

If the lost lamb got a party, and all the neighbors get called over for a missing coin, imagine what kind of bash-of-the-century God throws for a runaway child come home. Once again, we see climactically that for Jesus *lost* does not mean lazy, letdown, or loser.

Lost means loved.

CHAPTER 9

Welcome Home

How might we be shaped by God's reckless love? What does it mean to be formed by the Father's extravagant embrace? When I think of that, I think of Misha's story. Jim and Sarah welcomed Misha into their home when they decided to become foster parents. Misha was only a teenager, but she'd seen a lot: abandoned by her family, trafficked into the sex trade, and exploited for sex and money.

Jim and Sarah's first few days with Misha were great, but once that honeymoon period ended, everything became a struggle. Misha punched, kicked, screamed, fought, yelled, and threw things. Jim and Sarah bent over backward to make her comfortable, but the first few months felt as though they'd welcomed a cyclone into their home.

Sarah found it especially difficult. Misha paid loads of attention to Jim, lavishing praise and affection his way (this was how she'd learned to get attention from men). Even though Jim didn't reciprocate, it was hard for Sarah to watch. Misha even turned quickly to calling him "Dad." In contrast, she treated Sarah cruelly: shouting, blaming, ignoring, cursing, and calling her a barrage of names . . .

"Mom" wasn't one of them.

NIGHT ON THE TOWN

So after six months Jim and Sarah needed a break. They got a babysitter, dressed to the nines, and hit the town for the evening. They returned feeling rested and refreshed, having had a little space to just be a couple again and care for their marriage. The babysitter welcomed them at the front door and said everything went great. Misha had been pleasant all evening and was fast asleep.

Relieved, they went upstairs to get ready for bed. Jim walked into the master bathroom and let out a shocked, "Oh no! Sarah, don't come in here. You don't want to see this." He scrambled to gather cleaning supplies and deal with the mess before she got there, but it was too late.

Curious, Sarah charged into the bathroom and quickly discovered what the fuss was all about. Misha had taken Sarah's red lipstick and scrawled in massive letters all across the bathroom mirror and walls: "F*** you, Mom! F*** you, Mom! F*** you, Mom!" Jim's thoughts were racing: *Should we have stayed home? Did Misha think we abandoned her? How is Sarah going to survive this?*

He turned to Sarah and saw, surprisingly, that she began to laugh. Not a little laugh. Not a chuckle. But a slow and building roar.

It began as a rumble deep within, rising steadily up through her chest, until finally her mouth opened, the dam broke, and she roared hysterically. Sarah crumpled into a ball on the floor, a waterfall of tears streaming down her face, laughing as she'd never laughed before.

Jim was shocked, perplexed, and silent for a few moments. *Has she gone crazy? Lost it? Was this the straw that broke the camel's back?* Finally finding the words, he asked, "*What is so funny!?!*" Sarah peered out through tears of joy, fighting for breath, until finally, between the convulsions, she was able to squeeze out, "She called me Mom."

She called me Mom.

ANGRY PRAYER

I love how God loves our angry prayers. God's reckless love means we can come to him as we are, bringing everything before him. Unfortunately, we're often like Jim: we want to protect God from the raw, honest—and at times angry—emotions that are scrawled across the walls of our heart. So we sanitize our condition before we let God see it. If God can't stand to be in the presence of sin, we'd better clean the bathroom of our soul to make it more presentable before he steps inside.

But if we're honest with ourselves, we have moments where we're like Misha. We've been beat up and wounded by life, and if we held up a mirror to our souls, there are times we'd probably find our own profanities scrawled in red. We know our heavenly Father's busy running the world and all, so we try to keep it together and figure things out ourselves. Maybe we'll occasionally work up the courage to leave a tidy little sticky note on the corner of the bathroom mirror, with a safe, "Sorry, Dad. I had a little bit of a bad day."

But here's the thing: God is like Sarah.

God's not only big enough to handle our prayers; he wants us to bring 'em. Trusting God's reckless love means we can bring the fullness of who we are before him—even when it's ugly (and let's be honest: it often is)—trusting that our heavenly Father is *for* us. God takes joy in the simple fact that we trust him enough to call out his name—even when we're a mess inside.

The trouble is, it's often easier to vent to our friends or write a fiery blog post about God, than to bring our troubles to God. This can become a danger when we use our anger or confusion to build a platform for ourselves in distance from God, rather than bring it to him. God has given us the vehicle of prayer to approach him with the fullness of who we are.

I love this about the Psalms, the historic prayer book of God's people. The songwriters are willing to lament and struggle with God, to bring it all: the good, the bad, *and* the ugly. Here's the thing, though: When they *bare their hearts* before God, they bare them *before God*. When they *struggle* with God's faithfulness, they bring their struggle to *the One who is faithful*. When they raise their fists and cry out, "*Why?*" they unleash their frustration upon the *Who* delighting to uphold and embrace them—the One who is, at a deeper level than they may even realize, their hope of redemption and salvation.

Because they trust he's big enough to take it.

More important than the content of our prayers is *the One to whom* our prayers are addressed. Now, as we experience the Father's embrace, we gradually grow in bolder trust, the content of our prayers more seasoned with holy grace. If Misha is still saying, "F*** you, Mom!" ten years later, there's probably a problem, and if there's no growth in our life with God over time, we should pay attention. But this is a gradual change that works its way from the inside out over the long haul.

And the first step is to come as we are.

Perhaps the greatest sign of our lack of trust in God's love for us is a weak prayer life. Trusting God does not mean we sanitize our prayers so as not to offend; it means we trust God is good enough to receive us in the raw. *Not* trusting God ignores him and looks the other way, or puts on a facade and pretends around him. Trust vulnerably enters the reckless love outstretched to embrace us.

Our heavenly Father loves us when we're happy and loves us when we're sad . . . so when we scream and throw a tantrum and scrawl our red-raging anger all over his bathroom walls, unleashing the outburst of our fallen, broken lives, I think he falls to the floor in a heap of roaring laughter, rejoicing through a mess of tears:

"She called me Dad."

WELCOME HOME

When God's reckless love embraces you, you want to share it with the world. But how do we share it? How do we extend our heavenly Father's embrace to our neighborhood? My friend Jillana's taught me a lot about this. Jillana's family has adopted a number of children through foster care. Years ago, she rallied other foster families in our church to dream: "How can we mobilize the body of Christ to serve our city's most vulnerable children?"

They formed a ministry called Welcome Home.

They started simple, inventing Welcome Boxes: our church's children filled cute photo storage boxes with toys, games, and crayons, and placed a flashlight and a loving, handwritten note in each one. These boxes were for every scared child who'd just entered foster care so that boy or girl would know that he or she is loved. In the process, our church's kids learned about God's heart for vulnerable children. Before we knew it, families and home communities throughout the church were making Welcome Boxes and asking about foster care.

Next, the Welcome Home team said, "What if we did 'Extreme Makeovers'?" Our local child welfare offices were run-down, with bullet holes and shattered windows, collapsing couches and broken toys, and paint that hadn't been updated in decades. If space communicated value, we were not doing a good job letting our city's most vulnerable families, served by tireless workers with no funding, know they were loved. So Jillana rallied our church to blitz the offices with fresh paint, new furniture, fun toys, art, lighting, and loads of love.

Then, they dreamed, "What if we started a Foster Parents Night Out?" Now, every month foster parents from across our city, like Jim and Sarah, drop their kids off at the church. We send them on a date night to get some much-needed rest and refreshment, while we throw the biggest bash you can imagine for four hours on a Saturday night to love on these kids like there's no tomorrow.

A movement was born. People started coming out of the woodwork wanting to foster or adopt. More than twenty-five families from our church now welcome vulnerable children into their homes, with a support network and classes providing a Christ-centered approach and relational support.

Other churches wanted in, so Jillana's team expanded the umbrella and called it Embrace Oregon. As of today, more than 100 churches in our city are involved. Together as the body of Christ, we've made more than 12,000 Welcome Boxes, outfitting every child welfare office in the Portland–Metro area. Together, we've done 12 Extreme Makeovers on these offices, totaling more than $250,000 contributed directly by churches for our city's most vulnerable families. Together, there are now nine Foster Parents Night Out events at churches across our city with more than 250 volunteers serving nearly 500 children a month.

And more than 160 families have arisen to welcome vulnerable children home.

This is just one example of how we as the body of Christ can extend our heavenly Father's embrace.

A BETTER BROTHER

When Jesus tells stories such as the parables of the lost sheep, the lost coin, and the prodigal son, he is ultimately telling stories about himself. Jesus is the reckless shepherd who leaves the safe bet of the ninety-nine to go after the risky one. He is the frantic woman up all night, tearing the house apart to find that one darn coin. And Jesus is a different kind of older brother. Let me explain what I mean.

In the first two parables, God is the searcher: Reckless Billy and Crazy Annie on the hunt for what they've lost. But in the prodigal-son tale, where is the search? We could say it's in the Olympic Father's eyes, looking out on the horizon for any sign of his child, and bolting out of the gate at first sight like a thoroughbred at the races.

But Jesus sets up something more here: a critique of the older brother.

Unlike Reckless Billy and Crazy Annie, the older brother never went looking for Joe in the distant land. The valedictorian Goody Two-shoes didn't embody the reckless pursuit of God. And Jesus' story ends with the older brother out in the darkness, refusing to enter the party, clinging to his pride in the backyard, while the lights and laughter of the kingdom celebration are raging inside the father's home.

Which provokes the question: Which son is really lost?

In the older brother, Jesus confronts the Pharisees of his day, who saw the lost as those outside the pale of God's favor and called the dirty to clean themselves up and get their act together if they wanted God's face to shine upon them once more. They not only didn't pursue; they resented Jesus when he did.

Every time the Pharisees see him, he's got gangsters, prostitutes, and other people of dubious reputation swarming around. Jesus was known for hanging out with the riffraff: tax collectors, political revolutionaries, and swarthy, blue-collar fishermen. So they have a holy huddle, grumble and growl, then slip Fox News a press release to let loose their public arrow of accusation: "He takes in sinners and eats meals with them, treating them like old friends."[1]

This is the setting, what's happening just before the *lost* parables.

So Jesus confronts them, telling three tall tales of Reckless Billy, Crazy Annie, an Olympic Father . . . and the relentless love of God. Jesus inverts what they mean by *lost*. For Jesus, *lost* means God is coming after you. It speaks more to the heart of our Creator than the state of people. If our Owner wasn't looking, we wouldn't be lost. We wouldn't be missing if God didn't want us back. This story is about the Great Searcher, and the declaration that under his gaze of love, we are the *sought after*.

And Jesus puts his money where his mouth is. He knows we've

gone missing; he's seen our face on the milk cartons, so he sets out on his mission "to seek and to save that which was lost."[2] Unlike the older brother, Jesus leaves the Father's house and lays down the comfort and prestige of heaven, to pursue us in the distant land and live homeless and wandering in our war-torn earth. Jesus proclaims the kingdom of the Pursuing God and goes willingly to be rejected, mocked, and ultimately crucified . . .

All to bring us home.

Jesus is a better older brother, who reveals that *lost* doesn't mean *idiot*, *fool*, or *outsider*. It means *pursued*, *valued*, and *sought after*. Let me say it *one more time*, just in case you've missed it: *lost* means loved.

KEY IDEA

Caricature: Lost means you need to go find God.
Gospel: Lost means God's coming to find you.

CHAPTER 10

Dumb Farmer

HOW (NOT) TO PLANT A GARDEN

"What kind of soil are you?" Luke asked.

"That's a weird question," I responded. "I'm actually not made of soil. I'm a combination of about 99 percent oxygen, carbon, hydrogen, nitrogen, calcium, and phosphorous."

I don't think that's the answer he was looking for.

We were in Jesus' famous parable of the four soils, where a farmer—we'll call him Bob—is planting a garden. Farmer Bob "went out to sow his seed,"[1] scattering some seed along the path, some on rocky places, and some among thorns. All those seeds don't do so well, but some land on good soil and give rise to a good crop. I've found many people jump immediately to the question, "Which kind of soil are you? Rocky, thorny, or good?" but jump over an earlier observation: *This is a dumb way to plant a garden!*

STRANGE STRATEGY

What farmer, in his or her right mind, wastes precious seed along the road, scatters it over rocky gravel, or plunges it deep in the thornbushes? Jesus' audience was an agricultural society. They lived much closer to the land than we do today, and would have picked up on this irony immediately. Their initial reaction would likely have been, "Why the heck is he planting the garden *that* way?"

That is one *weird* farmer.

I once planted a vegetable garden in our backyard. Before I began, however, there was a gravel driveway smack-dab in the middle of where I wanted our garden to be. It had to be removed. Imagine instead if I had just gone out back and started showering my seeds all over the gravel driveway, tossed my kernels into the overgrown weed patch nearby, and dumped my remaining grains across the adjacent paved street.

My neighbors would think I was an idiot.

So is God a bad farmer? Why is he so extravagantly wasteful? I would suggest this: God is generous. Fill-up-the-bowl-till-it's-overflowing-and-spill-it-all-over-the-world *generous*. God throws his gospel, the good news of the presence of Jesus, across the land far and wide. God gives to all who will receive . . . and to those who won't. God showers his goodness upon the thorny soil, in the words of the beloved Christmas carol, "far as the curse is found."[2]

God throws down joy on our rebellious, rocky hearts.

God gives himself, in Christ, to the world.

THE GENEROSITY OF GOD

When we begin our consideration of the parable of the sower by recognizing the generosity of God, we still eventually come to the question, "Which kind of soil are you?" But it takes on a different shape and meaning. The four soils do not represent postures for performing but responses for receiving. The gospel proclaims God is a generous farmer, and the issue we're faced with is not how to make God happy, but rather how to enter the happiness of God.

When we start with questions like, "Which kind of soil are you?" it can lead to a self-defeating kind of moralism. *Have I been good enough? Jumped high enough? Made myself pliable enough to please a performance-based God?* We can gaze at our spiritual belly buttons all day long, wondering whether we've tilled ourselves into rich enough soil to please the frugal farmer . . . and scowl when we find ourselves a rocky, thorny path full of dust and weeds.

But Jesus starts with the Generous Farmer, the God-who-sucks-at-planting-gardens-because-he's-just-so-gosh-darn-generous. This leads to different questions, the kind that revolve around grace: *Will I receive his goodness? Do I have ears to hear the God who beckons me in love? Do I prefer the rocky, thorny paths that have led me far from home, or am I willing to be embraced by the big-hearted Father who pursues me in the distant land?*

Love changes you. When you let God's generous goodness take root deep down in your bones, you can't help but bear good, luscious, life-giving fruit for his world. When my wife and I started dating, friends said my face glowed. I had a spring in my step. I was still doing the same everyday things, but there was a fresh vibrancy to them. And I'd leave little love letters, plan special dates, and tidy my place up when she was coming over. I couldn't help myself. It was a joy.

Devotion grew not from duty, but desire.

If we claim to know the Generous Farmer, there's a healthy place for self-evaluation. Am I petty and prideful? Filled with malice, envy, and greed? If so, there's a problem. If we claim to follow Jesus, but our lives bear no fruit and show no signs of transformation, we should take notice that something's probably wrong. If the Generous Farmer has showered his grace upon us, yet we're stingy and self-absorbed, it raises the question of whether or not we've truly received.

This isn't to say we'll be bursting with strawberries and melons the next day. Gardens take time. Plants don't pop up overnight; the seeds need to soak in the soil for a season. Some of us need space to stop striving, put down our Christian activities, and rest in the generosity of God for a while. But when we do, in time you can't help but let it grow through you. That's the nature of God's love.

So over the long haul, it's healthy to ask: Is God's generosity spreading through me? Am I growing in the goodness, holiness, and justice that mark Jesus' kingdom? Do I increasingly love God and care for others, providing life-giving nourishment to God's hungry world?

FOUR RESPONSES

Jesus gives us four ways we can respond to the Generous Farmer. First, the soil "along the path" pictures a person distracted by other things. The seeds fall but don't penetrate the hardened ground, like one whose heart has become calloused against God. Infatuated with the idol of what people think, absorbed in the newsfeed of the day, and just *making ends meet*, the individual never lets the kingdom of God invade his or her soul.[3]

The seeds simply sit on the street, stone-cold and dormant, until the birds eventually come and suck them up, as the Enemy "snatches away what was sown in their heart."[4] Pursuing idols can distract us from our Creator's pursuit of us. We can run after shiny things and miss the best thing right in front of us, as God's lavish generosity piles up in pools on our unreceptive soil . . . only to eventually be washed away by the incoming tide of distraction.

Second, the seed falling on "rocky ground" represents those who receive God gladly . . . at first. They get excited, jump up and down on the spiritual trampoline, and declare how great God is—for a while. But God's lavish generosity doesn't sink deep down into the soil of their souls; it doesn't take root. "Since they have no root," Jesus tells us, "they last only a short time. When trouble or persecution comes, they quickly fall away."[5]

Over the years I've noticed something strange: those who are the most enthusiastic about God up front are often the least reliable in the long term. Over and over I've seen new folks roll into town saying, "Jesus is amazing! I want to plug in, serve, and lead." But soon after they're nowhere to be found. Once the rubber hits the road, they don't show up. When the initial burst of energy is gone, the fireworks fizzle out.

In contrast, the best long-term leaders are often unassuming at first. They're humble, calm, even unsure of themselves. They're not pressing for position or searching for the spotlight. They don't need to use ministry to prove something. Their transformation is a process: continually relying on God because they know they haven't "arrived." The goodness of God is gradually sinking deep into their lives.

Those reluctant to lead are often the best leaders.

Third, the seed that falls "among the thorns" is someone who sticks around but with no transformation. Such a person goes to church, attends Bible study, and identifies publicly with the people of God. This type of seed sinks deeper beneath the surface than the seed that falls on the other soils. But ultimately, Jesus tells us "the worries of this life and the deceitfulness of wealth" are like weeds that "choke the word, making it unfruitful."[6]

Some folks hang around the Generous Farmer but have no generosity. God wants more for us than going through the motions; he wants to set us in motion. God's love should revolutionize our lives. Jesus' grace propels us, by its very nature, into his world as agents of his kingdom. The Holy Spirit sees the hunger around us—a hunger for truth, a hunger for justice, and yes, actual hunger for real food—and wants to meet this hunger, to feed and nourish the world through us.

Fourth, the "good soil" is someone who receives the kingdom and is transformed. Jesus says the good soil gave rise to "a good crop—a hundred, sixty or thirty times what was sown."[7] When our empty hands are filled to overflowing, they can't help but give. When our insecure hearts experience the affection of God, they can't help but love. When divine goodness digs deep into our lives, it bears fruit . . . from the inside out.

God's generosity makes us generous people.

When I think of this "good soil," of letting God's lavish generosity take hold in our lives and spill through us all over the neighborhood, I think of my friend Bien, a rural Vietnamese farmer. Let me introduce you to her.

CHAPTER 11

A Mighty Oak

Bien is one of my heroes. She oversees HIV support groups for about fifteen hundred women in Vietnam. "I shouldn't be here," she told me when we first met. "I should be dead."[1]

Bien first learned she was HIV-positive about ten years ago, when she saw her husband wither away before her eyes and realized he had AIDS. She was six months pregnant at the time. Her husband had gone to Hanoi regularly as a migrant worker, like many men in the village. While he was in the worker camps, prostitution and drug abuse were rampant. He contracted HIV there and, without realizing it, passed it on to Bien when he returned. A week before their child was born, he died.

This was devastating in multiple ways. On a personal level, Bien was heartbroken: she grieved the loss of her husband and realized she was now facing the same fate. She was angry: he'd obviously gotten AIDS through either drugs or prostitution, and the sense of betrayal was huge. She was scared: What would happen to her children when she was gone?

On a community level, Bien was isolated: no one would come near her anymore. People were afraid of catching the mysterious disease: "If she breathes on me, will I get it?" Family and friends stopped visiting her home. What is more, Bien had no income: she had become the sole breadwinner for her children, but no one would buy her vegetables in the market anymore or hire her for work.

She was heartbroken, isolated, and desperate.

Bien's story is all too common. AIDS-infected women are often modern lepers. Isolated from family and friends afraid of contracting the disease, they end up battling their illness alone, cut off from support and resources that can help them live healthy, fulfilling lives.

Fortunately, Bien attended an HIV class through a church in Hanoi. She learned more about the disease she had—including how to fight back with antiretroviral medications to stay alive— and also discovered she was not alone. Other women from her village were also there, suffering and surviving in the shadows. Bien said, "Hey, let's band together," and rallied them into a support network.

They cared for one another. When one of the women got sick, the others would come over to help cook, clean, and care for the kids. They educated the neighborhood: it had been easy to ignore just Bien, but suddenly twenty-five women in the village were visible—people wanted to learn what they were dealing with.

As the local understanding changed, they began getting hired for work again. They were able to provide for their children and participate fully in the life of the community. And then something else happened that would revolutionize the group.

Bien met Jesus.

DEEP ROOTS

It was Bien's trainer from the HIV-ministry who introduced her to God. "She shared the gospel with me," Bien says. "It was the first time I met Jesus." Touched by the goodness of God, Bien responded deeply to the healing message of Jesus, devouring everything she could learn about him.

The seed took root in the soil of her life.

Bien became the first follower of Jesus in her village. She began sharing God's love with her group, and many said, "We want to follow him too." Neighbors saw the transformation and said, "We want Jesus too." Pretty soon, Bien was leading a church of forty people in her home.

Quickly, however, trouble came. Some saw Christianity as a threat, so local officials went house to house and warned, "Unless you renounce Jesus and shut this thing down, we're going to shut off your HIV medication," essentially threatening them with death. Many bailed, saying, "This isn't what I signed up for."

But Bien and many others stayed. The choice was clear: give up Jesus and save your life, or remain with Jesus and die. I asked Bien why, when she had been so afraid of dying upon first learning she had HIV, she was no longer. "What changed?" She explained:

> Before I was so scared of dying. But now I know it means going home to be with the Father. So now we are very confident and no longer afraid, because we know that our Lord controls everything, and we are safe in his care. We encouraged one another, saying, "Christ is our true reward." It was hard, but Jesus strengthened us to withstand the persecution.

The rocks and thorns of persecution could not choke out her seed in the soil.

Slowly things got better. Friends from Hanoi snuck HIV medication from the city. And the church's reputation improved. "God calls us to love and serve our neighbors," Bien said, so they started small businesses for vulnerable families, a support center for prostitutes, and a drug rehabilitation program for addicts in the region.

Neighboring villages wanted HIV support groups too, so Bien helped launch more than forty groups for fifteen hundred–plus women in the surrounding province. Within a few years, Bien was lifted up by the government to oversee HIV work in the entire province. And Bien can't help but talk about Jesus; she's seen many come to follow him and new churches spring up all over the area.

Bien not only withstood rocky resistance and thorny circumstances; she allowed the seed of God's kingdom to take root deep down in her life, bringing loads of life-giving fruit bursting forth from the surface.

UNLIKELY HEROES

Here's the thing that's crazy to me: if you would have gone back to Bien's village ten years ago, checklist in hand, looking for a change-maker, she's probably not who you'd choose.

- ✓ *Vocation?* Farmer.
- ✓ *Income?* Poor.
- ✓ *Education?* Weak.
- ✓ *Influence?* None.
- ✓ *Health?* Sick.

According to our usual standards and metrics, she would've been the last kid picked. But here's the thing: God loves taking the last kids picked and making them the center of his story.

God likes unlikely heroes.

We see this throughout the biblical story. God takes Israel, a nation of slaves getting their tails kicked on the outskirts of the empire, depicted as the last, least, and weakest of the ancient world, and sets them at the center of the nations to display his glory to the mighty, ancient, bloodthirsty, wicked, powerhouse empires. God picks David, the runt of his brothers, who nobody thought worthy of inviting to the party while he's out with the sheep, to be the greatest king in Israel's history and the great-great-ever-so-great grandfather of Jesus.[2]

Jesus picks his twelve disciples, and let's just say they're not the ancient cream of the crop. Tax collectors, fishermen, and revolutionaries whose faith is a mess. When we want to start a movement, we get the wealthy, influential, and powerful, but God does precisely the opposite. As Paul observes, God loves using the weak to shame the strong, things considered foolish to upend the wise.[3]

God's generosity looks *irrational* to the world's eyes—not only in *how* generous he is, but in *who* he uses to spread his generosity. If we had more time, I'd love to tell you about the prostitutes and disabled who've started thriving small businesses in Hanoi and are spreading the good news of Jesus to their neighbors. I'd tell you about the ex-con drug addicts and tatted-up gangsters who've become some of the strongest preachers in the city. They didn't bring God their résumés; they brought their willingness to receive.

Many would have looked at Bien as only a *recipient* of ministry, but God saw her as an *agent* of ministry. God's goodness can bear fruit in unlikely soil. It's not about how flashy our garden looks on the outside, but about whether we're willing to receive his kingdom on the inside.

The Generous Farmer loves tilling soil that many others would overlook, and bearing powerful, life-giving fruit through them for his world.

After Jesus tells the parable of the four soils, he compares the kingdom to a mustard seed, which, "though it is the smallest of all seeds, yet when it grows, it is the largest of garden plants and becomes a tree, so that the birds come and perch in its branches."[4]

God can grow big things from small places. Where the world sees only mustard seeds, seemingly small and insignificant, God sees potential for mighty movements. God wants to fill his world with life, fruit, and shade, to care for his world through his people. So when Jesus' love takes root, get ready for fruit.

The Generous Farmer is the Father, who lavishes his life upon the creation he loves. Jesus is the seed that goes into the ground, in his death and burial, to bring forth new life through the power of his resurrection. Their Spirit takes root deep in the soil of our lives, bringing us to die to ourselves and live unto God, bearing fruit for the neighborhood. The Father, Son, and Spirit invite us to join their gardening project, to lavish their life upon the landscape of our world.

To become their generous fools.

CHAPTER 12

Selling the Farm

Perhaps we should start calling Matthew 13:1–23 the parable of the Generous Farmer rather than the parable of the four soils, to emphasize the holy extravagance we must respond to. We tend to emphasize our need to be good; Jesus emphasizes the goodness of God. And when his divine delight takes root in us, it's worth more than anything.

The parable of the Generous Farmer comes in a string of other parables that play off one another. Shortly after, Jesus compares the kingdom of heaven to a treasure hidden in a field. When the treasure hunter found the fortune, "he hid it again, and then in his joy went and sold all he had and bought that field."[1] Like a pirate finally discovering that X marks the spot, he burned down the ship he sailed in on to have it.

Jesus drives the point home with a second, similar story. A merchant's on the hunt for fine pearls, out traveling on the road: "when he found one of great value, he went away and sold everything he had and bought it."[2] What do these two stories have in common?

Both the treasure hunter and the merchant find something so precious, so worthy, so valuable, it's worth giving up everything to get it.

So they sell the farm.

GOD OR US?

Now, here's an interesting question: Is the treasure-hunting merchant a picture of *God*, or of *us*? I think it's both. On the one hand, the Pursuing God comes boldly after us, discovers us in the distant land, and gives all that is most valuable to have us. The Father loves us enough to give his most valuable, prized possession, the deepest treasure of his heart: his Son. The Son loves us enough to give his very life, to be rejected, mocked, and murdered, to take on our sin and death. The Spirit loves us enough to give himself, pouring God's love into our hearts and filling us with God's very presence, to unite us through Christ to the Father.

God "sells the farm" to bring us home.

Jesus is a treasure-hunting merchant.

And we're the buried gold.

On the other hand, God is worth everything. There's nothing more precious, no one more worthy, nowhere more valuable. Is there anything you'd sell everything for? Empty the bank accounts, offload the car, and throw your house on the market just to have? Anything worth your comfort, your reputation, your very life?

My friend Dr. Minh gave his house to become the first Christian medical clinic in Hanoi. *Who gives their house!?* I can't imagine giving my house. Pastor Dao Van Vinh's small church built roads by hand for weeks, serving their village with hard labor to connect their community to the surrounding area. Other churches in the region bring food, bury the dead, and build homes for the vulnerable—though they themselves live in extreme poverty.

Bien, whom I introduced in the last chapter, says Jesus is worth everything. "I'm so grateful for my HIV," she shocked me one day by saying, "because without it, I wouldn't have met Jesus." *What?* That floored me. I cried when she said it. *You're telling me that the most tragic, traumatic event, the bomb that blew your life apart— you're grateful for?* Bien has encountered the goodness of God in the face of Christ, and believes there's nothing more valuable in the world.

He's worth selling the farm for.

When Bien risked her life for Jesus, many probably saw her as just a dumb farmer. But she had a secret: she'd found something worth giving it all for. And God sees her faith as beautiful. The Generous Farmer's extravagant goodness has taken root deep in the soil of her life, deeper than the rocks and weeds can get to. And it's grown to bear generous fruit spilling out into the world around her.

I want to be like Bien, willing to sacrifice everything if it means faithfulness to Jesus. Because Jesus is the buried treasure worth burning down the ship we sailed in on. Jesus is the fortune in a field worth selling the farm for. Jesus is the pearl of great price, worth giving it all to have.

He's worth it.

BECOMING THE BRIDE

When Jesus finds us, he takes that pearl of great price and wraps it around our hearts like a wedding ring. What's your favorite image of Jesus? Bien says that for the women with HIV, it's Jesus as the groom pursuing us as his bride:

> Many of the women have experienced deep unfaithfulness by their husbands, and great rejection by their community. But Jesus is a faithful husband who loves us deeply, pursues us strongly, and cares for us greatly. He lays down his life for us, calls us his beloved, and makes his home with us. We love him more than anything.

When I first came to Hanoi, years before I met Bien, I was looking out over the city and had a vision. I was asking God what he was up to, when I saw a magnificent hand coming down out of heaven, holding a diamond bracelet. As the hand drew closer, a few dozen hands reached up from the city, gradually joined by hundreds more, then thousands—coalescing together and forming into one large arm reaching up into the sky.

Meeting in the skyline over the city, the hand from heaven wrapped the diamond bracelet around the wrist of the upstretched arm. I asked God what this meant, what he was doing, and could swear I heard him say, *"I'm calling out my bride."*

The Generous Farmer is looking for a wife. The good news is this is not just for Vietnam; this is for us. The Spirit of God wants to wrap like a diamond bracelet around our hearts, filling us with holy love and making us fit for the coming wedding. Jesus' life becomes a pattern for our life, as the Spirit unites us to his perfect humanity and sanctifies us as we grow in the ways of his kingdom. Jesus wants to bind us in union with him forever, bringing us with him into the glorious home of our generous Father.

God is calling out his bride.

KEY IDEA

Caricature: Jesus emphasizes how to be good.

Gospel: Jesus emphasizes the goodness of God.

PART II

Taking Down the Corporation

CRUCIFIXION

CHAPTER 13

Lion and Prey

COSMIC CHILD ABUSE?

The cross is the climax of God's pursuit, but what's happening at the cross? The Christian tradition has held that Jesus is bearing our punishment in our place, but what does this mean? It has become common in some quarters to characterize the cross as "divine child abuse," or at least traditional understandings of it. A friend recently asked me, "Do you think God killed Jesus?" We were at a conference where nearly every speaker said something to the effect of, *I used to believe in a God who kicked the snot out of his Son on the cross, but now I've come to see that God is love and would never do such a thing. We killed Jesus; God didn't.*

This is a horrible caricature of historic Christian doctrine. But what does it mean to say Christ bore our punishment in our place? How do we make sense of themes such as sacrifice and wrath in relation to the cross? How is this all driven by divine love?

Let's return to the Artist in the painting image with which we opened this book. Remember that moment when the creator absorbs the death, destruction, and decay of his masterpiece into himself? I would suggest that this can serve as a guiding image for this section as we explore the crucifixion of Christ. As the Artist soaks in the destruction of his masterpiece, all of these themes like sacrifice, punishment, and wrath are entailed, and contrary to the caricatures, they are all driven by God's love for the redemption of his world.

Let's dive in and see how.

SAILING INTO THE STORM

A good place to start is to recognize that Jesus is an active agent, not a hapless victim. He is not coerced or manipulated to the cross against his will. Jesus boldly declares, "No one takes my life from me; I lay it down of my own accord."[1] Jesus goes of his own volition to accomplish *his* purposes. He is taking down the destructive power of sin, death, and hell.

Jesus is a lion; the cross is his prey.

Jesus "set his face [toward] Jerusalem" long before his execution and, like an arrow streaming toward its target, made his way toward Zion to atone for the sin of the world.[2] Jesus is constantly saying things like, "the Son of Man must suffer, be rejected, and be killed,"[3] while the disciples, confused and blind, rebuke him, saying, "May it never be!"[4] While we see the cross as a detour, Jesus sees it as a destination.

Jesus sets sail into the storm to bring us home.

This confronts the tendency to see Jesus as an unwitting casualty caught in the wheels of fate. For example, one popular illustration pictures Jesus as a child who goes to work with his father at the railroad. The father sees a train coming, full of passengers, and needs to lower the bridge so the train can cross the river. Unfortunately, he sees his son playing under the bridge in the gears. With tears in his eyes, the father pulls the lever and crushes his son in order to save the people on the train.

This is a horrible analogy for a number of reasons. But a big one is that Jesus is depicted as a naive bystander, playfully minding his own business and passively unaware of what's happening around him. The Gospels, in contrast, depict the Son of God taking on flesh and emptying himself on our behalf, running toward the cross as a man on a mission. Jesus is like a pro wrestler who tackles the cross to body slam it. Also, Jesus is not a five-year-old. He's a grown man, and he knows what he's doing. While he truly agonizes and suffers, Jesus is thirty-three, emotionally stable, and goes to Golgotha to conquer our grave. Jesus is a jaguar out to devour death.[5]

The cross is not happening to Jesus; Jesus is happening to the cross.

And Jesus' motive is love. He is "the Son of God, who loved me and gave himself up for me."[6] Jesus goes to the cross compelled by affection, driven by desire, moved by longing. He sees the cross as an act of service, explaining his mission:

> The Son of Man did not come to be served, but to serve, and to
> give his life as a ransom for many.[7]

The cross is a signpost of divine love poured out for the world. Jesus points to the cross as a way of life, saying that those who love him are to "take up their cross" and follow in his footsteps, to lay down our lives in sacrificial love for others.[8]

A cruciform life is an act of love.

EXILE AND DEATH

If Jesus bears our punishment, a good first question to ask is: *What is the punishment?* If Jesus bears the penalty in our place, what is that penalty? When some people hear of divine punishment, they envision the Father punching Jesus in the face on the cross, or something like that. But when we zoom out to the broader lens of the biblical story, we see a different picture.

Exile and death *are* the punishment.

When Adam and Eve rebelled, exile and death were the punishment for sin. They were driven from the garden (into exile), where they received the punishment of which God had warned them: "when you eat from [the forbidden tree] you will certainly die."[9] East of Eden, they found themselves distant from the presence of their Creator under decay, destruction, and death.

It was the same in Israel's story. After her repeated rebellion, she was driven into exile: God's protective presence left the land, and Babylon invaded, demolishing the temple, ravaging the land, and carrying the people into captivity. This exile led to death: Ezekiel's famous vision of a valley of dry bones is a massacre graveyard under Babylon's brutal power, a picture of the "death of the nation" in hopes of restoration.[10]

Why does Jesus bear our exile and death? To better understand this, let's return to the early church's idea of *recapitulation* that we looked at earlier: that Jesus relives our story, being faithful where we've rebelled, to be established as the new head of humanity. Jesus relives Israel's story: his virgin birth reminds us of the nation's miraculous birth from Sarah's barren womb; his childhood years in Egypt recall Israel's early years under Pharaoh; his wilderness temptation relives Israel's desert testing; his life and ministry fulfill his people's kingdom calling to embody God's reign in the land.

Jesus faithfully bears Israel's story in his own life to redeem it.

In Jesus' rejection and crucifixion, he is bearing Israel's exile and death, living out this next major era of his people's story. Jesus *is* an Israelite, and as her Messiah he carries her story within himself in order to redeem it. As Jesus is cast outside the city, he is *recapitulating* Israel's banishment from the land. As he is crucified under the pagan powers, he takes upon himself her national destruction. Though personally innocent, he takes upon himself the exile and death of his people.

And Jesus bears *our* exile and death as the new Adam. As Paul observes, "Sin entered the world through one man [Adam], and death through sin, and in this way death came to all people, because all sinned."[11] Like Adam, we've all wanted to be *like* God rather than *with* God; we've all declared independence from the kingdom; we've all severed earth from heaven. Our distance from the Giver of Life gives rise to death. Sin's river flows downstream along the banks of exile and empties in its deadly ocean.

And death is the ultimate penalty. "Sin reigned in death,"[12] writes Paul, depicting evil as a king who rules over a dominion called death. Sin tears apart creation, back toward the nothingness from which it came. Our rebellion rips apart the world, unleashing the disruptive decay that's out to destroy the masterpiece.

But fortunately, Jesus bears our exile and death, Paul concludes, to exhaust its power, "so that, just as sin reigned in death, so also grace might reign through righteousness to bring eternal life through Jesus Christ our Lord."[13] So when the Artist absorbs the corruption in his masterpiece, when the Lamb takes upon himself the sin of the world, when Jesus endures our exile and death, he is receiving the penalty our rebellion has unleashed; he is bearing our punishment for sin.

Because exile and death *are* the punishment.

THE UNASSUMED IS THE UNHEALED

Why does Jesus need to? Couldn't he just wave a magic wand and fix everything? The early church had a saying, "The unassumed is the unhealed."[14] What they meant was that Jesus takes on, or assumes, the full weight of our condition in order to redeem it. If our world's distance from God is the problem, then God bridging that distance to unite us with him—in our condition—is the solution.

It is Jesus' union with us that brings our healing. If Jesus only had a soul with no body, for example, his union with us would only extend to our souls. But since we "have flesh and blood, he too shared in [our] humanity," Hebrews tells us, in order to assume the full weight of our condition. He was "made like his brothers and sisters in every way," to break the power of death.[15]

Similarly, if Jesus took on a body but never suffered temptation or pain, his redemption would not enter the depths of our distress with the same weight and power. So "he himself suffered when he was tempted," Hebrews goes on, in order to identify fully with us.[16] Through our union with him, he is now able to help us when we are tempted, lifting us up with his power as his people.

Jesus was made like us in every way except one: he did not sin. The Son does not join our rebellion against the Father. He was "tempted in every way, just as we are," Hebrews observes, "yet he did not sin."[17] Some might say, "If he didn't sin, then was he really like us? Aren't our mistakes part of what makes us human?" But as we saw earlier, this misunderstands the nature of the problem.

Sin makes us less human, not more. We're not talking about accidental mistakes; we're talking about willful insurgency. We were made in the image of God, to reflect his glory, yet when we reject and run from God, we scratch markers across the surface of our lives that efface this reflection. We dehumanize ourselves and diminish the glory of life we were given.

Irenaeus famously declared, "The glory of God is man fully alive." Jesus is "fully alive" without sin—and God's goal in Jesus is to make *us* fully alive, *more* human, not less. Jesus is *more* human without sin, not less, as "the image of the invisible God,"[18] radiantly reflecting the splendor of the Father in pulsating, life-giving glory. When we look at Jesus, we see the face of the Father clearly displayed.[19]

Jesus is true humanity.

And yet, though he had no sin, Jesus *becomes* sin for us.[20] The Artist absorbs our destruction, the Savior soaks up our death, to the point that he is identified with it. The fact that Jesus is spotless, blameless, without defect or blemish, is part of what makes him not only *a* sacrifice, but the *perfect* sacrifice, to bear our exile and death—and to annihilate it in the grave. The Deliverer takes in our decay in order to make us whole.

Jesus joins us in our distance in order to bring us home.

CHAPTER 14

Jesus Is a Wall Street CEO

A central conviction of Christianity is that Jesus died for us, but can an innocent person really be punished *instead of* the guilty? Many find this idea revolting. For example, imagine a convicted felon standing before the judge in a courtroom to receive her sentence, when an innocent person steps forward and says, "I'll take her place!" Would any judge ever do that, and substitute an innocent person in place of the guilty? Would we even want him to?

Sure, if my crime is a parking ticket, and the person wants to "take my place" and pay the fine—that works great. But if I'm facing life in prison for rape and murder, and the judge puts an innocent person in solitary confinement instead and lets me off the hook to roam the streets—what does that accomplish? Society is not protected; wrongs are not righted. There's a reason no real judge in a real courtroom today would openly allow this.

It would be unjust.

So what does it mean to say Christ "took our place" on the cross? When Jesus substituted himself for us, what did *substituted* mean? Let's take a look.

HUMANITY INC.

A good starting point the gospel gives us is *corporate identity*. Now, when we hear the word *corporate* today, we think of big, modern companies, like Walmart, Starbucks, and McDonald's. But the ancient idea ran much deeper. It comes from the root *corporal*, or "of the body." Families, societies, and nations saw themselves as bodies meant to function together.

Within the body, you were part of something bigger. You belonged to your community. You had a responsibility to your people. Corporate identity was not so much about being part of an economic machine as it was being part of a body of people. The *head*, or leadership, directed which way the social body moved. If the Roman Empire was a body, then Rome (and ultimately Caesar) was its head.

In the gospel, Jesus is our new head.

God exalts Jesus over Caesar as head of the nations; he's the King of Israel lifted up as Lord of the world; he replaces Adam as captain of creation. To use our "Artist in the painting" metaphor, Adam was originally placed at the center of the masterpiece to care for it. When he messed it up, God replaced him with Israel at the center, but she messed it up too. Now Rome's *striving* to be at the center of the painting—and all of them have been exceptionally poor stewards, unleashing destruction.

So God finally says, *"I'll take care of this myself"* and steps in for an un-hostile takeover: the Father installs Jesus as the new CEO of Humanity Inc.

As the head of humanity, Jesus *identifies* with us. Though *personally* innocent, he shares our *corporate* identity. He has bound himself in union with us: this is why he can bear our punishment.

Let's use an analogy. During the U.S. housing crisis, there was widespread anger at the shoddy banking practices, fat-cat executives, and corporate corruption that threw a sledgehammer into the global economy. Now, imagine Jesus is installed in the aftermath as the new CEO of one of the massive behemoth corporations guilty for the crisis; let's say Bank of America.[1]

The old CEO is out the door; a new head honcho is in town.

Now, Jesus is *personally* innocent: he wasn't behind the wheel when the ship got steered into the rocks. But he's taken the helm of a *corporation* that still has a debt. Bank of America, for example, was responsible for paying more than $17 billion in damages after the crisis. Nobody would say, "Well, that debt was under the old CEO. Bank of America shouldn't be responsible anymore, now that a new CEO is in charge—*he* didn't do anything." That would be ridiculous. Every time a company was guilty, they'd simply fire the leader to avoid responsibility. BP wouldn't have to clean up their oil spill, just replace the boss upstairs.

It would provoke national outrage as an injustice.

When Jesus dives into humanity, he takes responsibility for his body. He unites his life with us, shares in our destiny, and participates in our fate—in order to redeem it. That's why the courtroom analogy above falls short; it's individualistic. Jesus isn't simply replacing an individual with himself; he's taking responsibility for the body of which he's a part. Jesus steps in for Israel as her representative head, for Adam as our new captain, for Humanity Inc. as our rightful leader, and takes on the exile and death that was ours to bear.

So on the cross, it's not so much that Jesus is being punished *instead of* humanity as it is that humanity is being punished *in* Jesus. Jesus bears our exile and death, taking our penalty upon himself not as an innocent bystander, but as the head of his body. And he does it to exhaust its power and raise us to new life.

EATING THE COST

Why doesn't God just forgive the debt? If our Creator was truly generous, couldn't he just move on without repayment? Live and let live? Here's the problem: someone *always* eats the cost. Let's say, for example, your neighbor drives home drunk one night and crashes his car through your fence. In the morning, you wake up, discover the shambles, and (once he sobers up) tell him you forgive him: "Don't worry about the fence! All is forgiven."[2]

Now, forgiving him doesn't *remove* the cost of fixing the fence; it simply means you take it on yourself. He's not responsible for it anymore, yet either the fence will stay in disrepair or you'll pay for it out of your own wallet. Forgiving your neighbor doesn't do away with the bill or dissolve the damage; it means *you* eat the cost.

Zooming out to a larger level, the Wall Street analogy is again helpful. In the aftermath of the housing crisis, the banks were deemed "too big to fail," and the government *forgave* the debt, covering the most expensive bailout of human history. Though the banking industry had caused massive damage, the debt was forgiven. Forgiveness, however, did not mean the debt went away. It meant someone else covered it—in this case, the American people.

Indeed, there was mass outrage: Wall Street executives walked away with bulging bonuses, and corrupt banks got off scot-free, while the economy was left in shambles and the people were left footing the bill. Forgiving the banks didn't make the debt disappear. Someone always eats the cost.

At the cross, God is eating the cost. The Father, Son, and Spirit are forgiving the debt by dealing with it themselves. The Artist is absorbing the corruption in his masterpiece. The CEO is bearing the exile and death of Humanity Inc. The Savior is swallowing our sin in order to make us whole. Why can't God just forgive the debt? This *is* what is happening at the cross: God is just(ly) forgiving the debt—by personally covering the cost. God takes in the decay we've unleashed to extinguish it in the power of divine love.

I misspoke earlier when I said the White House gave Wall Street the most expensive bailout of human history. Actually, the most expensive bailout was when the Father established his incarnate Son as the new CEO of a corrupt corporation called Humanity Inc. and together, in the power of their Spirit, they took upon themselves the most outrageous debt-forgiveness plan the world has ever known.

THE CROSS AS DECAPITATION

Jesus' death is more than a crucifixion; it is a decapitation. Because Jesus is the head of humanity, when Rome pounds the nails through his hands, the empire of Adam is ousting the Lord of the nations. When Israel rejects God's king, the mob is murdering the mayor. When Humanity Inc. lifts the Creator up on a cross, the crew is throwing the captain overboard.[3] We slice the rope to let the guillotine blade drop, not realizing our own social body is on the chopping block.

Humanity is chopping off its own head.

And yet, from another angle it is a *re*-capitation. More than any other event, it is precisely here that the Son is being most intimately bound in union with us as his body, soaking in our sin-struck shame, bearing our exile and sharing in our death; absorbing the decay we've unleashed and taking our penalty upon himself; making our corrupted body *his* body in order to raise it through the power of his resurrection, exalting us through his new life unto glory.

We have our head back.

KEY IDEA

Caricature: Jesus bearing our punishment is an act of divine child abuse.

Gospel: Jesus bearing our punishment is an act of divine love.

CHAPTER 15

Muggers and Physicians

GOD OR US?

In the last few chapters we've looked at the Son's role in the cross; now we turn to the Father. Was the Father actively involved in the murder of his Son? This is at the heart of the divine child abuse caricature we looked at earlier. For some people the Father looks cold, calculated, and unengaged at the cross. Is God safe and protected, high up above in his distant abode, while Jesus endures mocking, torture, and death in sacrificial love for the world?

For some, the Son is a poet proposing to his bride, while the Father is a mathematician settling ancient accounts on the throne-room whiteboard.

The gospel shakes this caricature up like an Etch A Sketch, and redraws the lines in radically different directions. The cross is an act of the Father's love. When I think of God's love in the crucifixion, my eyes are drawn not only to Jesus, who loved me and gave himself up for me, but perhaps even more to the Father, who gave the greatest gift the world could ever dream of.

Let's take a closer look at the Father's role in the most excruciating event any parent can imagine: the death of his Son.

Who killed Jesus: God or us? Obviously, we did. Nobody disputes this. Jewish leaders pushed the sentence, the Roman Empire pounded the nails, and our sin is what he bore. The real question is whether this is an either/or or a both/and issue. Was God actively involved in some way?

Earlier, we saw that *Jesus* is actively involved: the cross doesn't just happen to Jesus; Jesus happens to the cross. The Son of God is taking on the destructive power of sin, death, and hell—to conquer it. Can something similar be said of the Father? Is the Father absent or present in the death of his Son?

ABSENCE AND PRESENCE

I would suggest that exile is a helpful lens through which to look at this. We've seen that Jesus is bearing our exile on the cross. Israel understood her exile as arising from *both* the absence of God (from one important angle) *and* the presence of God (from another). Let's see how this worked.

First, Israel saw her exile as the result of God's *absence*. God relentlessly pursued his people throughout her history, but Israel repeatedly worshipped idols and unleashed injustice—becoming more and more corrupt. God sent prophets and messengers to call her back, but the people killed the prophets and rejected the messengers, preferring to live on their own and essentially asking God for a divorce.

So finally, God left town.

Catching his wife in bed with another man one too many

times, God packs his bags and vacates their home. In a famous passage, Ezekiel sees God's glory departing the temple, the place where God dwelt most intimately with his people. With suitcase in hand, God walks out of the "bedroom," exits the temple courts, and leaves the building. It's as if God is saying, *"I'm tired of her cheatin' ways. She wants her other lovers; she can have 'em. I'll take up shop in a heavenly hotel, and she can sleep around down here with whoever she wants."*

The unrequited Lover gives his wayward wife the separation she craves. This is the climax of Ezekiel's prophecy.

God's glory departs the temple.

Without God's protective presence, Babylon invades. God's presence was what kept her safe from invasion in the first place. God was her Defender from the mighty empires that surrounded her. Now, with her husband away, the cruel lovers pounce. With the King gone, Babylon swoops in to seize his kingdom: the pagan empire destroys the temple, sets fire to Jerusalem, lays waste to the land, and takes the people into captivity in a land far, far away. Israel is given her lovers, handed over to what she's chosen.

Exile arises from God's absence.

And yet, from another angle, God is also *present*. In a sweeping turn of phrase, God calls Babylon his "sword," her king "my servant," her armies his armies "to bring disaster on the city that bears my Name."[1] What?! This is crazy. How is God present in the godless, brutal butchers desecrating his holy home?

God declares he is at work in this event: chastising his people, driving them from the land, giving them over to what they've chosen, in hopes that the experience of destruction downstream will shake them to their senses and drive them back to the life they were made for—with him.

So Israel saw Babylon as God's "iron yoke" and "cup of wrath," doling out the paycheck her injustice and rebellion had earned.[2] "I am raising up the Babylonians," God says, "that ruthless and impetuous people." The prophet Habakkuk responds, "You, LORD, have appointed them to execute judgment; you, my Rock, have ordained them to punish."[3] Second Chronicles recounts this logic of exile:

> The God of their ancestors, sent word to them through his messengers again and again, because he had pity on his people and on his dwelling place. But they mocked God's messengers, despised his words and scoffed at his prophets until the wrath of the LORD was aroused against his people and there was no remedy. *He brought up against them* the king of the Babylonians.[4]

The Babylonian captivity is the sovereign judgment of God. Throughout the prophets, God repeatedly says *he* is the One sending them into exile, driving them out of the land, carrying them away, scattering them, and giving them over to the destruction they've chosen.[5] God is actively involved in his people's removal from the land. The prophets reveal that when God seems to have left the building, he may be most powerfully at work.

Here's the thing to recognize, however: though God and Babylon are both involved in the same event, their motives are starkly different—even diametrically opposed. The mighty empire simply wants to tear Israel down, while God ultimately wants to lift her up. The pagan power strives to distance the people from

God; God's endgame is to draw them to him. It's as if God and Babylon are driving together through Phoenix, but God's final destination is to get to Los Angeles, whereas Babylon's simply aiming for Death Valley.

The same event is oriented toward two very different goals. And God is ultimately in the driver's seat.

Exile arises from God's presence.

FORSAKEN AND INDWELT

In Jesus' death, this same imagery is at play as he bears our exile. On the one hand, the cross arises from the *absence* of God. At the climax of Jesus' crucifixion, he cries out, "My God, my God, why have you forsaken me?"[6] The Father's protective presence has left the building, the glory has departed the temple of Jesus' body, and his Son is now vulnerable as the pagan powers invade to tear down this Most Holy Place, to desecrate the sanctuary of his flesh and bone, to demolish him to rubble and carry him down to captivity in the grave.

Jesus is forsaken, the temple of his body destroyed.

The cross arises from God's absence.

And yet, from another angle, God is *present* in the crucifixion. When Jesus cries out, he cries out to *My God!* And you don't cry out to someone who isn't there.[7] More so, Jesus' final words are of trust: "Father, into your hands I commit my spirit."[8] As Jesus breathes his last, he entrusts himself to his Father and looks to him for vindication on the other side of the grave. As we murder God's Son, the Father's arms receive the tattered, lifeless body of his beloved child.

God is present at the cross.

Here's what's crazy, however: God is *doing something* through this event. The Father is present not only *over* his Son, but *in* his Son. At Golgotha, Paul declares, "God was *in* Christ reconciling the world to Himself."[9] In Jesus' darkest hour, the Father is actively present accomplishing something—the reconciliation of the world. Colossians declares in a similar vein:

> God was pleased to have all his fullness dwell in [Jesus], and through him to reconcile to himself all things, whether things on earth or things in heaven, by making peace through his blood, shed on the cross.[10]

God is dwelling *in* Jesus, working *through* Jesus, actively present at the cross—and his endgame is reconciling the world.

God's motives are radically different, however, from ours: we are out to crush the Son, while the Father is bearing our destruction in him to exalt him as Savior of the world. We kill Jesus to tear him down while God is at work uniting us to him, tearing our corrupted body down in him to ultimately build us up and lift us up through him. We are striving to keep our world distant from God, while God is—in the very same event!—drawing our world most intimately close to him. The Father is present *through* his Son and *in* his Spirit at the cross, working to bring us home.

A DIFFERENT MOTIVE

This question of motive is important. Two people can perform the same act for very different reasons. Both a mugger and a physician may slash me with a knife, but with opposing purposes. The mugger's purpose is selfish; the physician's altruistic. One seeks to steal; the other to heal. In the event of the cross, God's motives are not like ours.

We are the muggers; God is a physician.

How can this be? That we seek to destroy and God to heal—*in the very same event?!* This may sound strange to us, but it is not unique in the biblical story. I think one of the problems is that we tend to approach this as if only one agent can be the cause of an action. The Hebrew worldview, however, has room for divine agency in and through human affairs. We've already seen this at work in Israel's understanding of the Babylonian exile. Another classic example is the life of Joseph, whose brothers beat him up, sell him into slavery, and tell their father he's dead.

Joseph goes into *exile* in a distant land; God seems *absent*.

In Egypt, Joseph is repeatedly mistreated and maligned. His life is one long punch-in-the-face after another. And yet, God exalts Joseph through these tragic events to the heights of Egypt's empire, where Joseph prevents mass starvation in a severe famine, saves his family from destruction and death, and exalts God's name in the godless powerhouse that ruled the day.

Joseph goes ahead of his people into Egypt, *pre-capitulating* Israel's experience in slavery in advance, carving out space for his family to bear God's blessing to the world. At the end of the story, Joseph embraces his brothers and, looking back on his life, tells them, "You intended to harm me, but God intended it for good to accomplish what is now being done, the saving of many lives."[11]

Joseph sees God as *present* with him in the tragic events of his life, though with *very* different motives from his brothers— indeed, opposing motives. They were out to destroy him; God was working through it for "the saving of many lives." His brothers' purposes were truly wicked, rebellious, and evil; God's endgame was redemptive, positive, and good. They were muggers performing a robbery; God was a physician performing surgery.

In the very same event.

Jesus was, like Joseph, mistreated and sold into captivity by his brothers (Israel), where he was beaten and crushed by a pagan empire (Rome), and enslaved in a foreign land (the grave). And yet, God was not simply absent or watching from the sidelines through all this. He was at work for our redemption: the Father united his Son to us in our famished and failing estate, in the midst of our arrogant empires, in order to save the world through him.

Jesus is our greater Joseph. As the resurrected King, he now stands before us, the brothers and sisters who betrayed him, and offers the reconciling embrace of forgiveness. We can hear Jesus echo the ancient words of his ancestor Joseph, spoken now to us regarding his death:

> You meant it for evil, but God meant it for good, to accomplish what is now being done, the saving of many lives.[12]

God and we are both involved in the same event, though with radically different motives—in fact, opposite motives. Jesus views the tragic event under which he suffered, the cross, as *both* the cruel power of our sin *and* the sovereign, saving action of God, in a way that magnifies his Father's goodness and love. God intends good; we intend evil. While we seek to destroy his Son, the Father is judging evil in order to deliver us through him.

So the cross is the revelation of God's sovereign, self-giving love. God is taking on the destructive power of sin, death, and the grave. The Father is working through his Son and in his Spirit—for the reconciliation of the world. The Pursuing God is finding us in the distant land, to bring us into his divine life and carry us home.

CHAPTER 16

For God So Loved . . .

If God's love is not the primary thing we see displayed at the cross, like fireworks exploding in the sky, then we're not looking through the same lens that Jesus does. In perhaps the most famous verse of Scripture, Christ declares, "God so *loved* the world that he gave his one and only Son . . ."[1] The Son sees the Father's overwhelming affection for the world in his death on that rugged tree. The cross displays God's love.

Jesus is not alone. Consider these words from Paul and John, the most prolific apostles of the New Testament:

> God demonstrates his own love for us in this: While we were still sinners, Christ died for us.[2] (Paul)

> This is love: not that we loved God, but that he loved us and sent his Son as an atoning sacrifice for our sins.[3] (John)

Paul and John were well aware that an irrationally angry dad beating up his child was an act of brutality, not of love. But they flip this picture right side up: an overwhelmingly affectionate Father endures the affliction of his Son under the terrorizing blows of his enemies—and somehow, through the astonishing power of God, the Roman Empire's brutal instrument of torture is turned into a miraculous instrument of love.

God so loved, that he gave. Yes, the cross puts our human brutality on full display, but it also reveals something greater: the love of the Father. Jesus is the greatest gift the Father has to give. And perhaps the most startling revelation is not just *that* he is given, but *to whom* he is given: to us, not as God's buddies, but as his opponents; not as the heroes, but as the villains; not as those seeking him, but as those running away. "When we were enemies," the gospel declares, "we were reconciled to God through the death of His Son."[4]

The cross costs the Father the most precious, priceless, valuable gift he has to give—given for us. And the reason the Father's willing to pay the price is love. While Jesus endures the cross, God endures something greater.

The Father endures the death of his Son.

LOSING A CHILD

There's no greater pain than losing a child. Ask my friends Jim and Marilyn, whose twenty-six-year-old son, David, was killed in the Iraq War. Or Chris and Courtney, whose beautiful newborn daughter, Olivia, died the day she was born. They would tell you there is no agony more unbearable, no tragedy more heartbreaking, nothing they've experienced more heart wrenching, than being separated from their beloved by the grave.

Watching your child suffer is brutal. Our family went through the most difficult time we've yet experienced this last year: my five-year-old daughter had a psychotic break. Aiden didn't recognize us, and spent every waking moment screaming and shrieking at the top of her lungs, hitting, biting, and violently convulsing in a way that looked as though she were possessed. She'd wear herself out until she fell asleep, then wake and start all over again.

I spent ten days with her in the hospital. I was there with her the whole time, though she often didn't recognize me. When the nurses put needles in her arms, I held and tried to comfort her though her eyes stared at me in confusion. When she was strapped to a bed, fighting with everything she had, I stayed by her side though her vacant stares broke my heart.

The doctors didn't know what was happening. Her condition came out of nowhere. Had someone abused her? Did we fail to protect her as parents? Worst of all, we didn't know whether it was permanent. We thought we might have lost the little girl we knew and loved for good. I've never cried so hard in my life. I sobbed uncontrollably for days and days on end. I can honestly say I think the experience was harder on me than on her.

I would have given anything to take her place.

The greatness of my love for her gave rise to the greatness of the pain to see her suffer. Anyone who knows me would tell you Aiden is the apple of my eye. Something could happen to me or my wife and, though I love my wife more than anything and value my own life as well, the pain could not have been any greater than watching Aiden hurting. To see my little one so vulnerable, my firstborn threatened, my best little buddy and sweetest, darling girl attacked—the overwhelming vastness of my affection for her gave rise to equally overwhelming grief.

Most parents can imagine no greater threat than the destruction of their own child. I've sat on deathbeds with the dying, walked with survivors of sexual trafficking, soaked in the aftermath of genocidal war zones—and each of these has wrecked me. But I've never been so destroyed as when gazing into the eyes of my own beloved child while she suffered.

The intimacy of my affection only intensified my heartbreak.

Aiden's now fully recovered. Our medical team eventually discovered it was an extreme autoimmune response to a virus in her system, and she got better over the ensuing months. While she remembers blurry bits and pieces of the experience, the whole nightmare is vivid in my mind. And I've found a deeper empathy for parents like Jason and Alyse, whose four-year-old son, Justus, is fighting for his life in an ICU ward with viral encephalitis, as I write this.[5] Or families I've sat with as a pastor over the years, whose children fight for their tiny lives against leukemia, struggle to overcome sexual abuse by a trusted relative, or adjust to being disfigured from a tragic accident.

Every one of those parents would give anything to take their child's place.

PASSION AND AFFECTION

So why do we think the Father is cold and distant at the cross? Now, there are some obvious differences with God. The Father knows he will be able to raise his Son. As Creator, he is distinct from creation, with sovereign power assuring that the grave will not have the last word. Also, the Father does not have a physical body like ours, with adrenaline rushing through his bloodstream and synapses firing in the emotional centers of his brain. God does not passively suffer events in the world the way we do and will not be overwhelmed by the cross in a way that compromises his sovereignty.

And yet, in active love he endures the death of his Son.[6]

Perhaps one reason people today misperceive the Father as unengaged is that historically the church has taught that God does not "suffer passions"—but this doctrine is often misunderstood.[7] The word *passion* means something different today than it used to. When we say things like, "I'm passionate about making music," or "I'm passionate about mentoring youth," we often mean an active affection or desire for something good. A person with no passion is considered cold and lifeless.

The words *passion* and *affection* sound like synonyms.

But historically, *passion* and *affection* were used very differently, almost as opposites. Passions were seen as negative, while affections were positive. To be overwhelmed by your passions was to be passively impacted by your circumstances in such a way that compromised the integrity of your character, that made you desire to sin. So when someone murders their loved one in a "crime of passion," or "loses their temper" in the heat of the moment, there's a sense that the person is overwhelmed by an emotion.

Affections were *active*, while passions were, as the name suggests, *passive*. A father could have great *affection* for his son, providing, nurturing, and caring for him (which is a good thing), yet when his son comes home having wrecked the family car, the father could become overwhelmed with angry *passion* and abusively beat the snot out of his son. He might say later, "I don't know what came over me," or "I lost myself."

So when the church has said God can't "suffer passion," it doesn't mean God is cold and lifeless but rather that God doesn't lose himself and become an abusive jerk. No matter how bad we get, God doesn't act out of character or fly off the handle and inappropriately lose his temper. Far from being distant or "emotionally unengaged," God has *great* affection for his world.[8] God *is* holy love and loves us more than we love ourselves. God is overflowing with joy and goodness, and nothing we do can make him stop being good.

God is *always* life, light, and love—in everything he does. So even when God gets angry, he doesn't blow a gasket and go berserk, overwhelmed by the situation, but rather is *appropriately* angry at those who stand unrepentantly opposed to his goodness and against his patient purposes for the world. No matter how horrendous our actions become, we cannot act upon God so as to change the integrity of his character.

In the words of respected theologian J. Todd Billings, to say God does not "suffer passion" means:

> God has no disordered affections that could make his loving being and action ebb and flow. God's affections and actions are utterly consistent with his identity as the covenant Lord, thus the Lord who freely enters into covenantal relations with creatures is never blindsided or manipulated by them. Instead, God loves in fullness and has the appropriate relational, affective responses to creation: to delight in the goodness of creation and in obedience; to have compassion on the suffering and hear their cry; to grieve over the creation's self-destructive sin; and to be angry in response to evil, injustice, and wickedness.[9]

So at the cross, to borrow Billings's language, the Father "has compassion" on his suffering incarnate Son (who cries out as the innocent one in corporate identification as our head). The Father "grieves over" creation's self-destruction (borne in the flesh of his Son). The Father "is angry" at the cross (in response to our evil, injustice, and wickedness fully displayed). The Father "delights in" the cross (as it displays the obedience of the Son ordered towards the restoration of creation's goodness).[10]

The Father has a *massive*, multifaceted relation to the death of his incarnate Son. One of the reasons the cross is so profound is that it reveals the beautiful love of God from so many different angles (like the compassion, grief, anger, and delight mentioned above). Like a symphony when multiple instruments play in harmony, all these dimensions of God's affective relation to the world are revealed in power at the cross.

All of these angles are, to again borrow Billings's language, "the appropriate relational, affective response" of God's impassible holy love—the Father is not "blindsided or manipulated" by the cross, but acts in a way that is "utterly consistent with his identity as the covenant Lord." The Father does not "lose himself," but rather is *fully* himself—the life, light, and love of his being in relation to the multifaceted angles of all that he is sovereignly engaging and accomplishing at the cross.

PHYSICAL VS. RELATIONAL

Another reason some think the Father distant may be that we tend to focus only on the *physical* suffering of the cross. As Americans, we're fascinated with movies such as Mel Gibson's *The Passion of the Christ* that try to capture the horrific cruelty of the event. And it's true: crucifixion was designed to be particularly brutal. In using it the Romans were sending a powerful, public message through its excruciating pain: *don't mess with the empire.*

But if we become fixated on the physical brutality, we can miss a deeper reality: *suffering is relational.* This hit home for me once in Congo, with African pastors tortured during the brutal civil war there. They described the starvation and beatings, the electro-shock charges to their genitals, the heads dunked underwater and the mutilating cuts—I don't know many who've experienced worse *physical* suffering.

Yet they said the deeper wounds were *relational.* Torture sent the message, "You are worthless. You are dung. We find you so repulsive that we take pleasure in destroying you." This message spoke to their value and worth as human beings; it attacked their dignity as image bearers, as those loved by God. When the physical pain ended, the relational sting remained. The mutilation of their flesh only exacerbated the wound to their souls.

God's presence was with them, they said, in those darkest times. It is here, where the persecutors cut to the core of their person, that the powerful grace of Christ was doing its most signif-icant work in these deep places, to bring not only healing in them but forgiveness toward their enemies.

They taught me something important: suffering is more than physical. There is an important relational dynamic. When the rap-ist's attack is over, a woman must endure the emotional damage that can cast a long shadow on the road to recovery. When a child is ruthlessly bullied, the inner turmoil and insecurities can last long after the bruises have healed.

And one can suffer greatly when there is *no* physical pain. A lover whose spouse has betrayed, cheated, or left her or him knows this devastation all too well. There may have been no physical abuse, but the greatest pain is the abandonment and loss. In fact, there is perhaps no greater suffering than when someone you love is threatened, wounded, or taken away.

The greater the bond of love, the greater the loss.

If we only look at the cross through the restricted lens of physical suffering, then the Father may look cold, distant, and unengaged. The Father does not suffer the bodily pain of the cross: the nails do not go through his hands; his back is not whipped; his parched throat does not cry out, "I'm thirsty." Unlike the examples above, the Father is not being tortured like the pastors in Congo, bullied like a child on the playground, or passively acted upon by the world in a way that changes the light, life, and love that is his eternal existence as God.

Yet if we look through a more robust relational lens, things take on a new light. We see not only the passion of the Son, but the sacrificial love of the Father. The One of whom the Father said, "This is my beloved Son, in whom I am well pleased," bears our destruction in his flesh as he carries our sin and death into the tomb. As the Son goes into exile, he bears our distance in his humanity. The Father introduces this distance in order to bind the Son in union with fallen humanity and raise us with him from the grave.

They act in one accord, with an unbroken communion of will, in love for the world through the power of their Spirit, as the Father's greatest object of most intimate affection, the eternal beloved Son, is shredded to pieces and severed from earth into the grave. On Holy Saturday, while Jesus lies dead and buried, the living, loving Father looks upon the desolate earth that covers the face of his dead, incarnate Son.

The Father makes, I would suggest, the greatest sacrifice in the event of the cross. He does not passively suffer the world, but he does something much greater.

The Father actively endures the death of the Son.

KEY IDEA

Caricature: The Father is cold, distant, and unengaged at the cross.

Gospel: The Father endures the greatest sacrifice of all: the death of the Son.

CHAPTER 17

A Helicopter in the Forest

Could the Father have abandoned the Son? As Jesus lies vulnerable in the grave, what if God doesn't raise him? The Son trusts his Father, but what if he's wrong? The stakes are high: if Dad doesn't pull through, he's lost forever. This starts to sound similar to a question we explored earlier: *Could Jesus have sinned?* There the question was whether the Son could rebel against the Father. Here, the question is whether the Father could forsake the Son.

Once again, it all depends on what we mean by *could*. If we're talking about the *external circumstances*, as in, does the Father have the *opportunity presented* to abandon the incarnate Son, then the answer, of course, is yes. Jesus truly lies in the grave, and the Father is not forced by fate, compelled by creation, or manipulated by some force outside him to pull through.

But if we're talking about his *internal orientation*, as in, *would* the Father abandon the incarnate Son in the grave, then the answer, of course, is no. The Father is *for* his Son, *loves* his Son, *delights in* his Son—and will be faithful to him. God is not coerced from the outside but compelled from the inside, by his eternal affection, his faithful, unshakable character, his very divine nature—the Father is compelled by love.

And the same is true of the Spirit. We've focused on the Father and Son, but the Spirit is just as important—the whole Trinity is involved in this rescue operation.[1] The Father raises Jesus *through the power of the Spirit.*[2] And the Spirit is not coerced from the outside but compelled from the inside, by love. While the external opportunity is there to abandon, the Spirit will be faithful to raise Jesus, because the Spirit *is* holy, faithful, personal, unshakable love.

The persons of the Trinity are all on the same team.

SAME TEAM

Let's flesh this out with an analogy. Say a family is trapped in a forest fire, so a helicopter team undertakes a rescue. One fireman flies the helicopter over the smoky blaze to coordinate the operation and see the big picture. A second fireman descends on a rope into the billowing smoke below to track down the family and stand with them. Once he locates the family, he wraps the rope around them, attaching them to himself, and they are lifted up together from the blaze into safety.

In this rescue operation the first fireman looks like the Father, who can see the whole field unclouded from above to sovereignly orchestrate the plan. The second fireman looks like the Son, who descends into our world ablaze to find us, the human family, and identify with us most deeply in the darkness of the grave. The Spirit is like the rope, who mediates the presence of the Father to

Jesus, even in his distance, and raises Jesus—and the human family with him—from sin, death, and the grave, into the presence of the Father.

Of course, like all analogies, this one falls short. The Spirit is a person, not a *thing* (like the rope). And the Father, Son, and Spirit are not separate individuals but *the one God*, sharing a divine nature and essence as one being. Yet the point of the analogy is this: the rescue mission requires the interdependent action of all three persons. Each has a distinct and necessary role. And yet, zooming out, they are undertaking one united, joint action: the rescue of the human family. We miss what is happening if we pit Jesus against God, or God against Jesus. The Father, Son, and Spirit are working together at the cross, of one will and nature, in a united, joint action for the redemption of the world.

The cross is a triune act.

COMPELLED BY LOVE

Historically, the church has sought to safeguard this with a "covenant of redemption." The idea here is that before the creation of the world, the Father, Son, and Spirit enter into a covenant, or agreement, together on the plan of redemption, the rescue operation to bring us home. They're not caught off guard by our insurrection, wringing their hands and saying, "Oh no! What are we going to do now?" They anticipate our rebellion and, in triune love, are sovereignly for us from the beginning.

Jesus "was chosen before the creation of the world," to be the Lamb "slain from the foundation of the world." The Father "chose us in him before the creation of the world," through the Spirit, "who raised Jesus from the dead [and is now] living in you."[3] God creates the world knowing we'll set it ablaze, and dives in of his own accord. The Father, Son, and Spirit are well aware of the destruction we'll unleash, yet are for us from the beginning.

Speaking of this as a covenant, however, can run a danger: it can start to sound like a modern contract. The church has recognized three problems with this. First, a contract works by imposing consequences to keep unruly behavior in check ("I'll keep my side of the bargain if you keep yours! If not, I'll come repo your car.") The whole reason you enter a contract is you're worried your partner might not keep up to the deal, so you impose fines and penalties to keep him or her on the straight and narrow.

But there's no worry about this with God. They—Father, Son, and Spirit—are faithful because they *want* to be, not because they *have* to be. The Father is not pressured lest some heavenly furniture get repossessed. Jesus endures the cross "for the joy set before him," not because he's afraid he'll get fined otherwise.[4] And the Spirit doesn't need to be reminded about a piece of paper signed before the creation of the world. They're not coerced from the outside in; they're compelled from the inside out by their very nature and will as one God.

Compelled by love.

MORE THAN A CONTRACT

Second, a contract is often made between unequal parties. When a citizen signs on the dotted line with the king, a homeowner hires a contractor, or a person takes out a loan with a bank, there's a power imbalance at play, an inequality in what each person brings to the table.

But the Father, Son, and Spirit are equal. The Father is not coercing the Son: *"Go die for those rebels, whether you like it or not!"* The Son is not manipulating the Father: *"But please, Dad, just let me go save my friends!"* And the Spirit is not an innocent bystander caught up in someone else's agenda: *"What did I miss? What's going on here? What did you sign me up for?!"*

They enter this rescue plan together. In the words of Jonathan Edwards, it was an "agreement which the persons of the Trinity came into from eternity as it were by mutual consultation and covenant."[5] The Son and Spirit do not grudgingly submit to a Father forcing his hand like a stubborn general. Rather, they freely undertake our redemption. In the words of Amy Plantinga Pauw, an Edwards scholar,

> In the covenant transactions, the Father does not arrogate power for himself . . . Edwards did not portray the covenant as "a commandment from the Father to the Son, which he must submit to, and obey" . . . instead, consonant with his authority . . . [the Father] is appointed by the Son and Spirit to act as head in the plan of redemption as well. Nor are the Son and Holy Spirit compelled by the Father into subordinate roles . . . The Son and Spirit undertake their roles as agreed upon in the economy, and as a fitting reflection of their order of subsistence in the Trinity.[6]

They are compelled in unison as one God by love. They are, in the famous words of the Three Musketeers, "one for all, all for one."[7]

A third and final danger is this: contracts are entered into by individuals. But the Father, Son, and Spirit are not separate people meeting up at the local car dealership to sign a slip of paper together, then returning to their own homes. They *are* the one God. This is the famous theologian Karl Barth's critique:

> Can we really think of the first and second persons of the triune Godhead as two divine subjects and therefore as two legal subjects who can have dealings and enter into obligations one with another? This is mythology, for which there is no place in a right understanding of the doctrine of the Trinity.[8]

This gets us into the mystery of the Trinity, which we'll look at more later in this book, where the beauty of God's love is most clearly seen. But for now we can say this: while the language of *covenant* is helpful to highlight that the Father, Son, and Spirit are on the same team—not pitted against one another—the Trinity points us to something deeper: it is their personal union *within* their very life as God, their divine nature, not something external *outside* their life as God, that compels them in faithful love to undertake the salvation of the world.

CHAPTER 18

Destroy This Temple

If Israel was a corporation, the temple was her Wall Street headquarters—the pinnacle of her national body. Jesus stood in the temple courts and declared, "Destroy this temple, and I will raise it again in three days." *Yeah, right*, his listeners laughed. They rightly found this absurd: "It has taken forty-six years to build this temple, and you are going to raise it in three days?" But they missed something important, John tells us.

"The temple he had spoken of was his body."[1]

JESUS IS THE TEMPLE

Why did Jesus identify himself with the temple? The temple was the center of the people of God, the "hot spot" of God's presence, like Jesus, where the Creator dwelt most intimately in creation. We tend to think of it as tiny, like a regular building, but it was massive, taking up around a quarter of the city of Jerusalem. We tend to think of it as a religious site, but its significance was like Wall Street, Times Square, and the White House all rolled into one—the hub of Israel's political, economic, and social existence.[2]

The temple was the center of the kingdom.

And of the nations. Israel sat at the crossroads of the mighty empires, at the intersection of the trade routes between ancient powerhouses such as Egypt, Babylon, Assyria, and Rome. They traveled through her to get to one another. God placed Israel there to be a "light for the nations," a "kingdom of priests," living a life that displayed God as King to her neighbors.[3] And the temple was her headquarters.

Israel saw the temple as something like the umbilical cord of the world. God resided there as King, and from there his kingdom was mediated to the nations. This was where the Creator made his home in creation, and from which his presence extended to the earth. If Israel was at the center of the nations, the temple was at the center of Israel. So to attack the temple was to attack the world. Which is why Jesus got in so much trouble when he did.

CLEANSING OR DESTRUCTION?

When Jesus says, "Destroy this temple," he's just attacked the temple.[4] It's the famous scene where Jesus makes a whip, turns over tables, and drives everyone away. What's going on here? Jesus' actions are often referred to as the *cleansing* of the temple, but they're actually about its *destruction*. Let me explain.

When people say *cleansing*, they often think Jesus was upset because he didn't like things being sold in the house of God, "so get that bookstore out of the church lobby!" But the temple courts were *supposed to* have things for sale.[5] Jesus may have been angry at greedy vendors overcharging to exploit the "tourist trap," but this was not the primary issue.

Jesus' audience would have seen his actions as an *attack* on the temple, a prophetic foreshadowing of its coming destruction. In the Old Testament, prophets often gave dramatic performances as a visual sign of impending disaster. Ezekiel lay on his side 430 days and ate food cooked over dung to symbolize the coming captivity.[6] Isaiah walks around naked to depict Assyria leading captives away stripped and shamed.[7] Jeremiah smashes a clay jar before a crowd outside Jerusalem's walls to portray the city's coming destruction.[8]

Similarly, Jesus' actions are a prophetic sign of coming destruction.

God's coming judgment on the temple was a significant part of Jesus' message: because the people rejected God's messengers, killed the prophets, and ultimately would reject him, the Father's Son, the temple would be destroyed by the pagan powers and its people scattered among the nations.[9] Jesus regularly prophesied against the temple. In the vicinity of Jerusalem, he cursed a fig tree as a sign of the city's coming destruction for failing to bear fruit;

then he told his followers that if they had faith, they could simply speak the word and "this mountain," the Temple Mount they were approaching, would be "thrown into the sea," a metaphor for its coming destruction.[10]

In AD 70, Jesus' dire warnings came true. The Romans sacked Jerusalem, demolished the temple to rubble, and destroyed Judaism as it was then known. Within a generation of Jesus' death, the center of Israel's national life was gone, the temple destroyed. It's hard to overemphasize how significant this event was for Israel: the sacrificial system was brought to an end, her epicenter obliterated, and her national life as she knew it altered dramatically forever.

When Jesus turned over tables and drove people out of the holiest place in town, his audience would have seen this as a prophetic attack on the temple, a signpost of its coming destruction—and they would have looked back later in their generation to see that he was right.

Jesus is not picking up a bottle of Formula 409 to clean up the temple. He's grabbing a sledgehammer to tear it down.

NEW TEMPLE

Jesus fulfills the temple. He is where the Creator makes his home in creation, where the King resides at the center of the kingdom, where God's presence most intimately dwells—the umbilical cord that brings life to the earth. When Jesus stands in the sanctuary courts and declares, "Destroy this temple," he's speaking about the temple of his body—and he's about to be destroyed.[11]

Jesus' death *pre*-capitulates the destruction of the temple.[12] When the Roman soldiers lash Jesus' back, they are tearing God's dwelling place down, brick by brick. As the executioners hammer nails through his flesh, they are swinging a sledgehammer through the temple's sanctuary walls. When the centurion thrusts his imperial spear into Jesus' side, it is the final blow that crashes through the Most Holy Place and brings it to an end.

When Jesus breathes his last, the curtain of the Most Holy Place is torn from top to bottom, signaling God's bringing of the temple to an end.[13] The glory has departed. Jesus embodies the coming disaster he's foretold and draws the tragedy into himself. *"Tear it down,"* he says. "I will raise it again in three days."[14] Jesus is taking down the corporation, receiving in himself the demolition of the temple, bearing in his body the destruction of Israel and of Adam, in order to raise us to new life through him as the new temple, the fulfilled Israel, and the second Adam.

God raises Jesus as the temple rebuilt, the head of humanity, and the center of creation that brings life to the world. We have something better than a building of brick and stone to care for today; we have Jesus—the new temple—the place where God's presence most intimately dwells. In the new heavens and new earth, we're told the temple is no longer needed, "because the Lord God Almighty and the Lamb are its temple."[15] When the presence of God floods the world as the waters cover the sea, we'll look up to discover:

God's dwelling place is now among the people, and he will dwell with them. They will be his people, and God himself will be with them and be their God.[16]

In Jesus, the purpose of the temple has been fulfilled. God's home is with us.

CHAPTER 19

Dead Meat

J esus is more than just the temple. He is also the sacrifice. And
have you read the Old Testament lately? Why is there so much
dead meat everywhere? A quick look at Israel's sacrificial system can
make one wonder whether all those animal carcasses point to a bloodthirsty God who needs his pound of flesh in order to be satisfied. Is
God a malevolent carnivore with an insatiable taste for fresh meat?

Sacrifice seems barbaric today, so many people struggle to see
how it can point us constructively to Jesus' work on the cross. It
seems to revolve around our pursuit of God, not God's pursuit of
us. For example, if you ask folks how sacrifice works, I've found
you'll often hear something like this:

HOW TO SACRIFICE 101

If you mess up and make a mistake, God gets angry, runs
away, and hides in the universe somewhere. So:

1. Get your act together, pick up a sheep, and plug your way along to the temple.
2. Offer God an apology. When he sees you slit the lamb's throat, he'll realize you're really sorry. (*"Good, Joshua finally gets how bad he's really been!"*)
3. Wait while God's petulant rage cools down. Hopefully, your sacrifice will be enough to appease the distant Creator.

If you're lucky, God will come close and be with you again.

This sounds like us trying to find God, not God trying to find us, right? I would suggest, however, that we have it backward. Israel's sacrificial system was never about a God we must run after to earn his love, but a God who runs after us with sacrificial love; not about our cleaning ourselves up before God, but God cleansing us. Let's take a closer look.

THE CENTER OF A CELEBRATION

We don't sacrifice today. This sounds like a simple observation, but we're separated from the ancient world by centuries—this is a major reason sacrifice seems so weird to us. But *everyone* sacrificed back then. So let's clear some tumbleweed from the trail of history to get a clearer picture.

Back in the day, sacrifice was universal. From Egypt to Rome, China to the Americas, and giant civilizations to nomadic indigenous peoples—it was a staple of ancient life. In fact, on the historical scene we *today* are the oddballs.

Sacrificial animals were often at the center of a community celebration. Far from devaluing the animal, this often added a sacred significance. I think I got a sense of this once, attending an indigenous ceremony in which the elder offered a public prayer of gratefulness to the Creator for the sheep that was about to provide the community meal. Laying her hands on the lamb's head, she offered words of thanks and recognition that life is received from life given. The ceremony seemed to say, "Life is gift."

And the proper response is gratitude.

Then they ate the meat. This may seem too obvious to mention, but many seem under the impression that animals were just killed for the gods and then tossed in the trash. For Israel, the sacrificial system went a long way toward feeding the priestly tribe and providing for community celebrations. The irony is that throwing unused food in the trash is way more indicative of the modern West than the ancient world.

We still kill animals today, though most often without the recognition of life given or gratefulness. We are disconnected from the process. We get our meat shrink-wrapped in plastic and Styrofoam at Costco, cut into perfect proportions, sanitized, and clean. And we definitely don't treat their lives as sacred: we crowd our animals into jam-packed stalls far from the open fields, standing in their excrement, unable to move, and stuff them full of antibiotics to deal with the disease that floods their unlivable conditions.

We should be wary before too quickly pointing a finger at the ancient world; we may find a much larger mirror pointing right back at us. Our culture hasn't stopped killing animals; we've stopped remembering that life is sacred. We haven't lost the dead meat, simply the awareness that life is gift.

LIFE IS GIFT

And life *is* gift. We are not autonomous creatures; we must receive life to live. The Creator has inscribed this truth in the nature of our world. Even if one is a vegetarian, the head of grain must be beheaded from its stalk, the plant uprooted from its nurturing soil, the fruit plucked from its sustaining branch. The most honest way to receive life is to acknowledge that it is given. Our lives are not earned but received; our breath is upheld by gift.

When we deny this, we cut against the grain of the universe.

We are not our own; we belong to the creation that sustains us—and ultimately to the Creator from whom it has come. One wonders whether the *loss* of such ceremony has contributed to the Western world's exaltation of the autonomous individual *over* the world—no longer seeing ourselves within the Creator's interdependent web of creation, leaving us freer to exploit and consume regardless of ecological consequence.

For Israel, many of her sacrifices were simply ways of saying, "Thank you" and "I'm sorry."[1] For example, in Leviticus 1–7, the grain and fellowship offerings were ways of saying *thank you*, while the sin, guilt, and burnt offerings were ways of saying *I'm sorry*—and saying this together as a people to God. The food wasn't thrown away but rather provided for the Levites (the tribe of priests), and for the national celebrations (think of the biggest neighborhood block barbecue you've ever seen) with one another and God.

Community formation was in view—to be a people inscribed with humility and gratefulness before their Creator.

ISRAEL WAS UNIQUE

So far we've looked at some overarching themes, but Israel was unique from her neighbors in important ways. In the surrounding empires, the gods were often seen as violent and capricious, so sacrifice was a way to appease them—to get them to bless your crops, make you virile, and beat your enemies.

Israel, however, approached things differently. To them, sacrifice was not something you did to get favors from God; it was the way you entered into the favor God already had for you. And Israel got rid of the debauchery—or at least was supposed to. Ancient idol worship was filled with orgies, hedonism, and child sacrifice. Temple prostitution was common. Violent practices mirrored the brutality of the gods being appeased. Babylon's creation story, for example, had one god slicing another in half like a fish, then making heaven and earth from the two bloody filets—creation was a product of violence and sheer power.

Ritual practices could celebrate and continue this narrative.

For Israel, however, creation was gift. The Creator brings forth creation in love, and it is to be received and celebrated as such. There was a different underlying story at work. In place of gratuitous violence and hedonistic debauchery, Israel's practices were ordered toward loving submission under the Creator's life-giving reign.

THE END OF SACRIFICE

Another observation: Jesus is the reason we don't sacrifice today. This should probably be obvious, but many today don't seem to recognize that the first civilization in history to bring an end to sacrifice was the Roman Empire—and the reason was Christianity.

The gospel spread throughout the empire, and with the rise of the church came the downfall of the public altars. In the fourth century, as Constantine put an end to the sacrificial slaughter of Christians in the arena and stopped gladiatorial combat, he also removed the requirement of sacrificing to the gods to serve high-ranking positions in the empire, and he eventually outlawed civic sacrifice altogether.

What is shocking is that this was the first time sacrifice was removed from a major civilization, and it rippled out through the centuries into the world as we know it. If the White House were to open a summit with sacrifice today, the news outlets would be shocked and the public enraged. But this was the historical norm. As Peter Leithart observes:

> Constantine's reign marked the beginning of the end of sacrifice. . . . A desacrificed civilization has become so commonplace that we think it is the natural order of things. . . . Historically speaking, though, *we* are the aberrations. For millennia every empire, every city, every nation and tribe was organized around sacrifice. Every polity has been a sacrificial polity. We are not, and we have Constantine to thank for that.[2]

Christendom became the first civilization in history to abolish sacrifice. So the next time someone asks you why we no longer offer dead meat to the gods, you can explain it's not because we became more enlightened or rational or less encumbered by superstition.

It's because of Jesus.

Christianity's logic, however, was not that sacrifice was *bad*, but rather that it was *no longer needed.* The early church did not say, "What a horrible mistake! Thank goodness Jesus finally arrived to set us straight." They said, rather, "Jesus has provided the once-for-all sacrifice that sets our world aright." They did not point back at Israel and say, "Whoa, what a massive blunder all those lambs were!" They pointed instead at Jesus and declared:

> Behold, the Lamb of God
> who takes away the sin of the world![3]

How did Jesus take away the sin of the world? Let's move to the next chapter, where we'll take a closer look at the Old Testament sacrificial system and see how Jesus fulfilled it.

CHAPTER 20

The God Who Walks Alone

In the ancient Middle East, when two political parties were making an agreement, one important purpose of sacrifice was "sealing the deal." It was kind of like signing a contract. Let's say Great King Joe is negotiating with Little King Ben, saying, "I'll protect your people and land from invasion." Little King Ben responds, "Great! I'll pay taxes and send men to join your military." Great King Joe smiles. "Ladies and gentlemen," he says, "we have a deal!"

To seal the deal, they sacrifice an animal and share the meal together, formalizing the covenant and celebrating their relationship with one another. All is official now.

SEALING THE DEAL

This is the picture in Genesis 15, an important passage where God formalizes his covenant with Abraham. God is the Great King and Abraham the Little King. God has promised Abraham he'll bless him, make his grandkids into a great nation, and through them will bless and restore the world.[1] Abraham, however, still doesn't have any kiddos and is getting old—so he's understandably a bit concerned. Great King God understands his fears but confirms his promise.

And Little King Abraham believes.

As a sign of his faithfulness, God has Abraham bring some animals for a covenant ceremony. Abraham cuts the animals in half and lays the halves opposite each other to make a pathway between them. This may sound weird to us, but was common practice back then: the two parties would walk through the pathway together between the animals as a way of saying, "If I don't keep up my end of the bargain, may I get sliced up like these animals!" With Abraham, however, something strange happens next.

God walks through the animals alone.

Great King God takes a stroll on the covenant pathway by himself. The significance? God takes on sole responsibility for his commitment to Abraham's family. If Israel messes things up, makes a blunder of the relationship, and fails the covenant, Great King God says, "May I get sliced up like these animals if I still don't keep my word."

God will be faithful to his end of the deal, even if Israel is not to hers.

Can you imagine going to a car dealership to purchase a brand-new Ferrari, watching the papers drawn up to declare you the proud new owner of this fancy car—only when you go to sign, there's no dotted line for you at the bottom? The only dotted line is already signed—by the president of Ferrari. You're invited to contribute the payments and participate in the deal, but even if you don't, he'll incur the debt. The sole weight of responsibility for this hot rod remaining yours rests solely on the president being faithful to stand by his word.

A FOUNDATION STORY

Okay, why is this significant? This is a foundation story. Abraham's covenant is not just random; it occurs at the beginning of Israel's history and sets a paradigm for what's to come. This passage's language and imagery get picked up later in the Old Testament, laying a foundation for the temple, the priests, and the sacrificial system. Why did Israel sacrifice? One significant reason was to commemorate the covenant; that is, to celebrate God's commitment to their community.

Abraham is not pursuing God in this scene; God is pursuing Abraham—and through him, the world. The sacrifice does not signify Abraham's faithfulness to God; it proclaims the opposite: God's faithfulness to Abraham. It is not something Abraham uses to show God he's serious about their relationship; it's something God uses to show Abraham *he's* serious about their relationship.

For Israel, when the people brought their animals to the temple, they were not "sealing the deal" with God, but rather, celebrating the God who sealed the deal with them. Like Abraham their ancient ancestor, they split the animals before their Great King, who walks alone through the animals for them.

While the sacrificial system did many things, an important one was this: it reminded Israel that God was *for* them with an unwavering commitment. That however unfaithful they might be, God was going to be faithful to keep the vows he made to his bride.

And after? They feasted together in celebration. Following

Abraham's ceremony, God passed through the animals as a "smoking firepot with a blazing torch,"[2] preparing the animals for a feast. Great King God cooks a meal for Little King Abraham, and upon their sealed deal they sit down together to celebrate their shared hope for the setting right of the world.

THE BLOOD OF THE COVENANT

We're invited to a similar feast today. While we don't kill animals in our church services, we celebrate the death and resurrection of Jesus, feasting on the bread of his body and the wine of his blood. On the night he was betrayed, Jesus declared, "This cup is the new covenant in my blood, which is poured out for you."[3] Did you catch that word *covenant*? Jesus is making a new covenant, like Abraham's covenant so long ago. Great King Jesus is sealing the deal with us, his little people, not with the blood of animals but with his very own life, as he prepares to go to the cross.

In Christ, God is about to walk the path alone.

Jesus tears the bread in half as a sign of his broken body, and pours the wine as a sign of his life poured out. And he says, "Do this in remembrance of me."[4] When we tear the bread and pour the wine, we don't do it to show God how serious we are about him. We do it to be shocked afresh at how serious God is about us. We don't prepare the table to *give* something to God; we prepare it to *receive* life from God. We don't *create* the reality of the Eucharist; we *enter* the reality of the Eucharist.

We acknowledge: our life is received from his life given.

The word *Eucharist* means, literally, "to give thanks." In the early church, it was a celebration of Christ, who bore our death and brought us life. We come not only to a table prepared *by* Jesus, but to feast *upon* Jesus, to receive his life that forms us as a people. We come to encounter the living Christ, who conquered death on our behalf. And as we do, he forms us as a community marked by humility and gratefulness.

When I receive Communion, I love breaking a *big* chunk off the bread. As my teeth tear it apart, fracturing its wholeness into tiny scraps of what it once was, I encounter afresh how Christ was torn asunder in love for me. And as I drink a massive gulp from the chalice, swallowing its intoxicating waves deep into my parched and thirsty bones, I soak in the immense weight of his love poured out to bring me life.

I'm not taking Communion to show Jesus I'll be faithful to him; I'm celebrating the fact that Jesus is faithful to me. Jesus invites us to *drink deeply* from his life and to feast together upon his love, for it is he who makes us whole.

CHAPTER 21

Soaking Up Death

In this chapter we will look at sacrifice from one more angle.

Sacrifice is not something we use to clean ourselves up so God can stand to be with us again. On the contrary, sacrifice is something God uses to cleanse *us*, so that *we* can stand to be in *his* presence again. There's a famous scene in Isaiah that beautifully illustrates this.

Isaiah has a vision of God's throne room, from which God's reign radiated out to the ends of the earth. Isaiah sees God, the King of Creation, exalted high on his heavenly throne with his feet crashing down upon the earth in the Most Holy Place.[1] The foundations of the temple shake, God's robe floods the temple, and angels cry out:

> *Holy, holy, holy is the LORD Almighty;*
> *the whole earth is full of his glory.*[2]

Isaiah cries out, "Woe to me! I am ruined! For I am a man of unclean lips, and I live among a people of unclean lips, and my eyes have seen the King, the LORD Almighty."[3] Like an astronaut standing in the presence of the sun, Isaiah stands before the Creator of the universe—not from a distance but right up close—and is about to get blown away by the glory.

HOLEY SPACE SUITS

Okay, two observations. First, God is holy, as the angel song reminds us. But what does this mean? Some people think of holiness as "self-righteousness," like an uptight do-gooder looking down her stuck-up nose at all the filthy sinners polluting the air around her. But it actually means unique, dedicated to, set apart. Think of it like the sun: it's set apart in our solar system, unique; there's nothing like it. The sun does not need us to exist, but we need the sun to exist. The sun is powerful and radiant, and this radiant power is great from a distance, bringing life to our world, but get too close and you'd better have the right space suit on.

You could say the sun is holy.[4]

Similarly, God is unique. As Creator, he is distinct from creation. God is powerful and radiant, bringing light and life to our world. God does not need us to exist, but we cannot exist without God. God's character is true, pure, and good—and unfailingly so.

The sun analogy falls short, however, in an important respect: we were not made to live on the sun, but we *were* made to live in the immediate presence of our Creator. Our bodies are like space suits designed for the sun—we were made to dwell immersed in God's glory. "The chief end of man," as the Westminster Catechism reminds us, "is to glorify God and enjoy him forever." But our rebellion has torn the fabric, letting the cold, dark matter into our lives that leads to death.

Sin punches a hole in the space suit of our lives.

Our bodies are not the problem; sin is. To stand in the immediate presence of God in this condition is like waltzing too close to the sun in a ripped suit. This is why God warns people not to get too close to his immediate presence when they're not in the right condition. It's not that God's afraid of getting tainted, but that we can't stand the heat of potent divinity in our corrupted bodies.

God pursues Moses in the burning bush, but warns him, "Don't come any closer."[5] God gives the priests instructions to protect them from approaching in the wrong state. God's not worried that he'll be affected, but that we will—because sin can't stand to be in the presence of God. So like Adam and Eve's banishment from Eden to protect them in their corrupted state, God has us keep a certain distance from his immediate presence to protect us until our bodies are made fit for glory and restored in his kingdom.

RADIOACTIVE CLEANUP

This brings us to our second observation: Isaiah says he is "unclean." This is sacrificial language. In Leviticus, the sacrificial system is set up to deal with two types of *uncleanness*, or *impurity*. The first kind is *ritual* impurity: you could become ritually impure by touching dead bodies or being in contact with things such as mold, skin disease, or bodily fluids.[6]

This didn't mean you'd sinned or done something morally wrong, per se—it's not as though you killed someone or robbed a bank. We tend to think of spiritual impurity coming from doing bad things, but with ritual impurity something different was going on. The problem was, rather, being in contact with things associated with *death*. They could transfer their contamination to you because, unfortunately, death spreads.

In an age of disease and bacteria, ritual purity promoted health and community hygiene for ancient Israel. And it also gave an overwhelming sense that the Creator is a God of life, with an awareness that death and disruption are connected to our distance from him. As my friend Gerry likes to say, waltzing into the presence of God while ritually impure was something like me coming home from playing basketball a sweaty mess and trying to hug my wife. She plugs her nose and says, "You stinketh! Go take a shower." I haven't necessarily done something wrong, but I'm not in a good state for hugging my wife.

For Israel, you could go on with your life while ritually impure and follow God; you just couldn't "hug" God—entering the spaces of his intimate presence in the temple. If you're going to get right up in God's orbit, you needed to get clean first, with something to soak up the corruption off you like a sponge. So you'd wait a day, take a bath, then offer a sacrifice to absorb any remnant "death state" on you.

Ritually clean, you could stand again in the life-giving presence of God.

The second kind of uncleanness was *moral* impurity. A later section of Leviticus outlined violations against social justice, sexual integrity, and healthy relationships that would make one morally unclean. Such willful rebellion was, of course, the means by which death had entered the painting in the first place, the crack in the world through which corruption had invaded and infested the masterpiece.

So both *moral* impurity and *ritual* impurity had this in common: they were associated with death. And like darkness in the face of the sun, death could not live in the presence of God. In Leviticus, the sacrificial animals are like wool sponges: they absorb the "death" we're afflicted by and the "death" we unleash. The Creator grabs the wool sponge and scrubs off our death state, to soak up the junk in our lives and wash us clean—making us fit for life.

I've heard people compare God's presence to radioactivity, saying, "Don't get too close because it can kill you." But I think this gets it backward: God is not like radioactivity; *sin* is. Sin is the deadly force running amok in the masterpiece, the dangerous corruption in God's good world. We were *made* to dwell in the presence of our Creator. But God's life, light, and love are so strong that death and its toxic allies cannot stand in his presence.

So we can't just go whistling Dixie into the presence of life, light, and love while covered in radioactivity—we'll get blown away. Not because God is *against* life, but because of the dynamically vigorous extent to which God *is* life. God's radiance destroys radioactivity.

Notice with Isaiah how God's glorious goodness drives the scene. Isaiah doesn't say, "Oh no! God's really big and mean; I hope *he* doesn't beat me up." He says, "Woe is me! *I'm* unclean." The light of God's goodness reveals Isaiah's darkness. The purity of God's presence reveals Isaiah's uncleanness. The power of God's beauty unveils the wickedness in his people.

Isaiah is not afraid because God has a dark side, but because in God's presence the prophet sees more clearly that *we* do. Luckily, God is ready and waiting to wash us clean.

A BABY BATH

This brings us to the climax of Isaiah's encounter with God. An angel takes a burning coal from the altar, touches Isaiah's mouth with it, and declares, "See, this has touched your lips; your guilt is taken away and your sin atoned for."[7]

Okay, this is weird: an angel with a burning coal from an altar? What is going on here? This imagery also comes from the temple's sacrificial system. The curtains and sanctuary of the Most Holy Place were decorated with angels like these—not chubby little babies with wings, but powerful ministers of God who stood before his presence.[8] Just outside the Most Holy Place was an altar where sacrifices were made.

The coal taken from the altar is burning—a sign that a sacrifice has just been offered. The coal touches Isaiah's lips and, like a fresh burst of water washing through his soul, he is cleansed. Here's the important observation I want to draw our attention to: Isaiah is not using sacrifice to clean himself up so God can stand to be with him; rather, God is cleansing *Isaiah*—so that Isaiah can stand to be with God.

God is like a mother washing us babies in the bathtub. Sacrifice is not something we use to tidy ourselves up before a high-maintenance, distant deity. Rather, our Creator draws close and wraps us in his arms, soaking up the radioactive death that clings tight against our skin, and washing our beloved bodies clean.

Through Jesus' sacrifice, God washes us clean. Jesus is like Windex: he cleans the gunk off the window of our hearts so we can see our Father clearly again. He is also like a hazmat suit: he protects us from the radioactive gunk that would put us in a "death state." And finally, Jesus is like a shower: his holiness and righteousness wash us clean. Jesus fills in the holes we've punctured in our space suits so we can bask again in the life-giving radiance of God, and reflect that presence to the world.

Jesus takes our impurity upon himself to atone for it, and transfers his purity to us.

Jesus uses his sacrifice to cleanse us and make us whole.

KEY IDEA

Caricature: Sacrifice is how you clean yourself up so God can stand to be with you.

Gospel: Sacrifice is how God cleans you so you can stand to be with God.

CHAPTER 22

Fish on the Dock

We've looked at sacrifice; now let's look at wrath. I've found that one of the biggest topics some people struggle with is wrath. For example, there's a popular worship song that says, "Till on that cross as Jesus died / The wrath of God was satisfied."[1] Some have told me they can't sing this line in good conscience. *See?! God's beating up his Son. How is that loving?* Some popular voices have even called this a "monster God."

Against the caricature of a monster God, I want to share some insights that have helped me over the years. I believe the church is right to have historically held that divine wrath is involved on the cross, but what does this mean? Why does God get angry, and could he have just used some anger management classes instead? Was Jesus mistaken to call this Father good?

Let's take a closer look at how wrath arises *from* the love of God, rather than in contradiction to it—and is involved in the cross of Christ.

OUT OF WATER

Someone once challenged me with this example: Say there's a fish swimming in the water, and it decides to jump out of the water onto the dock. The fish is made to live in the water, of course, not on dry land—so it starts to flop around uncomfortably on the dock. Now, here's the question: Is the fish experiencing a *natural consequence* of its behavior, or is someone *punishing* it?

"Of course," we would all say, "a natural consequence."

Flopping around is not a penalty inflicted by someone else, but simply the expected outcome for jumping out of the water. A punishment, my friend continued, would be something like a person walking up on the dock with a stick and beating on the fish, shouting, "What are you doing out here? Get back in the water!"

His point was this: sin brings its own consequence. Distance from God leads to flopping on the dock. We see this in Scripture, so we should do away with wrath-and-punishment language, he suggested, because it makes God look mean. On the cross, Jesus experienced the *natural consequences* of our actions, he believed, not the wrath and punishment of God. Jesus was "flopping on the dock," so to speak, as he joined us in our distance from the Father, not "getting beat down by God with a stick."

I told him I understood the point he was making, but here's the thing: the fish flopping on dry land *is* a punishment. In the Hebrew worldview, take the guy with a stick out of the picture, and the fish wiggling uncomfortably on its own *is* a penalty. It is *both* a natural consequence *and* a divine punishment—at the same time. This can sound strange to our modern Western ears, so let's take a look at how this works.

INSCRIBED IN CREATION

The Creator designed the fish to live in the water. God ordered creation in such a way that the fish thrives in the lake and flops around on dry land. So when the fish rebels against its native environment, when it pushes back on its created purpose, it receives the due penalty encoded in God's ordering of the world.

From one angle, you could say the Creator has *handed the fish over* to the natural consequence of its action—by giving freedom and space to reject its created purpose. From another angle, however, you could simultaneously say the fish is receiving the *due punishment* inscribed in the created order by its Creator.

Now, fish generally don't have evil motives, and know their place is in the water—so let's turn the analogy back to us. There's an order to things: if I eat ice cream all day, I shouldn't be surprised when my body grows overweight and starts to break down. If I cheat on my wife, I shouldn't blame God when my kids are sad and my family falls apart. If I continually mistreat those around me and find myself lonely one day with no friends, it's nobody's fault but mine.

It's called getting what we deserve.

We experience natural consequences like fish out of water. I've loved watching *Mad Men* (which, sadly, ended recently), but the main character, Don Draper, is a train wreck in so many ways. He's a genius at his advertising job, but his lust for women, gluttony with alcohol, pride with work, and vanity in life leave him sad, broken, and alone at the end—with no one to blame but himself. He's an attractive fish, but he's flopping on the dock all the same.

And yet, these consequences are not disconnected from our

Creator. Things have been ordered toward justice by our loving heavenly Father. We're designed for "life, and . . . more abundantly,"[2] for *shalom*, or flourishing in right relationship, so we can thrive. Creation is a gift from a God who is *for* us. But what happens if we reject this right relationship? If we rebel against the Creator's ordering? If we tear at the fabric and rip at the flourishing of God's good world?

Throughout Scripture, God reminds his people that how we live matters—there are rewards and punishments, blessings and curses, compensation and consequences.[3] The Creator reminds us that swimming in the ocean of his good, loving, and just ways leads to thriving—this is the natural environment we were made for. But when we rebel against these ways, we're like fish jumping out of the water—leaving our intended environment and flopping around in the distance. There are good ways to live and not-so-good ways to live.

And the not-so-good ways can get you in trouble.

FLOPPING ON THE DOCK

Paul looks around in the Roman Empire of his day and observes:

> The wrath of God *is being revealed* from heaven against all the godlessness and wickedness of people. . . . God *gave them over* in the sinful desires of their hearts to sexual impurity. . . . God *gave them over* to shameful lusts. . . . God *gave them over* to a depraved mind.[4]

Notice how Paul's not saying here, "*If* you do these things, *then* God will eventually pour out his wrath on you." He says rather,

"*When* you do these things, God's wrath *is being* revealed against you." The emphasis here is not that the wrath of God *will one day* be revealed (though this shows up in other passages), but that it *is being revealed* today. And God's wrath shows up *in the very things* folks do.

Notice also how the phrase "gave them over" shows up three times, structuring the passage—after each one, Paul gives a laundry list of naughty behaviors we run after. God is giving the people what they want: distance from him. People are jumping out of the ocean of God's love into the dry and distant land of sin. When the fish gets its desire for dry land, its flopping around *is* the wrath of God. When Don Draper winds up isolated and miserable, he is receiving the due penalty for his pursuits.

God has an interesting way of showing his anger; he gives us what we want.

Thomas Aquinas, one of history's most famous theologians, observed how when we attack God's loving order, we unleash *injustice*, or disorder, into the way things are supposed to be. A husband's affair affects not only him but shoots a cannon into his marriage and family. Wall Street's bad loans impacted not only greedy bankers but threw a sledgehammer into the global economy. The BP oil spill not only hurt the company but wreaked havoc throughout the gulf. Sin lets loose ruin.

Think of the Artist in the painting image, with the dark decay we've unleashed in the painting. When creatures deface the masterpiece they're a part of, that they were called to steward, the destruction unleashed *is* punishment. Like ripples spreading out from the stone's splash in the water, sin ripples out, leaving devastation in its wake. The destruction we unleash infiltrates the created order, working its way through the painting and disrupting the harmony of the whole.

But sin also does something more. It impacts not only the world around us—it impacts *us*. For Aquinas:

> The order of creation is such that when we rebel against this
> order, we disorder ourselves, losing our interior order and justice
> to ourselves . . . When humans turn away from this divine love
> and refuse our debt of justice, humans lack the justice we were
> created to have, that is inscribed in the created order . . . the
> resulting *disorder* is itself a punishment.[5]

In other words, when we attack God's loving purposes for our world, it messes us up inside. When we reject the justice of his ways, we corrupt our character. We're like fish jumping out of the water we were made to live in, who wind up flopping around on the dock. This is why, for Aquinas, "sin itself then is *a* punishment—not the only punishment, but *a* punishment—of sin."[6]

So again, flopping on the dock is *both* a natural consequence *and* a divine punishment—at the same time. Part of the problem, perhaps, is that the phrase "natural consequence" is itself misleading. We tend to think of *nature* as something that exists independently of God. But the Creator gifts nature with its being, and sustains it with his very presence—so "natural" doesn't get us away from the Creator; it brings us before him.[7] The natural consequences we experience are mediated by God's sustaining presence in the creation we've disordered.

We start to see wrath in this picture not as God being mean, or vindictive, or as something opposed to God's holy love, but rather as an expression of God's holy love. Because God desires the goodness and flourishing of his world, wrath is the opposition of God's holy love to that sin which defaces and destroys his good creation, by trying to distance it from him. Like the prodigal son who squanders his inheritance in the distant land, our self-imposed distance from the Father *is* a punishment.

Because we were made for the ocean of God's love.

JESUS ON THE DOCK

So what about Jesus? Remember the Artist in the painting image, when the creator soaks the dark decay into himself like a sponge? This *is* an image of Jesus bearing wrath for sin. Jesus is taking upon himself our disorder, absorbing the destruction we've unleashed into creation, in all its immensity, in order to make us whole.

And while this disorder is the natural consequence of our collective sin, it is simultaneously something more—the punishment inscribed in creation for severing it from the Creator and desecrating the masterpiece. The dark, destructive decay *is* the wrath of God.

So when people hear *wrath* and envision God punching Jesus in the face on the cross (or to use the fish-on-the-dock imagery, the Father walking up on the pier with a stick and beating the snot out of his Son), we can see why this image is unhelpful. But our discussion thus far puts this question in a new light and helps us do justice to the biblical language: Jesus "flopping on the dock" *is* his bearing the wrath of God. No stick is necessary.

Jesus leaves his native environment swimming in the ocean of the Father's eternal love, to join us in our distance and "flop on the dock" in agony on the cross, being bound in union with us as our new head, to bear the deadly devastation we've merited in running from the God of goodness and life. Why?

To ultimately bring us diving back with him into the ocean of God's eternal love.

CHAPTER 23

Furious Love

In the last chapter, we began a discussion of a much-misunderstood term: *wrath*. This brings us to an important question: Is God *angry* at sin? The discussion thus far could sound mechanical, as if wrath is simply a cold calculus of cause and effect with no personality or emotion involved. And if God *does* get angry, what about love? Is God's wrath *opposed to* his love?

Miroslav Volf, a theologian and public intellectual, shares a powerful reflection that can help us get started. Living through the horror of the war in Yugoslavia, he reflects:

> I used to think that wrath was unworthy of God. Isn't God love? Shouldn't divine love be beyond wrath? God is love, and God loves every person and every creature. That's exactly why God is wrathful against some of them.
>
> My last resistance to the idea of God's wrath was a casualty of the war in former Yugoslavia, the region from which I come. According to some estimates, 200,000 people were killed and

over 3,000,000 were displaced. *My* villages and cities were destroyed, *my* people shelled day in and day out, some of them brutalized beyond imagination, and I could not imagine God not being angry.

Or think of Rwanda in the last decade of the past century, where 800,000 people were hacked to death in one hundred days! How did God react to the carnage? By doting on the perpetrators in a grandparently fashion? By refusing to condemn the bloodbath but instead affirming the perpetrators' basic goodness? Wasn't God fiercely angry with them?

Though I used to complain about the indecency of the idea of God's wrath, I came to think that I would have to rebel against a God who *wasn't* wrathful at the sight of the world's evil. God isn't wrathful in spite of being love. God is wrathful *because* God is love.[1]

THE MOTIVE IS LOVE

God gets angry *because* God loves. When a child is blown to bits in a shelled Croatian village, the Creator is furious. When a neighbor is hacked to death by a Rwandan machete, King Jesus is riled up in a rage. When we don't treat people as they ought to be treated—as objects of God's beloved affection—the Great Lover gets upset!

And God's anger is not just for genocidal war zones. It shows up much closer to home.[2] The heavenly Father was livid when our foster son's dad abandoned him and mom kept him hopped up on meth those first nine months in the womb. Jesus was up in arms when our friend had that affair and tore his family apart. And

God's angry at me when I hurt people he loves—which has been more often than I'd like to admit.

This highlights another problem with the caricature: Jesus gets angry too. Divine wrath belongs not only to the Father, but to the Son and Spirit as well. Because Jesus is God, and because Jesus is love, he gets rightly angry at our evil that tears apart his world.

Jesus' eyes are wide open to all the horror and tragedy we unleash in his beautiful world. As the popular slogan puts it, "If you're not angry, you're not paying attention." Well, God is paying attention. There's plenty of destruction in our world that *should* upset us. As D. E. H. Whiteley observes, "the opposite of love is not wrath but indifference."[3] Fortunately, God is not indifferent. But too often *we* are.

When we pay attention to the plight of our neighbors, taking our eyes off our own selfish pursuits, we should be moved by the hurt in our community, the injustice in our city, the devastation in our world. There's an unrighteous anger, but there's a righteous kind too. Righteous anger is helpful in motivating us to action.

And it is driven by love.

The real question is not why God would ever get angry enough to intervene, but why God waits so long. I've come to believe it has something to do with God being more patient than we are, and his patience with the destruction we unleash is itself a form of grace. But his patience will not last forever. When our sins have piled up to heaven, the reckoning day comes.

God walks down the pier with a stick and beats the fish.

I explored themes like this more in my last book, looking at God's *social judgment* in Old Testament holy war, New Testament governmental violence, and God's coming judgment on the empire of Babylon. We also looked at Jesus' images of God arriving as king to set fire to his rebel city, as father to boot the wedding crashers at his son's marriage, and as landlord to punish the tenants who've murdered his messengers and thrashed his vineyard.[4]

And all of these arise *from* God's goodness and love, not in spite of it.

Examples like these highlight another problem with the fish analogy: it's individualistic. One fish and a guy with a stick. It's a picture of "me and God," but in the biblical story, we're inherently social: there's *a bunch of* fish. Some fish are plucking other fish out of the water against their will, or preventing fish that are trying to jump back in from reaching the water. The wicked prosper and the righteous suffer. There's power dynamics: some are big king salmon using their power against little baby minnows. There's social dynamics: some are schools of fish in historical conflict with other schools of fish. There's moral dynamics: some fish learned they were made for the water; others were born on the dock.

The "me and God" story doesn't do justice to this complexity.

And this complexity is strongly at play when God gives the fish a beating—in the biblical story, the fish is often a society, or a stubborn fish in negative relation to other fish. As Swedish theologian Anders Nygren observed, "Only that love which pronounces judgment on all that is not love is in the truest sense restoring and saving love."[5] God's love is not a trite sound bite but an invasive mission to rescue, rebuff, and restore.

So even God's wrath as "beating the fish" arises from his love for the world, not in contradiction to it. Yet while I believe God's anger shows up like this at times, let's stick for now with the flopping-on-the-dock image, because I think there's more this still has to teach us about God's furious love.

TAKING IT PERSONAL

God is *personally involved* in his creation. God encourages his people, in places like Leviticus 26, to understand that if they swim in the ocean of his ways, they will thrive. But he also warns them, "If you reject my decrees and abhor my laws and fail to carry out all my commands," or in other words, if you jump out of the environment you were intended to live in, "then I will do this to you . . ."[6] God doesn't just say these natural consequences will unfold; he says:

> *I will do this to you.*

God refuses to depersonalize the consequences of sin. As Creator, he's established them, and through his ongoing providence holding creation together, he is involved in executing them. So we shouldn't minimize these judgments as just simple cause and effect—as if Jesus is a driving instructor who says, "If you drive off the side of the road, you'll get hurt," then proceeds to watch from the sidelines as a spectator. God, in essence, says, "If you stand against the flourishing of my world, *I myself will walk against you.*"

In the Leviticus 26 passage, God goes on to describe the curses that will come upon those who choose distance from God, making clear that they are ultimately about exile. If Israel stubbornly and persistently disobeys, God will "set his face against her" and the curses that will unravel involve enemies invading, cities being laid waste, and the land being devastated. The "curse of the law" is, ultimately, exile.

All creation is sustained *through Jesus* and *in the Spirit*, so it is *through Jesus* and *in the Spirit* that these judgments are enacted.

This should remind us of God's good character driving the scene. As Fredrick Buechner observes, when God pronounces curses,

> it seems less a matter of vindictively inflicting them with the consequences than of honestly confronting them with the consequences. Because of who they are and what they have done, this is the result.[7]

This honest confrontation is driven by God's love, but it is God doing the confronting.

So Israel was comfortable seeing events as both "we did this" and "God was punishing us." In 2 Kings 17, for example, Israel's king makes dumb choices that lead to Assyria's invasion, and the passage depicts the ensuing exile as a *natural consequence* of her bad foreign policy and foolish decision making. Yet the passage goes on to describe the same event from a different vantage point: God "was very angry with Israel" for her horrible behavior over the years, so through this event he "removed them from his presence," sending her into exile for her blatant, long-term, unrepentant sin.[8]

Exile was seen as both *natural consequence* and *divine punishment*—at the same time. Israel did not see these as contradictory; what's surprising is how comfortably and frequently this language shows up throughout Scripture. In the Hebrew worldview, there is a symmetry between our running *for* distance from God in rebellion, and the destruction that naturally unravels *in* our distance from God. The disorder we unleash in the world is itself an important aspect of the Creator's judgment.

This language of exile, curse, and wrath all works together. Since exile is "the curse of the law," to say Jesus bears our exile is, by its very nature, to say that he bore the curse of the law. As Paul declares, "Christ redeemed us from the curse of the law by becoming a curse for us."[9] Jesus bore Israel's exile as her king, and our exile as our Savior, exhausting the power of the curse and rising again to restore his people—and the world—through her.

DRINKING THE CUP

This context of exile helps us understand how Jesus sees himself as bearing the wrath of God. Throughout Jesus' ministry, he predicts he will be "rejected" and "delivered over to the . . . Gentiles," both Old Testament phrases for being handed over to the wrath of God.[10] When Israel continually rejected God, he finally turned the tables and "rejected" her, "handing her over to the Gentiles," whose gods she'd adopted and ways she'd chosen. Under the dark, destructive powers of exile's empires, she "drank the cup of God's wrath" as she flopped on the dock in her distance from him.

During Jesus' crucifixion, he is *mocked, forsaken*, and *darkness* hangs over the land, all Old Testament images for the wrath of God.[11] The simple fact that he dies is significant, for as New Testament lecturer Peter Bolt observes, "death itself is the manifestation of God's wrath."[12] And it's not only *that* Jesus dies, but *how* he dies—both Jews and Romans agreed that death by crucifixion was a sign of being under God's curse.[13] Israel's law declared, "Cursed is everyone who hangs on a tree."[14] Jesus bears the curse of the law under exilic wrath in order to redeem us from it.[15]

On the night before his crucifixion, Jesus prays whether "this cup" might be taken from him—*the cup* was a major Old Testament reference for "the cup of God's wrath."[16] Israel saw her exile as drinking this cup, but God's fury would not last forever—the cup would eventually be empty. When his anger subsided, the cup fully poured out, God would return for her and the end of exile would come. Isaiah held out hope for the day when God would say,

> Behold, I have taken from your hand
> the cup of staggering;
> the bowl of my wrath
> you shall drink no more.[17]

The end of exile would come. Israel would be reconciled to God.

Jesus sees himself as drinking this cup of divine wrath on the cross, bearing the weight of Israel's exile in his humanity in order to bring her home. Jesus is the head who drinks the cup that hangs over his body of people.

And he drinks it down to the dregs.

Jesus bears the curse of exilic wrath afflicting creation in its distance from the Creator. He soaks in the dark, destructive decay we've unleashed in the masterpiece, to the point that he *becomes* the curse he's absorbed as he carries it into the grave—to restore the masterpiece by flooding it with the presence of God.

CHAPTER 24

Unraveling Creation

I want to look at how Jesus absorbs not only our personal and social destruction, but our cosmic destruction as well. So here's a question to consider: Does God go a little overboard sometimes? Take Noah's flood, for example, or Egypt's empire getting crushed. These events are *massive* in scope, involving water, fire, and darkness. Some critics depict them as cosmic temper tantrums. They can definitely look at first glance as though God is "beating the fish" (see chapter 22), but upon closer inspection I would suggest Israel understood these events as being much more like "flopping on the dock."

Only in this case, creation is the fish.

CREATION AND CHAOS

When we push the world away from its Creator, it unravels. Let's start with Noah's flood. This story is intended to be read within the broader context of Genesis as a whole—this is how ancient Israel read her Bible. And if we go back a few chapters in Genesis, the waters have already made an appearance. In the beginning, God created the world out of a *dark, watery chaos* (called the *tohu va wohu* in Hebrew).[1] We go to the ocean today and say, "Oh! It's so beautiful," but the Israelites were afraid of the sea. The Hebrew tradition saw its tumultuous waters as dark, turbulent forces associated with primordial chaos.

Out of this chaos, the Creator brings forth space for life. One of God's first acts, in Genesis 1:6, is to "separate water from water": the picture here is God's powerful hands parting the turbulent forces, chiseling out space for the sky, making room for an atmosphere in which we can live and breathe.

God's first three acts of creation are similar; he *separates*: light from the darkness, sky from the waters above, and land from the waters below. God is carving out conditions for life with light (so we can see), sky (so we can breathe), and land (so we can live). While God carves out these life-giving spaces on the first three days, he then *fills them* on the next three days: with sun, moon, and stars (for the light); fish and birds (for the waters below and sky above); and animals and people (for the land). God *separates* space for life, then *fills* it with life.

The Creator is ordering creation, lovingly setting boundaries to keep the chaos at bay so that life can flourish within.

I know some people struggle with whether the Hebrews took this account literally or figuratively, and whether it's compatible with modern science and evolution. I believe it is compatible and, for those who want to pursue this further, I highly recommend John Walton's excellent book *The Lost World of Genesis One*.[2] But the point for our purposes here is simply this: when we get to the Flood, it is depicted as creation collapsing back in upon itself.

The boundaries are being broken.

The waters above are crashing back down upon the sky. The waters below are rising back up, as the land recedes beneath their surface. The light of day is swallowed by darkness. The spaces carved out for life are being invaded, the structure of creation collapsing, as the earth is dragged asunder, back into the *tohu va wohu*, the dark, watery abyss from which it came.

Creation descends into chaos.

DRAGGING DOWN THE SHIP

So is God causing the Flood, or are we? Once again, as we've seen throughout this book, we tend to approach this as an *either/or* question, but the Hebrew worldview is much more comfortable with a *both/and* answer. And once again, the temple and exile themes we've already explored can help us understand how.

Israel viewed creation as a cosmic temple, intended for God's indwelling presence.[3] Adam is depicted as its priest, called to "work" and "take care of" its garden. These words, *work* and *take care of*, are paired together in only one other place in the Bible, to describe the role of the priests in the temple.[4] Sacred gardens were common features of ancient temples, and Israel modeled their temple on the garden of Genesis, intending it to be a microcosm of creation.[5]

Creation is a temple; humanity its priests.

The Flood can be seen as caused by, like the temple's destruction later in Israel's history, the departing of God's presence. On the threshold of the Flood, God says, "My Spirit will not contend with humans forever," giving the impression that God is getting ready to depart.[6] And when God packs his bags and leaves, without his protective, sustaining presence the temple of creation is vulnerable.

The Spirit of God is like a central construction beam that holds the structure of creation together, or like the air that creates space inside a balloon by filling it, sustaining the space of our home so that life can flourish within. So when the Spirit of God evacuates the building, giving us the distance from God we crave, the structure of creation collapses in upon itself.

Things fall apart.

Like Babylon's forces of chaos later invading Israel's holy land and destroying the temple, the Flood's forces of chaos sweep in upon the earth and tear down the temple of creation. We've commandeered its steering wheel and rammed the ship into the rocks, away from God, dragging it down beneath the turbulent waters from which it came.

The Flood arises from God's *absence*.

And yet, from another angle, God is actively *present* in the Flood. Though we tend to think of the Flood arising from God's anger, Genesis actually emphasizes God's grief. Why is God heartbroken? He is sad because the earth is "filled with violence."[7] We should probably picture something like genocide here. In the early chapters of Genesis, violence is sin's chief characteristic, and a senseless spiral of generational violence has now spun out of control and "fills the earth."

So when all that's left are the "kings of the hill," standing atop the graveyards of their conquered masses, the rains start pouring down. We tear the human community apart, and God is sad. We fill the earth with blood; so God fills it with water. And washes it clean.

As with Israel's exile, God is *actively* involved in the event. Similar to God calling Babylon's pagan forces "my armies," the Flood's chaotic forces are seen as the sovereign judgment of God. But similar to God having a different purpose than Babylon's, these forces of chaos simply seek to unravel and destroy, while God has a different agenda: he is out to wash and make new. Out of the *tohu va wohu* that rushes in, the Creator will "separate the waters" again, creating space for life to reign once more.

The Creator's sovereign action is oriented toward new creation.

TEARING DOWN EGYPT

Egypt's plagues are also depicted as an unraveling of creation. The first few plagues are directed at the water, the next at the land, and the final ones at the sky.[8] There is a movement here: from sea to earth to heaven, as creation unravels around the oppressive empire. As Egypt rebels against God, seizing creation from Creator and pulling the reins toward its boastful chest, it tugs on the cord that unwinds the world.

Like a spool unraveling, things begin to fall apart.

The plagues start slow and build gradually, giving the empire time to repent. But Pharaoh, as a representative head for his recalcitrant people, refuses. While Egypt spirals downward into growing destruction, the plagues ultimately climax in darkness, death, and water—the primordial elements of chaos, the *tohu va wohu* from which the Creator brought forth the world.

The empire crumbles back into the abyss.[9]

Scripture looks at this as both God's *sovereign judgment* and as Egypt being *handed over*. Psalm 78, for example, describes the climax of the exodus as both God "unleash[ing] . . . his hot anger" with "wrath, indignation and hostility," and as Egypt being "[given] over to the plague," and coming under "a band of evil, destroying angels."[10] Israel was comfortable moving seamlessly back and forth between these active and passive angles.

We unravel creation; creation unraveled is God's punishment.

And as Egypt caves in upon itself, God once again "separates the waters." The Liberating King parts the Red Sea to guide his ragamuffin slaves out from under their oppression. The Redeemer parts the turbulent waters of the *tohu va wohu*, using the same imagery from Genesis 1 to depict this as a *new creation*, making space for life as he guides his people toward the promised land rising up in the distance and from the forces of chaos crashing down behind them.

God is Light, Life, and Love. Move from the Light; pull your world toward darkness. Run from Life; encounter death. Rebel against Love; sink into the collapsing of a self-contained world. This unraveling *is* the punishment inscribed in a creation ordered for the indwelling presence of its Creator. When our mutiny pulls creation away from the Creator, and he pulls back his sustaining presence, the whole structure flops around on the dock.

Creation unravels.

God is good. Remove God's goodness and his good world falls apart. The irony of the fish-out-of-water analogy is this: our predicament is the opposite. We were made to live on *dry land*, to flourish with our Creator in the good earth he's made, but we continually dive away from God, down toward the chaotic waters of oblivion—and drag the world down with us.

At the cross, Jesus takes all this head-on: our *personal, social,* and *cosmic* judgment. He comes under the dark, destructive decay we've unleashed, crashes under the turbulent waves of the *tohu va wohu,* grasping our hand deep in the depths below as he receives our unraveling of creation into himself—until it unravels him. The One through whom the world was made is himself unmade.

And yet, once he has identified fully with our tragic condition, grasping our hand and uniting himself with us in the depths below, the Father parts the chaotic waters of the abyss once again, raising his Son from his baptism in the grave, and leading us in the wake of his Spirit behind him, the resurrected head of humanity and firstfruits of the new creation.

KEY IDEA

Caricature: Wrath contradicts God's love and is inappropriate for his character.

Gospel: Wrath arises from God's love and deals honestly with our world.

---

INTERLUDE

Sunrise

Every Easter, my friend John roasts a lamb over a spit. A group of us show up late Saturday evening, watching over the lamb together through the night. Every hour or so, we turn the spit and reflect on the death of Christ. With every turn, we read resurrection passages from Scripture and authors throughout history. Together in that backyard, surrounded by darkness and cold, we anticipate the coming sunrise.

Then, on Easter, we feast.

People come flooding from the church and the surrounding neighborhood into the home. Usually around forty to fifty folks arrive, bringing the finest wine, savory salads, and scrumptious desserts. But at the center of the feast is the lamb, and all are invited to receive from the life at the center of the party. Some know Jesus, others do not, but for those of us who follow Jesus, we celebrate the One whose life was given that we might live.

It's one of my favorite annual traditions, anchoring my year in the sacrificial love of Jesus, the Lamb once slain, who forms a community through the power of his resurrection marked by new life offered freely to the world in the hope of his coming kingdom. And just when the flood of suffocating darkness presses most powerfully upon us, in breaks the coming of the dawn.

PART III

Rising Up from the Waters

RESURRECTION

CHAPTER 25

Communion of Love

Say the word *Trinity* and many people roll their eyes. We've been talking about the Father, Son, and Spirit, but isn't the Trinity just a strange, abstract, and irrelevant doctrine? My daughter is in kindergarten, and she's already learned that 1 + 1 + 1 most definitely does not equal 1.

When I became a Christian, people tried to explain the Trinity with crazy analogies: *God is like an egg: there's yolk, white, and shell, but it's one egg.* Or, *God is like water: there's ice, liquid, and steam, but one underlying substance.* I found these images more confusing than helpful. Fortunately, God is not like an egg in my frying pan or a pile of ice cubes in my freezer.

There is, however, an image I love: Andrei Rublev's famous *Trinity* icon. A masterpiece of Russian art created in the early 1400s, it's become the most significant icon for the Trinity in the Catholic and Orthodox traditions, and also had a tremendous impact on me.[1] As we explore Rublev's icon together, we'll find that far from being abstract or irrelevant, the Trinity is the foundation of the gospel's most beautiful proclamation.

God is love.

A WINDOW INTO THE HEART OF GOD

A word about icons: some people worry about "worshipping" them, but icons don't depict God directly.[2] They depict scenes and characters from Scripture and are intended to be viewed more like a window than a painting, meant not so much to be looked *at* but *through*, using color, symbolism, and imagery to give us a glimpse into the story of the gospel and the heart of God. Especially in times when most people were illiterate, icons were able to communicate truths visually about God on a broad and popular level that was easy to understand and remember.

Rublev's icon comes from a scene in Genesis 18, where Abraham shares a meal with three angelic visitors. In the passage, we eventually learn that Abraham is actually having a meal with God, and these visitors give him the promise of a son through whom God will save the world.[3] Rublev depicts this meal scene, and uses it as a window into the life of the Trinity.

Let's start with a look at their colors. The Spirit (on the right) is clothed in blue like the skies above and green like the grass below. The significance? The Spirit moves through heaven and earth, sustaining all things—the atmosphere we breathe and the ground beneath our feet—and bringing life to the world. All things hold together in the Spirit; were God's presence to completely depart, creation would fall apart.

The Son (in the middle) wears reddish brown like earthen clay, and blue like the heights of the sky we look up to. This speaks to Jesus bearing flesh and bone, being fully united with our humanity and the earth from which we are made (the red), yet fully divine, bearing all the transcendence of heaven above (the blue). Jesus unites divinity and humanity in his very person, reconciling heaven and earth.

And Jesus wears a gold sash over his shoulder, a sign of his

royal authority that reminds us, "the government will be upon His shoulder."[4] The Son of heaven is the King of earth, the desire of the nations, and the hope of the world.

The Father (on the left) appears to wear all colors. The garment's fabric seems almost transparent, changing with the light. A patch of blue underneath reminds us of his transcendent divinity as our heavenly Father, yet we are struck more by the radiance of his clothing. God is beyond description, yet fills the universe through his Son and Spirit, fulfilling all things in himself.

Next, notice the radiance around their faces and how everything that touches them is gold: their seats, wings, and chalice. God's presence communicates value. All things are made precious, perfect, and holy in their midst. It is not that the Trinity *has* valuable things; rather, things *become* valuable in their midst. The Father, Son, and Spirit shine brightly in their light, life, and love, bathing all who soak in their presence with the radiance of their glorious goodness.

HOLY LOVE

Notice their *posture*. This is perhaps the most significant feature of the icon. Each person is bent outward away from himself, his gaze arched toward the others in love. The position of their hands, the openness of their bodies, the look on their faces, all communicate a giving toward and receiving from the others.

The Father, Son, and Spirit are not grasping for power and attention *from* one another, but rather giving glory and attention *to* each other. This speaks to a major theme in Jesus' teaching: that the Father seeks to glorify the Son, the Son seeks to glorify the Father, and the Spirit brings glory to them both.[5] Rather than seeking to build their own platform against one another, they lift up one another:

You take the spotlight!

No, you!

In Jesus' longest recorded prayer, the main theme is the Father, Son, and Spirit glorifying one another in the love they've had from before the creation of the world.[6] Let's stop here and reflect for a minute. How are the Father, Son, and Spirit one God? The church has used a fancy Greek word, *perichoresis*, to explore this. It means "mutual indwelling" and comes from the image of a circle dance—combining the words *peri* ("around") and *chorein* ("make room for")—think of three dancers moving "around" one another and "making room for" one another. In their rapid, harmonious movement, it can be hard to tell where one stops and the other begins.

The Father, Son, and Spirit *mutually indwell* one another. Jesus declares, "I am in the Father and the Father is in me";[7] the Father actually *indwells* Jesus' identity, and vice versa. Their identities are intertwined, overflowing into one another. Jesus even goes so far as to say, "If you've seen me, you've seen the Father."[8] We not only look *at* Jesus, but *through* Jesus, to encounter the heart of the Father. Jesus is like a powerful icon through whom we see the face of God.

They define themselves in relation to one another. Without the Son, the Father would not be a father. Without the Father, the Son would not be a son. Without them both, the Spirit would not be their spirit. The Father, Son, and Spirit *are* God. As you look at the actions of Jesus, you're actually seeing the Father's movement in his world, in the power of their Spirit.

As if this indwelling couldn't get pushed any further, Jesus tops the cake, saying, "I and the Father are one."[9] The Father and Son are, in their Spirit, an eternal communion of holy love. This means God has relationship "in his very bones." The Father, Son, and Spirit are not three individuals who come together to hang out; they *are* the one God. They are bound up in, with, and for one another.

God is inherently relational.

WHY GOD CREATES

This confronts the caricature of our Creator as a large, lonely giant, kicking the cosmic curb and sullenly saying, "I wish I had some friends!" Some people seem to envision God making the world because he's bored and needs some buddies. There's a kind of codependency in this picture, where God is like that needy date who uses you to try and fill that hole inside or fix an identity crisis. And a codependent Creator will quickly resort to manipulation and guilt-tripping to get what he wants.

A *needy God* quickly becomes an obsessive stalker.

But God doesn't create us because he *needs* us; he creates us because he *wants* us. The Father, Son, and Spirit already *have* perfect relationship from eternity. They share affection, intimacy, and joy. They not only *experience* life, light, and love; they *are* life, light, and love. God is not just *a* being; God *is* Being, the ground of our existence. The Trinity creates the world in divine freedom, not to fill a need within but from an overflow of their divine love. We are each made as creatures to lavish their affection upon. They are not trying to get something from us; they are giving themselves to us.

Divine love gives birth to creation.

In the words of Augustine, "God did not create under stress of any compulsion, or because he lacks something for his own needs; his only motive was goodness."[10] God does not make us out of obligation, but out of desire. God does not have to *empty* himself to create, but from his expanding *fullness* shares his life with us. In the words of C. S. Lewis, "in God there is no hunger that needs to be filled, only plenteousness that desires to give."[11] We were created by the spreading goodness of God, and exist *for* this goodness—to live and subsist enfolded within the overwhelming, enveloping love of God. God *is* generous goodness.

This is the God we are raised to. We are not only created *by* this God, but redeemed *to* this God. Through the resurrection of Christ, we are drawn through faith into the circle of divine love and the overwhelming goodness of God.

CHAPTER 26

The Journey Home

G od enters the journey with us. Each of the three figures in Rublev's icon, which we began exploring in the last chapter, carries a walking staff, a sign that God travels down our dusty roads to find us and bring us home. What does this journey home look like? In the background landscape, behind the Father, Son, and Spirit, are a mountain, a tree, and a house. Each depicts a part of our journey into the heart of God. Let's take a look at how.

A MOUNTAIN, TREE, AND HOME

The mountain is behind the Spirit. The Spirit of God finds us in the rocky, distant places, and guides us along paths that may be steep and difficult, but ultimately brings us through these treacherous trails to a high place, the "mountaintop experience," where heaven and earth meet. As the Spirit guides us up the trail, the mountain is arched toward Jesus: the Spirit's goal is to lead us to Jesus.

Jesus sits before a tree, which spreads its shade to offer rest and refreshment from the heat of the sun and the difficult journey. We are reminded of the Tree of Life in Eden, where we were created to receive life in union with God, and of the cross, where Jesus transforms our death-dealing curse on that forsaken tree into life-giving power through his resurrection, reestablishing the Tree of Life and breathing the winds of Eden back into creation.

Jesus *is* the Tree of Life who replants the garden of God.

The tree is also, like the mountain, bent to the left, toward the Father: Jesus brings us home to the Father. Notice how the Father's house has a tower, rising high above everything else, giving the Father a sovereign view of the whole land below. Its door and upper window are open, facing outward toward the world. In the words of one observer, our Father's home is

> the goal of our journey, the beginning and end of our lives . . .
> Its door is always open, it has a tower, and its window is always
> open so that the Father can incessantly scan the roads for a
> glimpse of a returning prodigal.[1]

Our heavenly Father's posture is one of open embrace, inviting us into life together with him. This is not Mr. Clean barring the windows and slamming the gate to keep our grubby hands from muddying up his house. This is our heavenly Father welcoming us with arms wide open, beckoning our broken world to enter his healing embrace. The Father pursues us through his Son, in their Spirit, with the goal to bring us home.

THROUGH THE SON, IN THE SPIRIT

The icon is meant to be read from left to right: from the Father, through the Son, to the Spirit. The early church held that God always acts through his Son and in his Spirit. Irenaeus, one of the earliest church fathers, described Jesus and the Holy Ghost as the "two hands" of God, always present in all his works. So, for example, at creation God spoke the world into existence through his Word (saying, "Let there be!"[2]) and in his Spirit ("hovering over the waters"[3]).

Jesus *is* this Word through whom the universe was spoken into existence, the very Voice of God, and the Holy Spirit is this Spirit in whom our world has come to be, the very Breath of God, now indwelling our hearts. Similarly, throughout the Old Testament, the "word of the LORD" and "Spirit of God" come to prophets, priests, and kings, bringing God's action to bear in the world.[4]

The church has used a clunky Latin phrase for this: *opera ad extra indivisa*. It means all of God's actions in the world, or operations on the outside (*opera ad extra*) of his life as God, are works of the Father, Son, and Spirit together, undivided or indivisible (*indivisa*) as the whole Trinity. So, for example, the Father does not create the world alone, or the Son redeem by himself, or the Spirit sanctify as a solo project. The whole Trinity, all three persons, are involved together in everything they do.

This means when Jesus dives into our world, the whole Trinity is involved. Jesus is sent by the Father, as the "Word become flesh" in "the power of the Spirit."[5] Jesus arrives not as a *new* thing, but as the eternal Son of God to *do* a new thing. Jesus doesn't just point us *to* the Father; he *is* the action of the Father in our world.

Jesus regularly says he does "only what he sees his Father doing," and speaks "not [on] my own" but only what "the Father who sent me commanded me to say."[6] And Jesus works in the power of their Spirit, "anointed . . . with the Holy Spirit and [with] power," as he travels throughout the land, "doing good and healing all who were under the power of the devil, because God was with him."[7] Throughout Jesus' life and ministry, the Father is acting through his Son and in his Spirit.

A PERSONAL UNION

Now, here's the thing: this doesn't change in Jesus' crucifixion and death. The Father is acting *through* his Son and *in* his Spirit for the salvation of the world. Together, they're taking on the sin, destruction, and decay we've unleashed in order to restore their masterpiece. The cross doesn't happen to the Trinity; the Trinity happens to the cross.

The cross is a triune act.

Earlier, we saw how the church has used a *covenant of redemption* to highlight that the Father, Son, and Spirit are on the same team—not pitted against one another. While helpful, we also saw how the church has recognized that this language has some limits: it can sound like a contract entered into by three separate individuals. Here, we see why this language falls short. The Father,

Son, and Spirit are on the same team not because they entered an agreement *outside of* themselves, but because of who they are *inside of* themselves: they *are* the one God.

So the reason they don't abandon one another is not because they got together to sign a piece of paper back in eternity: *Oh yeah! Shoot, I forgot about that contract. Is there a shredder around here somewhere?* It's because of their personal union, their "mutual indwelling" as Father, Son, and Spirit, their loving communion as one God. They don't break the divine dance because of *who they are.*

The Trinity is bound together by something much stronger and more beautiful than a contract; they are bound together by their unbreakable union as God, an eternal communion of holy love. One in three; three in one. Together, they are at work at the cross, finding us in the distant land to bring us home.

Rublev depicts this with a chalice.

THE CHALICE

At the center of Rublev's icon, on the table, is a chalice. It is a picture of Christ's sacrifice for us, the Eucharist of his body broken and blood shed to bring us home. Inside the chalice is a slain animal. In the Abraham story of Genesis 18, a "choice, tender calf" was chosen for the meal.[8] In the gospel, Jesus is "the Lamb, who was slain,"[9] elected from before creation to atone for sin and restore us to the table.

The chalice belongs not only to Jesus, however, but to the Trinity as a whole. The cup stands at the center of *their* table, inviting us into *their* fellowship. The chalice embodies the Father's sacrificial self-giving, in and through his Son and Spirit, to bring us into communion with their very life as God.

The table upon which the chalice sits is actually an altar. If you look at the base of the altar, you will see a little square opening. This is the space where, in the Russian Orthodox tradition, pictures of the saints are kept. The significance? We are welcomed to the meal, invited through Christ's sacrifice into fellowship with God.

Notice also how the Father, Son, and Spirit create space for us to enter. If you think of the icon as a clock, they are at the 9:00, 12:00, and 3:00 positions. But space is opened up in the 6:00 position, at the front of the icon, inviting us as the viewer to enter the circle of divine hospitality and join in the feast. God wants to do life with us.

We are invited to enter the life of God. In Christ, Peter tells us, we become "participants of the divine nature."[10] This doesn't mean we *become* God—we are still creatures, not Creator. But it does mean we *participate* as creatures in the very life of our Creator: the Spirit of God dwells *inside* us, binding us in union *with* Christ, and bringing us *through* Christ into the embrace of the Father.

The Spirit surrounds and indwells us as the bride, lifting the veil before our eyes so that we see Christ, our Groom, revealed before us, and through our union with Christ, we enter the household of the Father, being surrounded and indwelt by the very life of God. This is our salvation: to be indwelt by God within us (the Spirit), united to God before us (the Son), and embraced within the life of God surrounding us (the Father). Our salvation is none other than the very life of God.

We enter their eternal communion of holy love.

CHAPTER 27

Life into Death

COULD GOD EXPLODE?

Jesus' resurrection raises a radical question: If he was not raised, what happens to the Father and the Spirit? If the Son is permanently in the grave, does this not thrust a stick of dynamite into the very heart of the Trinity and blow up their communion as God? If the Father, Son, and Spirit *are* the one God, through their union in and with one another, then is it not only creation that is threatened with annihilation at the cross, but our Creator as well?

The Father would not simply begin again on his own. *Oh well! Guess I've got to start over.* The Father's identity is bound up with his Son; their union in the Spirit is unbreakable. They *are* the one God. This makes the gravity of the question immense: If the Father does not resurrect Jesus from the grave, could God explode?

STRONGER THAN DEATH

This starts to sound similar to a question we explored earlier: *Could Jesus have sinned?* There the question was whether the Son could rebel against the Father; here the question is whether the Father could have abandoned the Son to the grave. Once again, it all depends on what we mean by the word *could*. If we're talking about the *external circumstances*, then yes, the Father has the opportunity presented to abandon the Son, to leave him in the tomb. But if we're talking about his *internal orientation*, then the obvious answer is no—the Father *could* have but *would not* have, because he *loves* the Son, and because together in the Spirit they are the one God. The reason God could not have been destroyed by the cross is bound up in the very divine nature: God is love.

And God's love is stronger than death.

The Son *could not* be lost, *will not* be lost, *cannot* be lost—not because the external circumstances aren't there, but because the Father *will* be faithful to raise him in the power of their Spirit. This illuminates what's at stake in the cross, however. From the outside looking in, at a human vantage point, we are faced with the question, *Will the Father raise the Son?* From this outside-in perspective, it is not just the survival of creation that seems to hang in the balance, but the existence of the Creator. Not just the object of redemption, but the triune Redeemer as well.

And yet, observing the cross from the inside looking out, there is nothing at stake from the vantage point of impassible triune love. The Father, Son, and Spirit love the world, but their love for the world overflows from their love for one another, and their love for one another has primacy within their eternal life as God.[1] They cannot be acted upon so as to abandon one another. Though they choose a course of action that is so unprecedented, so extreme, that it brings God near the point of dissolution, yet as the Father tackles the cross through the Son and in the Spirit, taking on all that it represents, they remain sovereign and cannot be acted upon so as to abandon one another because of the invulnerable supremacy of triune love.

WORD OF LIFE

One is almost tempted to say that the Father and Son's *communication* is severed, however, because we experience death as the severing of communication. My friend Terry passed away years ago, and one of the hardest realities of his death is that I can no longer talk to him, interact with him, or hang out with him.

Our face-to-face encounter has been interrupted by the grave.

So we might be led to think the Father and Son experience a break, or suspension, in the relationship they've had from eternity. It could appear their *communication* is severed, or ruptured, while their *communion* of will remains unbroken.

Yet this will not do—because the Son *is* the communication of the Father. He is the Word of life spoken into our death. Like the beginning of creation, when the Father spoke his divine word "Let there be!" into the chaotic void of nothingness, and brought forth life in the power of his Spirit, so similarly here again the Father speaks his divine Word, Christ, into the unraveling of creation we've unleashed, the chaotic *tohu wa vohu*, the darkness, dissolution, and death of our grave, in order to bring forth life and new creation in the power of his Spirit.

As the Son goes into the grave, he *is* God's communication

into our alienation and death, present to his Father in the power of their Spirit.

This is why the church has historically said that Christ suffers *in his humanity* on the cross, bearing our destruction in his flesh, while yet *in his divinity* he remains present to the Father even as he descends into the tomb. As the Son bears our distance from God into the depths of the earth, he simultaneously bears the life-giving power of God into our distance.

The eternal Son of God endures the conditions of our mortality under the weight and power of sin, as the life-giving Word of the Father spoken into our destruction in the grave.

SOVEREIGN LOVE

What about the Spirit? We've talked a lot about the Father and Son, but the role of the Spirit here is crucial. The Father sends his Son into the world on a mission "anointed . . . with the Holy Spirit and with power,"[2] a mission that goes crashing through the cross into our grave in the power of that same Spirit.[3]

The Trinity is not caught by surprise at the cross, but actively engages it. In the language of the New Testament, the Father "offered . . . up" his Son; the Son "offered up Himself" to the Father, and does so "through the eternal Spirit."[4]

The Spirit accompanies Christ into the grave, bridging the distance the Father and Son offer up between each other. In holy love, the Spirit mediates our forsakenness, exclusion, and death from the Father to the humanity of Christ that bears our sin, such that the Father and Son's distance from one another becomes a mode of their presence to each other.

The Trinity is bringing our sin, death, and destruction into their communion in order to conquer it in the power of divine love.

On the Spirit's role, if we go back to the helicopter rescue example we used earlier, consider that point where the second fireman descends by rope into the deepest part of the smoky blaze, identifying the family and binding himself in union with them through the rope. In the analogy, the rope is a metaphor for the Spirit—through the Spirit, the Son is binding himself in union with us as fallen humanity in the grave, as he bears our judgment for sin.

And similar to the firefighter still being connected to the helicopter above by the rope, the Son is still bound to the Father through the Spirit, even as he enters the "heart of the blaze" in our distance in the tomb. The Father is actually working through his Son, in the power of their Spirit, bringing life into our death, judgment upon our sin, and binding him in union with us toward the goal of our restoration.

The Father, Son, and Spirit are still singing their same song of holy affection, but it is played out here in a minor key, as they envelop and overwhelm our suffering and death in the humanity of Christ, communicating their divine love within their unbroken communion of will.

Again, like all analogies, the firefighter picture falls short. The Spirit is not a thing, like a rope, but a person, and the Father is not simply hovering above, but personally at work in the death of his Son. And the Trinity is infinitely more unified than this picture can portray because, as we've seen in the last few chapters, the Father, Son, and Spirit *are* the one being of God. They are more than three friends hanging out and working on a project together; their communion is substantial, with a shared nature and will.

The point of the analogy, however, is that they are not divided, torn asunder, or severed by the grave. Rather, the death and resurrection of Christ is perhaps more than any other event where the unity of the Trinity and depths of divine love are most profoundly revealed. The Father is, through the Son and in the Spirit, reconciling the world.

The Father, Son, and Spirit remain sovereign through the event of the cross. The Son is sovereign over the grave, even as he lies dead in it—because the Father and Spirit will be faithful to raise him. The Father is sovereign, even as his Son marches toward Golgotha—because Jesus will not join humanity's rebellion and will be faithful unto death. The Spirit is sovereign, even when entering the grieving and groaning of creation to apply the work of Jesus to our broken world, because the Father and Son will receive the world he brings.

The hope of the world is God's sovereign love.

INVITED TO A FEAST

God is one. The Christian doctrine of the Trinity holds that, though God exists as three persons, they share the same being and substance. So at the cross, as pastor and author Tim Keller observes: "God did not, then, inflict pain on someone else, but rather on the Cross absorbed the pain, violence, and evil of the world into himself."[5] In the words of theologian Adam Johnson, "through Jesus Christ the triune God brought the reality of sin into his own proper life, that he might deal with it in and through himself."[6] Or as Benedict XVI, the former pope, puts it:

> God himself becomes the locus of reconciliation, and in the
> person of his Son takes the suffering upon himself. . . . God

himself "drinks the cup" of every horror to the dregs and thereby restores justice through the greatness of his love, which, through suffering, transforms the darkness.[7]

The greatest pain Jesus endures is not the whips, the insults, or the nails; it is his separation from the face of God, mediated by the Spirit. People have died worse deaths. Don't get me wrong: crucifixion ranks right up there with the world's worst ways to die—it was horrific, but others were crucified too. And if we're talking about sheer physical pain, it has been beat.

What makes Jesus' death so horrible is not simply its physical brutality, but who he is—the eternal Son of God—and who he is in relation to: the Father. If the Father, Son, and Spirit have existed from eternity as a holy communion of love, and if suffering is at its core relational, then there is no greater suffering imaginable for the incarnate Son than the distancing of this relationship.

From an inverse angle, the Father endures the cross. While the Son suffers death, the Father endures the death of his Son. The Father does not feel the physical pain of the nails pounded into Jesus' hands on Good Friday, but the Father endures the torture, mocking, and crucifixion of his most beloved Son under our cruel hands. And on Holy Saturday, as his Son lies dead in the grave, the loving Father gazes upon the desolate earth.

And yet, there is an unbroken communion of will. The Father will be invulnerably faithful to raise the Son, as the Son has been impeccably faithful to the Father, together in the power of their Spirit. The cross and resurrection most powerfully reveal the Trinity because they display their faithful love to one another amid our darkest depths. The Father, Son, and Spirit take in our suffering, shattering, and death in order to overwhelm it with the life, light, and love they share as the one God.

To return to Rublev's icon: the chalice at the center of the table is filled with the blood of Christ, and it marks the time the Father, Son, and Spirit took on our sin, death, and destruction in order to overwhelm, conquer, and destroy it through their communion as one God in the power of divine love. The "chalice of the cross" that sits at the center of the Trinity can only be properly understood within the broader surrounding circle of extravagant self-giving that characterizes their invulnerable communion as God.

The cross and resurrection reveal the radical extent the Father, Son, and Spirit are willing to go to bring us home. The sacrificial chalice sits within their circle of divine love . . .

as they invite *us* to sit down and join them for a feast.

KEY IDEA

Caricature: The Trinity is an abstract doctrine with no relevance for today.

Gospel: The Trinity changes everything—the Father, Son, and Spirit are a holy communion of love who invite us to participate in their eternal life.

CHAPTER 28

Bad Bridge

We are now in a good position to take a look at one of the most controversial questions for Christianity today: Is Jesus the only way to God? The exclusivity of Christ is one of the biggest challenges many have with the faith. It can sound arrogant and closed-minded. I've heard many conversations over the years, for example, that go something like this:

> **Christian:** Jesus is the only way to God, not Hinduism, Buddhism, or Islam. So if you want to go to heaven, this is the road you must take.
>
> **Skeptic:** How can you think your religion's right and everyone else is wrong? Don't you realize how arrogant that sounds? You should grow up and accept that all roads lead to God.

Notice how both the Christian and the skeptic: (1) assume this is primarily a conversation about world religions; (2) use the image of a road; and (3) make the traveler moving along the road us. I want to suggest that the way we frame this conversation is often backward. Jesus isn't the one and only way we go out into the universe to find God. The gospel moves in the other direction.

Jesus is the unique and decisive way God has come to us.

ROAD OR DESTINATION?

Consider, for example, the famous bridge analogy, used in popular tracts and thousands of evangelism conversations over the last few decades. In the analogy, God and humanity are separated by sin and, like the Grand Canyon, the chasm is too big for us to cross. Fortunately, Jesus went to the cross to build a bridge so we can travel to the other side and be with God again.

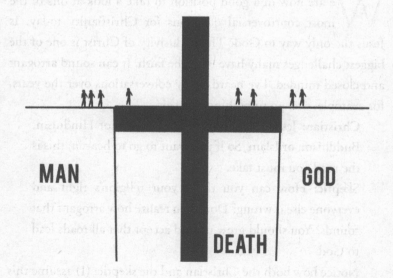

My friend Scott created a humorous cartoon to point out a problem with this analogy that often goes unnoticed: travelers run into an unexpected problem while trying to cross this bridge—because the shape of a cross is probably not the best architectural design for trying to cross a canyon.

Does anyone have a ladder?

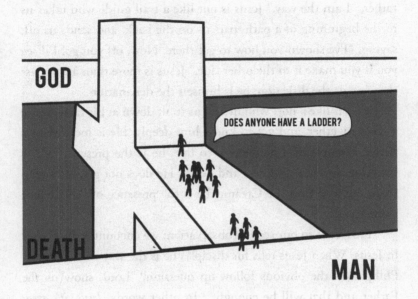

Scott's picture is funny, but I think it highlights a deeper underlying problem with this analogy: the direction of travel. We are the ones trying to get to God, wanting to jump over the chasm, but God's backed too far away. We desire to leap across the divide, are trying to build bridges across the Grand Canyon, but we'll plummet to our deaths because God keeps moving farther into the distance.

We're pursuing God, but God's running away.

As we've seen throughout this book, however, the gospel story moves in the opposite direction: God is the one pursuing us—we're the ones running. The cross is not a mechanism we use to get to God, but the way God has come to find and raise us. Let's take a closer look at the context when Jesus says he is *the way.*

Jesus famously declares, "I am the way and the truth and the life. No one comes to the Father except through me."[1] Here's three observations. First, Jesus doesn't say, "I will show you the way," but rather, "I am the way." Jesus is not like a trail guide who takes us to the beginning of a path, pats us on the back, and sends us off, saying, "I've shown you how to get there. Now, off you go! I'll see you if you make it to the other side." Jesus is more than a compass showing us the direction; he is himself the destination.

Jesus is like a host who invites us to sit down at his table, share a meal together, and get to know him deeply. He is more than a heroic example of a better way to live; he is the presence of life breaking into our darkness and death. He does not give us a map to go out and find the Creator; he is the presence of the Creator come to us.

This leads to our second observation: we encounter the Father in Jesus. When Jesus tells his disciples he is the way to the Father, Philip asks the obvious follow-up question, "Lord, show us the Father and that will be enough."[2] In other words, *Jesus, it's great that we're buddies and all, but God's still over on the other side of that canyon. So just show us how to go find the Father, and that will be good.* Jesus' response is at the center of the Christian faith:

> Don't you know me . . . even after I have been among you such
> a long time? Anyone who has seen me has seen the Father. How
> can you say, "Show us the Father"? Don't you believe that I am
> in the Father, and that the Father is in me?[3]

"What has Jesus been smoking?" we might ask. The Father is *in* Jesus? Jesus uses this language a lot, telling his disciples that in his life and ministry, "it is the Father, living in me, who is doing his work," and even goes so far as to say, "I and the Father are one."[4] At first glance, this can sound really strange and mystical: *I'm in him; he's in me; we'll come make our home in you; then you'll be one as he and I are one.* What's going on here?

This is the language of *union*, of *mutual indwelling*, that we looked at earlier in exploring the Trinity. It's relational language that shows up throughout the New Testament. Jesus not only says the Father is in him, but extends this imagery to his followers, saying he and the Father will "make our home with them" by sending their Spirit to indwell us.[5] Our being "in Christ" shows up more than eighty times in the New Testament.[6] Jesus is not only one with God; he invites us, through him, into union with God.

THE WAY THAT COMES TO US

Finally, Jesus is the way that comes to us. When Jesus says he's *the way*, he's *on his way* to the cross. In context, he's preparing the disciples for his death; his trajectory is set for Golgotha. The trail he is about to blaze, the path he's about to travel, the journey he's about to complete, is not one that pulls us out of the earth in escape, but one that plunges right into the depths of our grave and plants the flag of his kingdom in our world's heart of darkness.

Jesus arrives not with a ladder for us to climb out of creation, but a shovel he'll use to dig up the wicked root of our sin within creation. And in its place, he'll plant the sacrificial love of God, burying his own body like a seed deep in the death of our world, cracked open to bring new life rising up from creation's cosmic broken heart.

Jesus himself will spring forth from the earth as the resurrected

Tree of Life, welcoming all things back from the brink into the arms of God. Jesus is:

> the *Way* our world is reconciled to God
> the *Truth* of God's goodness outstretched to embrace resistant
>   rebels
> the *Life* that restores our God-haunted, sin-struck world, back
> into the presence of the Father

The cross is not a bridge we use to get to God; it is the flag of God's kingdom planted deep beneath the death-dealing soil of the cracked and barren earth we tread. It is the bridge through which God breaks into us. The resurrection is not a motivational talk to get our lives together; it is God's life-giving power breaking through the walls of our rebellion, spilling around the ramparts we've erected, to receive all who will be embraced by his reconciling goodness, to restore all who will repentantly submit to his kingdom reign, to flood the earth with God's glory when all things are made new in the power of Christ's victory.

Jesus is not a path we set out into the universe on to go find God.

Jesus is the way God has come to find us.

So to return to the question we opened this chapter with: Does Jesus being right mean everything else is wrong? Let's turn to the next chapter to find out.

CHAPTER 29

The True Myth

When most people talk about Jesus being *the Way*, they're thinking about things such as world religions and ideologies. Even if this is not directly what Jesus is speaking to when he says he's the way, truth, and life, are there implications for this? If Jesus is the unique and decisive way God has come to us, what does this have to say to the other paths and stories of our world?

Christ is the "true myth," in the words of C. S. Lewis,[1] an expert in ancient myths and stories. One of Lewis's major hang-ups with the Christian faith before his conversion was, *How can this one story be true and all the others false?* One night, however, a conversation with J. R. R. Tolkien (famous author of *The Lord of the Rings*) turned his world around.

That Jesus is true, Tolkien explained, doesn't mean everything else is false. Rather, Jesus *reveals* that which is true and false in our world.[2] Jesus is both *the way* God has come to us and *the truth*, the center of reality, the One through whom the world was made and in whom our life is sustained. So when we look upon Jesus, he sheds light on the meaning of existence and the structure of creation, as the center of the universe.

Our stories and traditions reveal, in many ways, our deepest longings, hopes, and desires. Our stories are projected from earth up to heaven, while Jesus bears an important distinction, coming from heaven to earth. In the words of Joseph Pearce,

> Tolkien explained to Lewis that the story of Christ was the true myth at the very heart of history and at the very root of reality . . . [where we encounter] God expressing Himself *through* Himself, *with* Himself, and *in* Himself.[3]

Jesus is the "True Myth," who does not annihilate all the dreams and aspirations embodied in our stories but rather, in some important ways, fulfills them.

Jesus is the fairy tale come true.

THE HEAVENLY MAGNET

I like to think of Jesus as a heavenly magnet: he draws out the good and refines out the dross from our cultural heritages. As the King of heaven and earth, it's too simplistic to say all the cultures of the world are inherently wrong or totally right in relation to him. Rather, everything stands in dynamic relation to Jesus as the King.

When I look at my own culture, there's a lot of junk that needs to go, but there's a lot of good, true, and beautiful in the mix too. I remember a time this hit home for me years ago, watching Spike Lee's *25th Hour* with my roommate, Tony. When the movie ended, he asked me, "What did you think?"

"It was all right," I responded. To be honest, I was tired after a long week of work and only half paying attention, lying on the couch, mostly trying to zone out.

"Are you kidding me?" Tony snapped back. "The gospel was in there."

As he walked me back through the storyline, I began to see: this was about second chances, redemption, and new life. The movie opens with Monty, the main character, stopping his car before a dog mauled in a dogfight, lying half-dead in the road. Monty plans to shoot the dog to put it out of its misery but, after looking him in the eyes, changes his mind and puts the dog in his car, taking him to a nearby clinic and adopting the dog as his own.

The dog was on its *24th hour*, so to speak, about to die but given a new day, a second chance at life, a *25th hour*. The dog becomes a metaphor for the rest of the movie, which follows Monty's last twenty-four hours of freedom before entering prison on a seven-year drug sentence. Like that dog, Monty and nearly all his friends are a mess on the brink of destruction, about to get run over by life, and desperate for a second chance, a *25th hour*.

In the final scene, Monty's father is driving him to prison and suggests they go west instead, into hiding, to start a new life. A fantasy sequence ensues where Monty daydreams about his life with this fresh start—it's a cry for redemption, a longing for a chance to start again. If movies are "modern myths," the stories we tell to make meaning of the world, then films like this have powerful places where the cry of the human heart and some of our deepest cultural longings intersect with the hope of the gospel.

Jesus *is* the 25th Hour.

Jesus stands on the brink of destruction in Gethsemane (like Monty, his friends, and that dog on the road), willingly entering our pit in his crucifixion and our prison of death, identifying with us all at the end of our rope. Yet Jesus' resurrection breaks the bars of our prison and brings us a *25th hour*, a new day, a second chance to the world through the power of his redemption.

GOOD, TRUE, AND BEAUTIFUL

Since that conversation with Tony, I try and watch movies now through a Christ-centered lens, attentive to the Spirit, looking for ways Jesus might be pointing me to him and displaying intersections where the gospel speaks to the heart of my culture. I'm amazed at how frequently Jesus shows up. My wife is tired of hearing me say things like, "Oh my gosh—that was just like the Trinity!"

Obviously, there's a lot of junk in our movies too. Dross that needs to be refined, thorns that need to be weeded out, things that Jesus stands against—and the trash is usually easier to spot than the treasure. But there's loads of treasure in those Hollywood hills too.

And this is much more than just movies. When I flip through the radio stations in my car, I'm amazed at how much dysfunctional junk clutters the airwaves. I became more attentive to the degrading lyrics when my young daughter began singing them back to me—many of our hit songs increasingly sound like soft porn. It was time to get an MP3 player. To paraphrase John Cusack's classic question in *High Fidelity*, I sometimes wonder for our culture: "Do we listen to pop music because we're miserable, or are we miserable because we listen to pop music?"

And yet, I *love* mainstream music. God has encountered me there with moments of total euphoria, creative explosion, and such grand epiphany that my heart bursts forth in praise. The artist or creator often has no desire or intention to glorify God—he or she may even hate God and stand in complete opposition to Jesus— but the Spirit of God is powerful enough to commandeer the work of even the most rebellious pagan and, despite that artist's intentions, still sovereignly speak through it to glorify Jesus. Sometimes simply the *structure* of the music itself can be treasure, while the lyrics intertwined with it are dross to be burnt away.

Jesus is good, true, and beautiful, and reveals in his presence that in our culture which is good, true, and beautiful. It can only *be* good, true, and beautiful by participating, whether its maker wants it to or not, in the structure of creation held by him at the center of the universe in the power of his Spirit. And inversely, the more we get to know Jesus, the more clearly we see the darkness, destruction, and decay—those things in our culture and tradition that lead to death. And there's unfortunately plenty of that to go around.

This of course goes way beyond the arts. In our culture-at-large, my eyes are increasingly drawn to Jesus when I see the doctors bringing health to my father's body, teachers pouring wisdom into my daughter, janitors performing microbiological warfare on enemies of my immune system, or entrepreneurs launching initiatives for the flourishing of our community.[4] Yet this is simultaneously the culture of the school-to-prison pipeline, millions of refugees in squalid camps from conflicts we've armed, millions of babies medically killed, and the greatest wealth disparity the world has ever known.

Jesus both confirms and confronts.

So it's not that we look around at our culture to find all the pieces that we like and then assume, "God must be like that."

Rather, as we get to know the Father better through his Word and in his Spirit, we become more attuned and attentive to the signposts that surround us.

Jesus is *the way* God has come to us.

Jesus is *the truth* that reveals.

Jesus is *the life* that renews.

ROMEO AND JULIET

But let's stick with story for a minute. My buddy Don says story itself is powerful *because of* God's story.[5] There are four main components to story, a common structure that authors and filmmakers use when trying to craft a powerful narrative. The first is *setting*: the location (where) and characters (who) of the story. The next is *conflict*: What is the problem that must be resolved?

Romeo and Juliet, for example, sets the main characters as two star-crossed lovers in the land of Verona, in the midst of a brutal family feud between the Montagues and the Capulets. This only sets the stage, however, for when Romeo and Juliet meet and fall in love. Yet their romance is doomed from the start by the warring factions that surround them. This is the conflict at the heart of the story.

Every great story has conflict (try to think of one that doesn't), a challenge that must be faced, an obstacle to be overcome. Some have tried making stories without conflict, and it just doesn't work.

As the conflict builds, third comes the *climax*: this is where the conflict reaches its highest pitch, where the stakes are fully raised, the final showdown takes place, and the outcome is to be determined. This is where Juliet drinks the potion, where Romeo fights

Count Paris, where the lover encounters his sleeping bride: Will she wake in time? Will they wind up together? Will their romance or the surrounding violence win the day?

Finally comes *resolution*: this is where the conflict is resolved, either through a happy ending (if things turn out well), or as tragedy (if things turn out badly). *Romeo and Juliet* is partly so powerful because it combines these two: it is tragedy because they *die* in each other's arms, but they die together in a way that brings an *end* to the violent family feud that surrounds them.

Okay, does this "structure of story" relate to the gospel? Christianity says there are four main components to God's story: *creation, fall, redemption, restoration*. Creation is like the setting, where the characters are introduced and placed in a location—we, the human characters, live out the drama on earth as the stage. Immediately in the story, however, conflict is introduced: the Fall gives rise to the challenge that must be faced, our sin is the obstacle to be overcome, and the bulk of human history takes place as the playing out and building rise of this conflict.

The human family is at war. God's love story with his bride is worked out amid this broader setting of a brutal cosmic feud. The gospel is a romance in the midst of a war zone.

The climax comes at the cross: where the stakes are raised and the conflict reaches its highest pitch. The Groom gives his life for the bride, the Artist receives the corruption in his painting, the King takes on his archenemy in sacrificial love for rebels—and goes into the grave to accomplish redemption. Like Romeo and Juliet, the Groom and bride are bound together in union through death.

Finally comes restoration: Jesus' resurrection turns the tragedy into a comedy, bringing forth laughter from the pit, victory from the darkness, joy from the wasteland, as a firstfruit of the restoration that is coming when his kingdom is established in fullness upon the earth—the happily ever after through God's eternal love.

THE STRUCTURE OF THE WORLD

Don taught me stories like *Romeo and Juliet* work because they participate in the narrative structure of God's story—whether they intend to or not. So it's more than just *themes* like sacrificial love, victory over evil, or second chances; it's the *structure* of the stories themselves. The myths we project from earth onto heaven resonate most deeply in the human heart when they participate in the nature and structure of the "True Myth" that God brings from heaven down to earth: Jesus and his story for our world.

Similarly with music, I'd suggest, it's not just *lyrics* but the *structure* of music itself that can bear witness. Have you ever been awestruck at orchestration? The three notes that simultaneously *are* one chord, with dominant and relative sounds in harmony? The symphony with the particularity of each instrument performing *as yet* one sound? While this is not "proof" of the Trinity, it makes sense for a world crafted by a triune Creator who is three-in-one, one-in-three, relational in his very being. There's a strong sense of *mutual indwelling* in music, of orchestration as an analogy of *perichoresis*, of the one and the many in mutual co-inherence, a relational world bearing witness to our relational God.

God is the Author and Orchestrator of our world. All things stand in relation to him. In making culture, we can look to our Creator for guidance in our vocations. Those in education can look to Jesus as Teacher; for those in medicine, he is Healer; for those in politics, he is King; for those in law, he is our Judge; for those in communications, he is the Word; for those raising children, God is our loving Father and nurturing Spirit.

Our world is grounded in God. "In him we live and move and have our being."[6] Jesus is the *way* God has come to us, revealing the *truth* that grounds creation, that we might have *life* if we receive him, allowing him to cast away the corruption and treasure the true as he refines us in his image.

CHAPTER 30

Upside-Down Kingdom

Jesus shows up in ways we wouldn't expect: the King is born in a manger. Our Healer is afflicted, our Savior destroyed by sin. We've talked about Jesus being *the Way*, but what are we to make of *the way* Jesus comes? And what does it mean for how we encounter him and follow in his dust today?

THEOLOGY OF THE CROSS

Years ago, I was struck by Martin Luther's "theology of the cross." In it, he contrasts what he calls a *theology of glory* with a *theology of the cross*. In a theology of glory, we want to ascend the sacred mountain, encounter our Creator in power, and "figure God out."

Here's the way I think of it: Imagine someone hiking in the mountains and thinking, *Wow. This is all very big! Someone powerful must have created this. This Creator must want me to behave. I'll walk upright to please this powerful god, make myself a better person, and gain access to his power.* We want to unmask God in all his brilliance and glory.

But God refuses to be found there, knowing it would only fuel our pride, our desire for control, and the corruption of our condition—because what we're really out for is *our* glory. We want to be like God rather than with God and under God. We want to approach him on our own terms rather than in submission to his kingdom.

So God intentionally hides himself from being discovered this way, and instead takes a different approach. He reveals himself in the opposites of where we'd expect: in weakness, suffering, and shame. At the cross, God is most powerfully revealed in affliction, rejection, and death. In Israel, God takes the last and least of the nations, identifies himself with this ragtag group of beat-up slaves, and encounters the mighty empires of the ancient world through them.

In the church, God doesn't start with the bold, bright, and beautiful to get his movement rolling, but takes the last kids picked and launches his revolution through them. As Paul puts it in 1 Corinthians:

> God chose the foolish things of the world to shame the wise;
> God chose the weak things of the world to shame the strong.
> God chose the lowly things of this world and the despised
> things—and the things that are not—to nullify the things that
> are, so that no one may boast before him.[1]

God breaks into our world in unexpected ways, not only in history but intimately in our lives today. Jesus encounters *us* in our affliction, meets us in our pain. God subverts our world by approaching us from the "bottom up" rather than from the "top down." And brings his resurrection power there.

SYLVIA'S STORY

My friend Sylvia is brilliant and was shocked at how Jesus showed up in her life. She had traveled the globe, garnered advanced degrees, cared passionately for people, fought against injustice, and wanted to make the world a better place. Eventually, she began to explore God, but couldn't overcome her intellectual objections to the faith. But she had experiences she could only describe as God's pursuit of her.

So she tried to follow up by beginning to read, research, and study. The more she tried to "figure God out," however, the more conflicted she became. Tired from the struggle, she'd become convinced it was a sham and collapse in frustration on her couch—and suddenly feel an overwhelming sensation of God's presence with her. She had experiences like this over and over again, frustrated at trying to figure God out but collapsing to find God coming after her.

Eventually, she gave in and received Jesus. She traded her pursuit of God for God's pursuit of her. This didn't mean she checked her brain at the door, but gradually, the questions she struggled with took on a new light. God became her starting point rather than a conclusion she reached on her own terms. She exercised, in the words of Anselm, *faith seeking understanding.*[2] And as it is when putting on a new pair of spectacles, from the perspective of God's upside-down kingdom, many things came into focus and began to make sense.

Over the years since then, I've seen Sylvia's life radically transformed by the relentless love of God. She's encountered Jesus in her scars and insecurities, the places she didn't have figured out. She's learned to see God approaching her "from below," through the way of the cross.

THE WAY OF THE CROSS

The name *Christian* basically means "little Christ," one following Jesus and becoming like him. But before the name *Christian* took hold, Jesus' first ambassadors were simply called followers of "the Way."[3] They wanted to walk behind Jesus and follow in his dust. What was this way? He summed it up for his disciples:

> If any of you wants to be my follower, you must turn from your selfish ways, take up your cross, and follow me.[4]

Jesus calls us to the way of the cross. The cross is not a way we break out of the world to get up to Jesus, but a way Jesus breaks into the world through us as his people. In the words of Tullian Tchividjian, Jesus forms us on this journey to be a people marked by

> giving rather than taking, self-sacrifice rather than self-protection, dying rather than killing . . . [to find] that we win by losing, we triumph through defeat, and we become rich by giving ourselves away.[5]

This is tough for our *culture of glory* to accept. We want to find God with our best foot forward rather than let God find us in the secrets of our darkest closets. We strive to minimize our suffering and make our best life now. We're addicted to self-help: always on to that next diet fad, that next fashion trend, that next project or philosophy to put our lives together, with Oprah and Dr. Phil as our high priests along for the ride. If we get ourselves together, maybe we'll get God in the process.

But God beckons from our brokenness, breaks in through the

back door, invites us to encounter him in our insecurities, sits in our suffering, waiting for us to join him there. And when his grace rather than our glory becomes the starting point, there's freedom to enter the world as it is, to not ignore or sugarcoat the pain but to call it what it is and graciously give our lives away for his glory there, as signposts of the upside-down, resurrecting kingdom.

Jesus is a one-way bridge moving contrary to our culture of glory. While we're striving to move up from earth toward heaven, climbing the social ladder to "make a name for ourselves,"[6] God is breaking in from heaven to earth, bringing resurrection power through the back door to name us as his own. We're invited not to set out and find God, but to stop running and be found. Not to strive harder and do, but to hear him say, "It is done!" To let the Father lift us on his back and carry us on the strength of his shoulders across the wasteland that surrounds us into the world he is making his home.

KEY IDEA

Caricature: Jesus is the one and only way we go out to find God.

Gospel: Jesus is the unique and decisive way God has come to us.

CHAPTER 31

Nazis and Whores

When we think of *who* God pursues, many envision the upright and uptight, the pretty prom queens and polished politicians, whose kids have good grades and homes have great views. But the King of the gospel goes after strange citizens for his kingdom; the Groom pursues an unlikely bride; the Father embraces unexpected children.

God goes after Nazis and whores.

Let's check out two of Israel's prophets, Jonah and Hosea, who beautifully—if ruggedly—capture the relentless heartbeat of the Pursuing God.

CITY OF BLOOD

I love Jonah. God tells him, "Go to the great city of Nineveh,"[1] and the reluctant prophet does a 180 and sets sail across the Mediterranean as far from Nineveh (and God) as he can go. I've heard people give Jonah a hard time for this, but *why is it* he wouldn't go? Was he shy? Just didn't like talking about God in public places? Actually, there's something more going on here: asking Jonah to go to Nineveh was like asking a Jew to enter the heart of Nazi Germany . . . and tell them to repent.

I'm not sure I'd go either.

Nineveh was not just any city; it was the capital of the Assyrian empire. The Assyrians were famous for devising gruesome methods of public torture, like skinning the conquered alive, or driving stakes through their rectums carefully enough to lift them high and keep them breathing for days, or orchestrating large public displays of skulls and mutilated bodies—all intended to frighten potential enemies and show off their sheer power.[2]

So "Jonah, go to Nineveh" was no small ask.

The prophet Nahum cries out against Nineveh, that she is a "city of blood, full of lies, full of plunder, never without victims!" She is a military city, filled with the sound of "galloping horses and jolting chariots! Charging cavalry, flashing swords and glittering spears!" She has "enslaved nations" with "endless cruelty" and within her are stacked "many casualties, piles of dead bodies without number, people stumbling over the corpses."[3]

Assyria was brutal . . . and she was after Israel. Assyria conquered Israel, destroying the Northern Kingdom's cities and carrying the people into captivity. This was the beginning of Israel's exile. Later, Babylon would polish off the job, laying waste to Jerusalem and the Southern Kingdom. Assyria was a beast, intent on devouring Jonah's people.

The prophet didn't want to stick his head in the lion's mouth, and I can't say that I blame him.

Add to this that Jonah wasn't ringing the doorbell with

flowers and chocolate in hand. He was bringing bad news, calling Nineveh's wickedness on the carpet, delivering a court summons for their impending judgment. Imagine you have a worst enemy who wants to tear your family apart, so you pay a visit to his home and critique his decorating, pull the skeletons out of his closet, and remind him that his house sits on stolen property—and it's time to pay the piper. Jonah would be vulnerable, exposed, and ready for the Assyrians to shoot the messenger.

THE BELLY OF THE BEAST

The most famous part of the story is, of course, Jonah being swallowed by a "huge fish." As Jonah makes his great escape and sails away, God hunts him down, sending a massive storm that riles up the high seas. Jonah's thrown overboard, and God provides a big fish to swallow him. Jonah spends three days and nights in the most uncomfortable hotel ever, essentially buried alive in the smelly belly of the whale. But the prophet cries out to God from the drowning depths of darkness, so God commands the fish, and it "vomited Jonah onto dry land."[4]

What's this all about?

When Israel heard this story, yes they would have heard *a rebellious prophet was swallowed by a big fish*. But they also would have heard something much more. They would have seen in Jonah a dramatic picture of their own story. Let me explain.

Beasts were, for Israel, an image of empire. And the sea, as we've seen, was a picture of primordial chaos (the *tohu wa vohu* that threatened to tear creation apart). The prophet Daniel described "beasts" that "came up out of the sea" as a symbol for Babylon, Rome, and other empires that raged against God.[5] These pagan powers devoured nations, assimilated them into their belly (under their authority), and perhaps most important, were a symbol of exile: the people of God lived under these bestial powers that raged in God's world.

So when Israel heard about a giant sea-beast rising up from the stormy waters of chaos to devour the prophet, they would have seen in Jonah a dramatic representative of their own story: a pagan empire arising to devour God's rebellious people and drag them into exile. Like Jonah, Israel was called to be a "light to the nations," to display God's glory to the surrounding ancient world. She was called to embody God's justice, an implicit critique of the wickedness in the bestial empires that crouched at her doorstep.

But Israel ran from that calling. Like the prophet doing a 180 on a boat, Israel fled from God and took on the ways of the nations. Like Jonah with the pagan sailors, Israel blended in with the idols of the nations rather than standing out as the people of God. Like Jonah on his way to Tarshish (the wealthy "Times Square" trading center of the ancient world), Israel ran on a materialistic pursuit of security and independence apart from God. Like Jonah asleep on the boat, Israel fell spiritually asleep, far from her calling and distant from God.

So God sent a "violent storm" that dragged Israel into exile.[6]

Assyria arose like a beast from the primordial forces of chaos, devouring Israel and dragging her down into the depths of destruction. The pagan empire consumed God's people, conquering the Northern Kingdom, and carrying them into captivity. Yet miraculously, God sustained his people in the "belly of the beast." Like a rebellious prophet crying out in repentance from the heart of the fish, Israel cried out in repentance from the midst of the exile, longing for God's restoration.

Jonah's story recapitulates Israel's story. The prophet is a representative for his people, who rebelled against their prophetic calling to be a signpost to the nations and went into captivity in the belly of a pagan empire.[7]

But God's not done with her yet.

Listen to Jonah's cry from the belly of the fish, and hear in it the national cry of Israel, bellowing in hope from the depths of exile:

> You hurled me into the depths,
> into the very heart of the seas,
> and the currents swirled about me. . . .
> I said, "I have been banished
> from your sight;
> yet I will look again
> toward your holy temple." . . .
> From deep in the realm of the dead I called for help,
> and you listened to my cry. . . .
> My prayer rose to you,
> to your holy temple. . . .
> I, with shouts of grateful praise,
> will sacrifice to you. . . .
> I will say, "Salvation comes from the LORD."[8]

God would ultimately deliver his people. Like Jonah being spit back onto dry land, the prophets saw exile as a picture of *death*, distant from the face of their Creator, but God would bring the nation back to life into flourishing before his presence, carrying her back into the land as his people.[9] Like Jonah, Israel would return from captivity and reclaim her prophetic destiny to call the nations back to God.

THE EMPIRE REPENTS

Perhaps the most fascinating aspect of Jonah's story is not surviving in a whale—*it is that Assyria repents!* Jonah enters the "Nazi capital" to preach its impending destruction, and to everyone's surprise, the empire responds: "The Ninevites believed God. A fast was proclaimed, and all of them, from the greatest to the least, put on sackcloth."[10] The king himself issues a decree:

> Let everyone call urgently on God. Let them give up their evil ways and their violence. Who knows? God may yet relent and with compassion turn from his fierce anger so that we will not perish.[11]

God went after Assyria, and when they responded, "he relented and did not bring on them the destruction he had threatened."[12] Okay, if you're Jonah, perhaps the only thing worse than waltzing into Hitler's headquarters and having your head blown off is having him fall to his knees and receive God's forgiveness. *They're repenting! You're letting them off the hook? These tyrants who've destroyed us, laid waste to nations, and devastated the world?!*

Jonah is livid; he wants revenge. In fact, Jonah tells us here the real reason he initially fled from Nineveh ran deeper than fear; it was bitterness: "God, I knew your love was so great you'd look for any chance to avoid their disaster."[13] Jonah didn't want any chance for them to repent and be spared. Perhaps Jonah's relatives had been killed, his village raped and pillaged, his own children laid waste at the hands of the Assyrians.

Forgiveness was too much.

So Jonah asks God to kill him: "Now, LORD, take away my

life, for it is better for me to die than to live."[14] God's enemy-love can feel like too much when *our* enemies are lavished upon as the recipients. So God gives him a little object lesson: a plant grows up over Jonah to give him shade outside the city—Jonah's happy. The next day, God has a worm eat the plant—Jonah gets sunburnt and loses it, exploding at God, "I'm so angry I wish I were dead."[15]

God confronts Jonah: *"Is it right for you to have so much concern for this plant, though you didn't tend it or make it grow, and I not have concern for this city of 120,000 people who can't tell right from wrong?"*[16] The story ends here, confronting Jonah—and God's people—on this note with a question: Will we share in God's extravagant, pursuing love, even for our brutal enemies who've torn our lives apart?

Because God's mercy is much wider and deeper than our own. Even for Nazis.

Let's take a look now at how to apply this today . . .

CHAPTER 32

Forgiveness Sets You Free

Unlike Jonah, whom we looked at in the last chapter, how do we embody God's reconciling love? My friend Célestin has taught me more on this than perhaps anyone I know.[1] Célestin endured the Rwandan genocide and its aftermath, as men in uniforms invaded his village with guns, grenades, machetes, and clubs. His mother fainted and, presumed dead, spent four hours buried beneath the bodies of her friends. They killed his father, four other family members, and seventy people from his church.

Célestin's community was destroyed.

ENEMY-LOVE

Everything in him raged against the killers; he was filled with understandable hate for those who had torn his world apart. Like Jonah, he cried out to God for revenge. Yet he heard God say, *"You see them as tribesmen instead of as brothers. You are becoming what you hate. You have been teaching others to forgive. It is time for you to forgive—without even knowing who did it."*[2]

Unlike Jonah, Célestin pressed into God's heartbeat of enemy-love. Over time, as God's forgiveness took root in his life, he found himself letting go of anger and bitterness. To his surprise he began to find freedom. Though his heart fought hard against it at first, Célestin says forgiveness sets you free:

> Forgiveness means you are not bound by the past, and you are not defined by what has happened to you. Healing does not take place until we forgive. The person who fails to forgive becomes a victim twice—a victim of what has been done to him and a victim of what he does to himself.[3]

Célestin says there's a difference between forgiveness and reconciliation. Forgiving the killers didn't mean hanging out with them or pretending that nothing had happened. Forgiveness is a posture toward those who have wronged you, while reconciliation is a process that requires the repentant involvement of the offender. "Reconciliation is a process," he said. "We have to build trust. We must begin the journey of trusting again. Reconciliation may require a third party to bring two people together—a neutral party who loves both of you."[4]

A year later, this posture was put to the test when he unexpectedly met the killers' family. They didn't recognize him, and the tumultuous storm of emotions grew and raged within his heart as he grappled with how to respond. After composing himself, he approached them, declared what had been done . . . and offered forgiveness. Face-to-face, they owned the wrong and received it.

Célestin embraced them.

He even asked their forgiveness for the hatred he'd held in his heart toward them. As they built trust, they began building community together as Célestin started a reconciliation ministry that brought Hutu and Tutsi together to process the genocide, seek biblical forgiveness, and link arms side by side in community development initiatives together.

Some didn't like it. Many of his people felt it was a betrayal to focus on reconciliation rather than justice. Célestin was beaten severely, interrogated, and tortured multiple times for suspicion of his motives, in working for the welfare of his "enemies." Reconciliation is not only hard; it's costly.

Over time, however, the ministry took hold and is now thriving in eight African countries. Célestin dives headfirst into war zones and conflict areas, like Sudan and the Congo, bringing leaders together from government, business, the church, police, grassroots initiatives, and more. Célestin walks boldly into the center of empires and, in the belly of the beasts, proclaims boldly the reconciling love of God.

POLITICS OF THE PURE HEART

Who do you have a hard time forgiving? Are you holding bitterness against someone who's wounded you? In our society there's a sense in which it's easier: we can just move away. That family member who annoys you? Move to another city and you only have to endure him or her at holidays. That friend who hurt you? Just stop calling and find new people to hang out with. That spouse who now feels more like an enemy at home? Sign the divorce certificate and start over.

We're a society that likes to think of ourselves as loving, but it's not because we deal well with conflict—we simply avoid it and move away. It's the luxury of a wealthy society, where we don't have to endure the Hatfields and McCoys in such close proximity as our ancestors once did. We don't need forgiveness; we just need *space*.

But this isn't biblical enemy-love. And as Célestin found, there's a freedom in forgiveness that we're missing out on. There's a beauty in reconciliation, a power in pursuing those who've wronged us. What will it take to enter this beautiful power? For starters, we might need to see ourselves as more than simply victims.

We often focus on Jesus welcoming the beat-up and broken (and we probably see ourselves in their faces), which is true and great, but we don't often focus on his message: how he called them to repent, calls *us* to repent. What is going on here? This is horribly offensive, to call *the victims* to repent. As Miroslav Volf asked, "Does he not have anything more comforting and constructive to say to 'the poor' than to insult them by calling them sinners?"[5]

But Volf goes on, observing our tendency to use the sin done *to* us to justify the sin done *by* us. In his own country's genocide, he details how narratives of victimization were used to justify the perpetuation of hate, retaliatory violence, and the ever-escalating cycle of brutality and slaughter against the "other." In what he calls "the politics of the pure heart," he concludes that while victims obviously do *not* need to repent for the evil done to them, yet still:

> victims need to repent of the fact that all too often they mimic
> the behavior of the oppressors, let themselves be shaped in the
> mirror image of the enemy. They need to repent also of the
> desire to excuse their own reactive behavior either by claiming
> that they are not responsible for it or that such reactions are a

necessary condition of liberation. Without repentance for these sins, the full human dignity of victims will not be restored and needed social change will not take place.[6]

Like Célestin, who recognized the hatred that had taken root in his own heart, we need the freedom of forgiveness. Like Jonah, we need healing not only for the sin done to us, but the sinful posture we want to justify in response.

A BETTER JONAH

Jesus is a better Jonah. In fact, he *uses* Jonah to point to his own mission:

> For as Jonah was three days and three nights in the belly of a huge fish, so the Son of Man will be three days and three nights in the heart of the earth.[7]

As the "perfect storm" swirls around Jerusalem, Jesus lets his own body be thrown overboard so the many might live.[8] The high priest, Caiaphas, walks Jesus down the plank and sounds a lot like Jonah's pagan sailors when he declares, "It is better . . . that one man die for the people than that the whole nation perish."[9] Jesus walks right up to the brutal, crucifying power of Rome's exilic empire—and lets it devour him. He identifies with those who've run from God and, as he's tossed into the chaotic waters below, he bears our exile and death.

The swirling sea of primordial chaos drags him into the darkness of the grave, as the *tohu wa vohu* consumes him in the bowels of the earth below—Jesus is swallowed by death.

But God's not done with him yet.

After three days in the tomb, the belly of the beast "vomits him out" onto dry land. Jesus is raised in power as a signpost to the nations. The ghastly graveyard of exilic empire is unable to hold him. The Resurrected King proclaims repentance and reconciliation to the very people who've blown his world apart.

Jesus is like Jonah, except he doesn't run from his calling. Jesus runs down the plank and takes a swan dive of his own initiative, plunging into the swirling waters below to bring us home. Jesus walks boldly right into the heart of the empire, to outstretch his arms in the reconciling embrace of enemy-love: "While we were yet sinners, Christ died for us."[10] And Jesus doesn't get angry and pout when rebels return to God, when Nazis repent and enter the kingdom, when enemies receive the embrace of their Creator—it's the reason he came in the first place.

Jesus is a better Jonah, who rejoices to bring us home.

CHAPTER 33

Blind Date

In Jonah, we saw God call the victim to pursue his oppressor, the ones without power to pursue the ones who've wielded power against them. But it also works the other direction. God calls his followers to join him in pursuing the beat-up, battered, and broken, the rebellious and disenfranchised, even if their lifestyle may cause a massive inconvenience. Let's look at the story of Hosea, who beautifully fleshes this out.

MATCH MADE IN HEAVEN

God has some exciting news for Hosea: *Come with me! I feel like playing matchmaker, and boy do I have the perfect girl for you.* Hosea has probably always dreamed of meeting "the one," finding that perfect romance to last a lifetime—and what better person to lead the search than God? So imagine the prophet's excitement as he takes God's hand downtown to meet his bride-to-be.

The prophet has probably bought into the popular notions of a "godly marriage," so he sees Sally walk by and asks, "God, is that her? Sally sings in the choir, always knows the right answers at Bible study. She's a *godly* woman, just right for a prophet." The Matchmaker smiles and says, *"Nope, not Sally."*

Next Barbara walks by. "That must be her, right? Barbie does her hair up all nice, is always on her way to the gym, turns all the heads, just like those magazine covers in the checkout line . . ." Hosea rubs his hands together like a schoolboy, while God patiently responds, *"No, not Barbara."*

The prophet turns the corner and feels a nudge in his rib: *There, that's her!* "What? Gomer?!" Hosea catches his breath. "God, I think you've made a mistake. I'm a *godly* man, a man of the cloth, I'm a prophet to the people, I'm a . . . And she's a prostitute, a harlot, a woman of the streets. Do you know what they do behind closed doors? Do you know how many lovers she's been with? Lord knows the infections she must have . . . how *improper* this all is! You're joking, right? Things just aren't done this way. The rumors will fly. *I'll* be on those magazine covers. What will the people think?"

"What will the people think?" God responds. *"That's precisely the point: I want the people to think, to see, to know . . . who I am."*

"You're going to be a picture of me."

GOD LOVES WHORES

Hosea is a picture of God, the Creator who bypassed the shiny, sexy superstar empires of the ancient world and entered into covenant with Israel, the last and least of the nations, beat-up and broken on the outskirts of Egypt's empire. God drew her to him, faithfully and lavishly cared for her, provided for and protected her from the surrounding empires. But she continually left him, ran after other lovers: worshipping idols, practicing injustice, and unleashing destruction in the land.

Gomer is a picture of God's people, continually leaving the warmth and security of a healthy home for the cheap hotel on the outskirts of town, selling themselves to the cheapest bidder only to find themselves enslaved to the cruel, abusive lovers who once spoke so sweetly. Fortunately for Israel, God can't give up on her: his love is too strong. So God tells the prophet to marry a prostitute, as a picture of his pursuit:

> Go, take unto thee a wife of whoredoms and children of whoredoms: for the land hath committed great whoredom, departing from the LORD.[1]

Prostitutes were looked down upon in the ancient Middle East, haunted by shame and social stigma. God doesn't take the glamorous Disney princess for a wife; he goes for the restless and discarded at the bottom of the social pile, taking the bruised and battered and saying, "That's my bride."

Because God loves whores.

CRAZY NAMES

The prophet and the prostitute have kids, and they give them the craziest names. I think it's wild these days when pop stars name their kids Apple or Moon Unit, but Hosea and Gomer have us beat. They name their first son *Jezreel,* after a horrible massacre site. This would be like a Native American family naming their precious baby boy Wounded Knee, or a Vietnamese family calling their child My Lai. Why such a brutal name? The significance is that God remembers the horrible massacre and will repay those with blood on their hands who were responsible.

Their next two children are named *Lo-Ruhamah* and *Lo-Ammi,* which mean "not loved" and "not my people." *What?* Talk about getting teased at school. Can you imagine hearing every day, "What's up, Not Loved? Hey, Not My People!"? The point? They're a signpost of Israel's adultery, a reminder of her unfaithfulness to God.

It might sound mean to name kids that way, but not to worry—it was short-lived. Changing names was common in biblical times, so before long their names were transformed to: "My People," "My Loved One," and "Children of the Living God." They became a signpost of God's reckless love, his pursuit that made them his people again, a promise of hope and restoration.

While Israel's being mistreated by her cruel, abusive lovers in exile, God starts planning a romantic date with her in the desert:

> *Therefore I am now going to allure her;*
> *I will lead her into the wilderness*
> *and speak tenderly to her.*
> *There I will give her back her vineyards,*
> *and will make the Valley of [Trouble] a door of hope.*
> *There she will [sing] as in the days of her youth,*
> *as in the day she came up out of Egypt.*[2]

It was in exile that Israel's heart turned back to God. It's often at the end of our rope that we're ready to fall into grace, as God uses the gnarly circumstances in our life to draw us to him. It's often when we experience the consequences and devastation of our sin that we find God encountering us, as our hearts grow inflamed with affection for the Savior we tried to leave behind.

Jesus comes after us in the desert, turning our wilderness of troubles into a "door of hope," a turning point through which we enter into intimacy with him. The Father begins to restore our "vineyards," growing new life and lifting us on his shoulders to carry us through the wilderness back to our home with him in the land. The Valley of Trouble can become a door of hope.

MEN IN HEELS

We tend to think of Jonah and Hosea as the heroes of the story, but in many ways they are the antagonists. God is the Hero trying to communicate his saving love, while Jonah's and Hosea's resistance must be overcome. God runs to Assyria, while Jonah running the other direction is the conflict in the story that must be resolved. God goes after his unfaithful bride, but Hosea must face the challenge of living out this countercultural act.

God pursues Nazis and whores, but his people often refuse to go with him.

God is not only teaching Israel and Assyria about his great love; he's teaching his prophets as well. Similarly, we tend to think of ourselves as the heroes who are going to bring God's love to others, but generally we are first and foremost the obstacles that must be overcome. We need to first taste the medicine we plan to offer, to experience God's transforming goodness in our own lives. But when you truly do, you can't help but give it away. When we are bound into union with the Pursuing God, we cannot help but become part of his pursuit of the world.

To marry Gomer, Hosea had to be willing to get uncomfortable. To identify with her, he was willing to be misunderstood. To embody God's redemptive love, he was willing to be inconvenienced and to put a public target on his back. Jesus was like this, known as a friend of prostitutes, tax collectors, and sinners, willing to be identified with, and inconvenienced by, those often rejected, abused, or forgotten by society.

This reminds me of my friends Tom and Howard, who asked years ago, "How can we identify with exploited women in our city?" Tom rallied hundreds of men to support the Sexual Assault Resource Center—a brave group of women who provide frontline support to victims of domestic violence and sexual assault in our city. There was a "Mile in Her Shoes" walk, where hundreds of men—including a large biker gang—marched in high heels through downtown Portland to identify with survivors and raise funding for frontline workers.

But this was only the beginning. Tom launched an organization called EPIK and began dreaming with Howard about ways to do more.[3] After years of prayerful involvement with frontline organizations, they launched an initiative at our church, in close cooperation with local law enforcement, to disrupt the sexual exploitation of children online. During an evening online patrol, their team posts ads together pretending to be girls soliciting for sex, crafting the ads to sound as young as possible. When the phone calls come streaming in, they run through a script: "Hi. My name is Howard. We have your phone number and it may be forwarded to local law enforcement for follow-up. We want you to listen while we share some information with you . . ."

They educate callers, unpack how the exploitation works, offer resources for sexual addiction, and demystify myths, explaining, "You're not helping put her through school." They identify the most frequent callers and pass their numbers on, as a sort of "anonymous tip" to the police department, who is able to correlate the phone numbers with names, addresses, and Facebook accounts, to let the callers know they were found responding to the ads.

I imagine these guys hope their wives don't pick up the mail that day.

In the first few months, Tom and Howard's team of ten guys tracked more than six hundred unique phone numbers. So they trained forty more members, and now as I write this they've tracked more than six thousand unique phone numbers, helping lead to multiple arrests of repeat offenders. The really crazy part came when they were invited to share at a major national anti-trafficking conference. After they shared, a team got up from two major universities who had been monitoring online trafficking in cities across the country. They explained how trafficking had remained constant in all major cities across the country.

Except one.

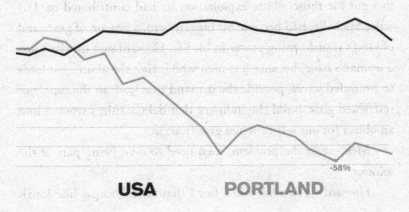

-58%

USA   **PORTLAND**

In Portland, they'd found a sharp, drastic, plummeting drop . . . right after Tom and Howard's initiative started. They hadn't known how to explain the drop or what caused it, until now. Tom and Howard's team received a large grant and an invitation from ten major cities, and is now hard at work training police departments, churches, and civic agencies on how to work together starting similar initiatives across the country.

WE ARE GOMER

I could say it all started when they walked a mile in the shoes of exploited women, but it actually started earlier. Howard would tell you it started long before that, when God convicted him about his porn addiction. He'd grown convicted that he was participating in something profoundly exploitative to women in our society. Jesus confronted Howard, and he went through a long season of dealing honestly with his addiction with the grace of his wife, the support of a small group, and the healing power of God.

It was coming out the other side that he wanted to give back, to fight for those whose exploitation he had contributed to. His wife, Michelle, had become his biggest hero, a beacon of grace and of God's transforming power in his life. Howard says this isn't just a woman's issue, because it is men who inflict the abuse that leads to wounded wives, provide the demand that leads to the supply of trafficked girls, build the industry that dehumanizes women into an object for our self-centered gratification.

Men create the problem; men need to own being part of the solution.

Howard's a hero of mine, but I share this because like Jonah and Hosea, we are first part of the problem before we become part of the solution. There's a danger if we only give Hosea a superficial reading and use the prophet as a picture of men-in-general coming in to rescue women-in-general. Hosea is not a picture of men-in-general; he is a picture of God. And Gomer is not a picture of women-in-general; she is a picture of all of us.

We are Gomer.

Howard is Gomer. You and I are Gomer. Howard says his wife, Michelle, was like Hosea in his life, displaying God's faithfulness to him amid his own unfaithfulness. And she says it was all because of the experience of God's grace in her own life. We are the unfaithful ones in need of our faithful God, who loves us despite our unfaithfulness, who meets us in our brokenness, who speaks softly to us in the desert of our destruction and delights to bring us home. I am a man, and I am the whore. Yet I am more than that—I've experienced the pursuing love of our Creator. I am a man, and I am also the bride.

MY MOTHER, THE WHORE

It's not quite right, however, to say *I* am the bride, for in the New Testament it is *we*, together as the people of God, who are the bride. Of course, the church is not very popular today, and sometimes for good reason. Like Gomer (and Israel), we've often run from God, pursuing sex, money, and power above him and being shaped in their image. A lot of our warts and pimples are showing; our skirt's been lifted and shame exposed.

The church is marked by unfaithfulness.

Yet God is faithful. Augustine famously said, "The church is a whore, but she's my mother."[4] I love this quote and the tension it expresses. On the one hand, we have this checkered history (and present), yet Jesus pursues us through her. I wouldn't know Jesus without his people, and neither would you. The church has carried the words of Scripture, the witness of the Spirit, and the sacraments of God through history right on down to us. Like Hosea, Jesus pursues his messy bride and identifies with us, even when it's in confrontation. Our hope as the church is not in our greatness but in the greatness of God.

We receive the presence of God through the people of God. As Cyprian of Carthage famously said in the early church, "you cannot have God for your Father unless you have the church for your mother."[5] We receive God's life through her, and from her womb in the power of the Spirit we are born into the presence of God.

Jesus is a better Hosea. He comes after us in our weakness, in our broken areas, the places where we don't have it all together. We don't have to perform for Jesus, to try and make ourselves into a shiny, sexy supermodel so he'll want to take us as his wife. Jesus delights to pursue us at our worst, to meet us where we are and take us as we are. As Luther observed, "The love of God does not find, but creates, that which is pleasing to it."[6] God isn't looking for the beautiful to give his love to; it's the reception of God's love that makes us beautiful.

Jesus comes looking not for our trophies, but our scars.

So there is a freedom to get vulnerable before God with where we're really at, our frustrations and disappointments, the areas we feel as though we're a letdown or we don't measure up. Those are precisely the areas where we find ourselves in need of grace, before a God who loves to give it. The beauty of the gospel is not that we make ourselves good enough for God to *need* us; it's that God *wants* us and finds us where we're at.

KEY IDEA

Caricature: God prefers the polished, pretty, and put together.

Gospel: God goes after Nazis and whores, victims and
oppressors, to make them his people and his bride.

CHAPTER 34

Vampires

Vampires are strange creatures. To sustain their existence, they must feast on the life of others. Without fresh blood, they waste away. This is the stuff of horror, of course, because their craving destroys their victim. And it's the stuff of pop culture: as Bram Stoker, *Buffy the Vampire Slayer*, and the Twilight series have taught us. We seem fascinated by vampires.

Ironically, Jesus makes his followers sound like vampires. Listen to this shocking imagery Jesus uses when issuing a challenge to the crowds:

> Unless you eat the flesh of the Son of Man and drink his blood, you have no life in you. . . . . Whoever eats my flesh and drinks my blood remains in me, and I in them. Just as the living Father sent me and I live because of the Father, so the one who feeds on me will live because of me.[1]

Are Jesus' followers like vampires? Yes and no, I would say. Yes, because we need his life to survive. Without it we'd waste away, like Count Dracula eventually crumbling to ash. Jesus gives his life sacrificially so that we might receive life from him. Jesus brings us back from the brink of death to thrive in the presence of God.

Yet no, because Jesus is no mere victim, but a sacrificial Savior who willingly gives his life that we might live. And no, because Jesus' resurrected life is inexhaustible: we cannot take away from his fullness, detract from his victory, or decrease his shining glory. As Jesus fills us, he does not lessen while lifting us to the greatness of life in him.

And once more no, because here's the major distinction that sets us apart from the vampires: Jesus makes us bearers of life, rather than death, to a world that he loves. When Jesus takes us to himself, he makes us *part of* himself. He doesn't just invite us to join a club; he makes us part of *his body.* The church is not so much a collection of individuals pursuing God together as, rather, the body of people through whom God pursues the world. Jesus continues to *embody* his outpoured love into the world—through us.

The Pursuing God makes us a pursuing people.

THE BODY THAT MAKES US A BODY

I love every week when we participate in Communion, or the Eucharist, while we worship as a church body. I've heard some people talk about the Eucharist as just a remembrance, or symbol, that Jesus died two thousand years ago—like that picture on the mantel of Grandpa, who fought in the war, a memory of an ancient sacrifice that impacted my life today. But it is *much more* than this. The point is not simply to practice a religious ritual, but to come to the living Christ at the center of our life as a people.

While Catholic, Protestant, and Orthodox have disagreed on the exact nature of *how* the Eucharist works, all the major traditions have agreed that Jesus is actually present through it.[2] In the power of Jesus' Spirit, his presence is alive with us today.

Now, normally when we eat food, we take it into ourselves. When I eat a taco, I ingest its nutrients and absorb its protein as fuel—that delicious carne asada and guacamole become part of me. But Communion works just the opposite: as we feast on Jesus, the bread of life, we are taken *into him*, absorbed and integrated into the body of Christ.

Augustine envisioned Jesus as saying:

I am the food of the fully grown; grow and you will feed on me. And you will not change me into you like the food your flesh eats, but you will be changed into me.[3]

As Jesus binds us into union with himself, we are brought into the body of Christ. Communion is not just an act between me and Jesus, but a participation in the people of God. As Orthodox theologian Alexander Schmemann observes, the original meaning of the word *liturgy* was "an action by which a group of people become something corporately which they had not been as a mere collection of individuals."[4] Jesus gathers us together and forms us as his people.

The Eucharist is the body that makes us a body.

Jesus gives us his body as gift. Yet usually we receive gifts as passive recipients, then take them away on our own. We unwrap that Christmas present, then head to our room to play with those Legos or that new remote control car by ourselves. But when we receive *Jesus'* body as gift, we are *brought into* the gift: we become part of the body of Christ we receive. Indeed, union with Jesus is wrapped up in the very nature of the gift itself.

We become Jesus' gift to the world.

Jesus takes us in his Spirit, breaks us like that bread, and pours us out like wine, giving our lives in sacrificial love to his world. In the words of Catholic theologian William Cavanaugh, the Eucharist is

> the heart of true *religio* [religion], a practice of binding us to the body of Christ which is our salvation . . . the stunning public *leitourgia* [liturgy] in which humans are made members of God's very body. . . . As members of the Body, we then become nourishment for others—including those not part of the visible Body—in the unending trinitarian economy of gratuitous giving and joyful reception.[5]

The Father embraces us through his Son, in the power of their Spirit, and pours our lives out for his world. Jesus continues to take on flesh and bone today, as he unites himself to us through his Spirit for the Father's glory in the world.

I AM NOT THE CHURCH

Communion confronts my individualism. I tend to think of the church as something like a bowling league or manga club: an affinity group for people who like the same things or share my same interests. But in Communion, I am being gathered into the global and historical body of Christ. I am bound with the Afghan villager and the Vietnamese businesswoman across national borders, united with my homeless neighbor and the CEO who runs my bank, drawn into life together with the soldier, the soccer mom, and the starving artist sitting in the pew next to me—the people of God in all our diverse array.

Jesus didn't die so I could hang out with my buddies; he died to reconcile a gloriously diverse humanity.

This confronts the individualistic way many Americans approach life with Jesus. For example, we often read the New Testament books as if they were written directly to us like personal letters. But as a friend once pointed out, "The *you*s of the New Testament are plural." What he meant was this: in English, we say *you* whether we're talking one-on-one to a friend in the coffee shop or to a large crowd onstage through a microphone—it can be read either singular or plural. When we come across the word *you* in our Bibles, we tend to assume it's singular, but most of the *you*s in the New Testament are plural.

The closest thing we have in English is *y'all*, Southern colloquial for "you all." It's too bad Paul wasn't a Southerner, because this emphasis would stand out more. Check out, for example, how a few popular verses might sound this way. Philippians 2:5 admonishes the church, "Have the same mind in y'all that was in Christ Jesus"; Colossians 1:27 rejoices in God's presence with the church as "Christ in y'all, the hope of glory"; Ephesians 2:22 says that in Jesus, "y'all too, are being built together to become a dwelling in which God lives by his Spirit."

The emphasis is less on "me" and more on "we."

God cares about our life together as his people. The *one another* statements throughout the New Testament also strongly showcase this dynamic: Romans 12:10 encourages us to "honor *one another* above yourselves"; Galatians 5:13 to "serve *one another* humbly in love"; and 1 Thessalonians 5:11 to "encourage *one another* and build each other up."

These commands are hard to do alone in a room by yourself.

Our Bibles read less as, *Hey Johnny, be good,* and much more as, *Hey y'all, be good to one another and watch how y'all are living as God's people together.* Jesus indwells *us* as his body. Discipleship is something that happens through his communion with us, as his Spirit forms us together as his bride.

This is a weird way to work. Wouldn't it be easier for God to just approach us directly, rather than going through his messy people? Lesslie Newbigin observes how we want to encounter God through the "skylight," opening our own personal window to the heavens above to have a direct one-on-one encounter with God. But God prefers instead to come through the "front door," encountering us through the neighbor who comes bearing the message and presence of Jesus.[6]

Why? What reason could God possibly have? It is because, Newbigin reflects, God is not as interested in millions of scattered, one-on-one relationships with isolated individuals as he is in building a body, forming a community, gathering a people to himself and through himself to one another. "How beautiful are the feet of those who bring good news."[7] God enters through our front door so that we can only receive him by receiving the presence of our neighbor.

We enter his body by receiving his body.

BAPTISM: UP FROM THE CHAOS

If Communion sustains us as Jesus' body, baptism is how we first enter that body. Baptism can seem like a weird symbol at first glance: *Getting dunked under the water? What's the point of that?* But like Communion, it is more than a symbol; it's a sacrament—a means of grace through the power of God's Spirit.

Baptism is, first and foremost, an identification with Christ in his death and resurrection. As Jesus went down into the grave to identify with us and was raised by the Father into new life, so we go down into the waters to be united with Jesus in his death, and are raised through the power of his resurrection.

"In the name of the Father, the Son, and the Holy Spirit," we are baptized into the very name of God. I die to myself under the death-dealing waters of sin and destruction, and as my head breaks forth from the surface of the grave and the fresh air rushes into my rising, gasping lungs, I find myself in the very presence of God. We are raised in the power of the Spirit, through the life of the Son, into the embrace of the Father.

We are raised unto God.

And we are raised into God's people. Baptism is entrance into *the church*. We rise not only into union with Jesus, but into the body of Christ in all its fullness. The two are simultaneous. We do not join our lives to Jesus, then go find a church. When we are bound to Jesus, we are—by the very nature of that act—bound into union with the church.

Union with Jesus means communion with his people.

While Jesus' death and resurrection are central, when we zoom out to the broader biblical storyline, baptism is loaded with more layers of meaning. The waters, as we have seen, are a Hebrew symbol for the primordial chaos, the *tohu wa vohu*, the state of disorder that sin wants to unravel the world back into. As we go under the waters, we identify with the trajectory of our sin: the nothingness of separation from God, the annihilation of the world in its distance from our heavenly Father, the unraveling of creation under our rebellion against the Creator.

And yet, God's gracious Spirit parts the waters once again. As in the beginning to make space for creation; as in Noah's day to bring forth restoration; as in the Exodus to bring slaves into freedom, the Creator parts the waters, bringing us out from the enslaving chaos of our life under sin and into the fresh space of kingdom life for his new creation.

Baptism is not only our entrance into God; it is God's entrance into us, and through us into his world. Some people think of the church as a fortress, a holy huddle clambering inside the defensive walls, trying to protect ourselves from the big bad world outside. We want to make sure we get "upstairs" to God and aren't left behind on earth below. But the life of the church works in the opposite direction.

As we are brought into the embrace of the Father, through the life of the Son, in the power of the Spirit, we are caught up through God's pursuit of us into God's pursuit of the world. We are no longer afraid of being tainted or inconvenienced by the messiness around us. We can dive headfirst into the sin-struck war zone of God's world to embody his life, hope, and sacrificial love.

CHAPTER 35

Kingdom in the Wilderness

After Israel's baptism at the Red Sea, when God parted the waters to bring her out of Egypt's deadly empire, her life with God in the wilderness was a messy process.[1] As the saying goes, "it took God one day to get Israel out of Egypt, and forty years to get Egypt out of Israel." The desert was a time of sanctification, of God forming her as his people, of Israel learning to rely on her King.

During this time, her "Communion" was manna, the heavenly bread that sustained her as a body in the wilderness. Interestingly, Jesus drew on this image of manna in the desert when he said to eat his flesh and drink his blood (the vampire saying we saw in the last chapter). Jesus fed five thousand people with miraculous bread, and they started saying, *Isn't this like Moses giving manna in the desert?* Jesus declares:

> I am the bread of life . . . the bread that comes down from heaven
> and gives life to the world. . . . Whoever comes to me will never
> go hungry. . . . Your ancestors ate the manna in the wilderness,

yet they died. . . . [But] whoever eats this bread will live forever. This bread is my flesh, which I will give for the life of the world.[2]

Jesus sustains us in the wilderness with himself.

JOURNEY TO THE PROMISED LAND

The church recapitulates Israel. Did you ever wonder why Jesus chose twelve disciples? Why not eleven, or thirteen, or forty-two? The number twelve is itself significant: it draws upon the number of Israel's twelve tribes. Jesus' audience would have seen him as reconstituting Israel around himself, centering the life of the people of God around his person. Now, if Jesus saw *himself* as one of the tribes, he would have only picked *eleven* disciples—leaving room for himself as the twelfth. But in choosing twelve disciples, Jesus places himself in the position of the electing God who chose the twelve tribes of Israel.

The people of God are being reconstituted around Jesus.

And he sustains them with his presence.

The fledgling church is dramatically depicted as a new Israel in the book of Acts. For example, whereas Moses ascended Mount Sinai in the Old Testament to meet with God and bring down the Law, Jesus ascends to God's throne in Acts and brings down the Spirit to his people. Whereas Israel waited upon God at Mount Sinai during Pentecost and, upon seeing God's presence as fire, retreated, the disciples wait upon God in Acts during Pentecost and, upon seeing his presence as fire, are empowered to boldly bear God's presence to the world.

Following the golden calf incident at Mount Sinai, three thousand rebels who rejected the Lord are cut down with the sword and killed by Moses' emissaries. Following the crucifixion of Jesus in the

New Testament, three thousand rebels who crucified the Lord are "cut to the heart" with the Word of God by Jesus' emissaries and receive new life. "For the letter [of the law] kills, but the Spirit gives life."[3] Shortly after Israel is formed as a new community at Mount Sinai, Achan deceptively plunders treasure for himself and buries the spoils with greed—and is struck down by the people. Shortly after the church is formed as a new community in Acts, Ananias and Sapphira deceptively keep treasure for themselves and, like Achan, greedily bury the money—and are struck down in the presence of the people.

The formation of the church mirrors the story of Israel.

This doesn't mean the church *replaces* Israel, but that it is *grafted onto* Israel, through her allegiance to Jesus the Jewish King, the messianic fulfillment of God's promises to bless the nations through the line of Abraham.[4] The church is bound in union with Jesus, the Davidic king, as her head, through whom God is establishing his kingdom in the world.

Like Israel in the wilderness, the church is in an in-between time: having left her allegiance to the Egypt-like empires behind her, yet still awaiting the full coming of the kingdom she travels toward. In the meantime, Jesus' presence travels with us through the Eucharist, the bread that sustains us in the wilderness of the world like manna from heaven. The church finds herself as a kingdom in the wilderness, on her way to the promised land.

CHRIST OUR LIBERATOR

Jesus institutes the Eucharist during Passover. On the night before his death, Jesus is sharing the Passover meal with his disciples (the famous last scene of Leonardo Da Vinci's popular masterpiece). The Gospels

make clear to highlight that this is during Passover. Why is this emphasis significant? On the night before his death, Jesus takes the bread and
wine from the Passover meal and reorients their meaning around him.[5]

The Passover celebrated God's deliverance from Egypt. In
Jesus' day it was the most popular festival of the year. Israel was
under Roman occupation, and the Passover festival not only *looked
back* to the exodus of Moses' day, but *looked forward* to the messianic King's rescue of his people from the hostile powers of the
world that stood opposed to his kingdom.

God's people were looking forward to deliverance.

Many thought it was perhaps *on* Passover that the great new
exodus would come. So every year the city was packed. Pilgrims
came from everywhere, crowding Jerusalem's streets, filling every
hotel, taking up every spare room, and pitching tents in the public
squares. Think Times Square on New Year's Eve—it was the bus-
iest holiday of the year.

All day long, the sound of Passover lambs bleating would echo
throughout the city. It's estimated that many thousands of lambs
would have been slaughtered by the priests on that day, their blood
running through the courts of the temple.[6] Can you hear the noise
of the lambs echoing through the streets and imagine the bustle,
commotion, and expectation in the city?

This sets the stage for Jesus: he *is* the Passover Lamb preparing
to be sacrificed. Luke emphasizes that Jesus' last meal is on the day
when "the Passover lamb had to be sacrificed."[7] As Jesus gets ready to
break the bread and pour the wine, he turns to his disciples and says:

> I have eagerly desired to eat this Passover with you before I suf-
> fer. For I tell you, I will not eat it again until it finds fulfillment
> in the kingdom of God.[8]

Jesus *is* the Passover Lamb at the center of the meal. He sees his sacrifice "finding its fulfillment" in the kingdom of God. This is *loaded* language: Jesus does not die to simply fill a privatized corner of our personal lives. He sees his death inaugurating God's judgment on the Egypt-like empires and hostile powers of our world opposed to his kingdom. Jesus sees his sacrifice liberating his enslaved bride toward the promised land of the new creation.

Jesus likely sees the Israel of his day as bound up with these powers, and himself as preparing the way for those who follow him to "come under" his blood as the Passover Lamb and avoid the coming judgment on the people of God (fulfilled when Rome destroyed Jerusalem and the temple within a generation of Jesus' death). The church rises forth into history, up from the waters of Israel's surrounding destruction and Rome's eventual collapse, as the body and bride of Jesus sustained in the wilderness on her way to the kingdom.

So today when we receive Christ's body and blood, we are to be formed as an embodied signpost of God's coming kingdom, in the midst of our modern empires that want to rule the earth without God. We eagerly anticipate God's coming salvation, to judge the hostile powers that stand opposed to his kingdom and establish the reign of Jesus fully in their place. The Eucharist, with all its Passover imagery, is a public proclamation that our Father is coming to reign through Jesus on earth as in heaven, and his kingdom shall be without end. The Spirit and the bride look up over the walls of Babylon and cry out, "Come, Lord Jesus, come."

We long for our coming deliverance: out of our empires, into his kingdom.

And that day is coming.

CHAPTER 36

Bigfoot Jesus

Jesus has big feet. Upon his resurrection and ascension, we're told God has "put everything under his feet."[1] That's a strange phrase—my feet are not the most sanitary of things; you would probably not want to rub your face up against them. So why does God put *everything* under Jesus' feet? As we shall see, all things coming under Jesus' feet have now become the hope of the world.

KING OF CREATION

"Under his feet" has two main meanings in the Old Testament. First, it means *authority over creation*. David marvels in Psalm 8, for example, that God has given us responsibility to care for his world. He sings:

> *What is mankind that you are mindful of them,*
> *[the son of Adam that you care for him? . . .]*

> *You made them rulers over the works of your hands;*
> *you put everything under their feet.*[2]

David then unpacks this "everything" under our care: *flocks and herds, animals of the wild, birds in the sky, fish in the sea*, climaxing in a cry of praise: "O LORD, our Lord, how [majestic] is Your name in all the earth!"[3] This is a "creation song," looking back at Genesis 1, where God called us to steward the earth he created.

Everything under our feet means we have authority over creation.

Notice something strange, though? This psalm's not talking about Jesus; it's talking about Adam—and us. When Paul quotes this verse, did he miss it? Forget he was in the Old Testament and make a mistake? Did he mean to say, "Adam," and accidentally say, "Jesus"? Actually, Paul is making a powerful observation—let's zoom out to the bigger story to see.

Adam was given authority over the earth, but we know things quickly took a turn for the worse. Our rebellion unleashed destruction into God's good world. Creation was disrupted; thorns and thistles corrupted; earthquakes and volcanoes erupted. As Romans declares, creation *now groans* under the weight of our sin, the heaviness of our feet, longing to be "liberated from its bondage to decay and brought into the freedom and glory of the children of God."[4]

Adam's disobedience brought bondage; Jesus' obedience brings liberation.

Jesus is the new Adam. He succeeded where we failed, faithfully bearing the death-dealing curse of our sin in order to bring the life-giving rule of God to the earth. The liberation of our groaning world has begun in Christ, through the power of his resurrection. God putting *everything under Jesus' feet* means creation has been placed under his authority. Our Resurrected King has redeemed

Adam's calling—and our calling—to establish God's redemptive kingdom.

Jesus has big feet; all of creation can fit beneath them.

His authority is over the world.

THE COMING VICTORY

"Under his feet" also has a second meaning: victory over one's enemies. King David wanted to build a temple for God, for example, but could not because of "the wars waged against [him] from all sides." Eventually, however, once "the LORD put his enemies under his feet," the land had peace and rest, and the temple could be built.[5]

During the war years there was a tension: King David *already* had the land under his feet (God had established him as king), but he did *not yet* have his enemies under his feet (there was opposition to his reign). Similarly, today there is a tension: God has established Jesus as his resurrected king over the earth, placing the land under his feet. But injustice still runs rampant—there are "wars waged against him from all sides"—God's will is not currently done on earth as it is in heaven.

Like King David, Jesus is enthroned and out to "build God's temple"—to flood the earth with God's presence—but there is still widespread opposition to God's kingdom that must be overcome. So Paul also uses "under his feet" in this *future* sense: not only that Jesus reigns over the earth today, but that "he must reign until he has put all his enemies under his feet"—and as Paul reminds us, "the last enemy to be destroyed is death."[6]

Jesus has already risen victorious over the grave today, and the fullness of his victory is coming.

EVERY SQUARE INCH

Jesus is exalted over all. In the famous words of Abraham Kuyper, "there is not a square inch in the whole domain of our human existence over which Christ, who is Sovereign over *all*, does not cry: 'Mine!'"[7] And this is not a greedy, selfish claim, like a toddler clinging for that toy he doesn't want to share and crying, "Mine!" It is the claim of divine love upon that which our rebellion has destroyed, the Pursuing God who comes to find us in our wreckage and, through the power of his presence with us, make all things new.

When we cry, "Jesus is Lord," it can sometimes sound as though it's just for us, as in "Jesus is Lord of my heart," a private, personal confession that has nothing much to do with the world at large. But everyone knew back in the day that "Caesar was Lord," and to say "Jesus is Lord" meant there was a new king in town, a rival to the throne. Jesus has been exalted not only over creation, but over presidents and politicians, economic and social systems, cultures and traditions.

To say "Jesus is Lord" is to place ourselves *under his feet* today, submitting our lives to his kingdom.

As we come under his feet, Paul says we actually become joined to "his body, the fullness of him who fills everything in every way."[8] As the church, Jesus wants to *embody* his life, *fill* the world with his light, *flood* all things with his love, through us today. As the body and bride of our Resurrected King, we're more than an inspirational poster or a sound bite slogan to *remind* people of Jesus; we are, rather, through the power of his Spirit, *the fullness* of Jesus, his actual presence, called to embody his life in the world—as we're brought with creation under the massive, glorious, resurrected feet of Jesus.

Jesus wants to fill his world through us. Heaven is breaking into earth. A people are coming under the rule of the King. Jesus takes us to himself as his body, in order to *embody* his presence in the world through us today. The Father is present through his Word and in his Spirit, gathering a people to him and pouring them out for his world.

We who *feed* on the body *become* the body.

We who *drink* the blood are *poured out*.

The Pursuing God *pursues* through us.

KEY IDEA

Caricature: The church is a collection of individuals pursuing God together.

Gospel: The church is a body of people through whom God pursues the world.

FINISH

All in All

God will be all in all. The Artist will restore his masterpiece through his own indwelling presence. The Captain at the helm of creation will steer the ship into its intended port. Jesus, the Temple now rebuilt, will fulfill heaven and earth by reconciling all things to God. This is the end of the pursuit, for its goal has been attained: the world will be filled with God.

The end of the world is the love of the Trinity.

This side of kingdom come, in a self-centered world, this love seems reckless—for it's willing to crash like a bull into the china shop of our lives and tear apart all the idols we've built in order to get to our hearts. In a world of "might makes right," this love seems irrational—for it works through HIV moms, once-deadbeat dads, and a homeless carpenter who died on a rugged tree. And in a world striving to keep its distance from God, this love seems obsessed—for it's a furious love that stops at nothing to hunt us down and get us back.

This love is dying to bring us home.

The incarnation, cross, and resurrection show us the radical extent God's willing to go to embrace, heal, and restore us. Golgotha, the "Place of the Skull," displays the opposition of God's holy love to the sin and evil that disfigures and destroys his good creation, while simultaneously displaying his willingness to bear the weight of that opposition himself to overcome the distance we've created.

The question we're faced with before the risen Christ is not whether we've done a good enough job going out to find God. The question is whether we're willing to stop running and be found. God wants to be with us, but do we want to be with God? Really? Are we willing to receive his mercy that makes us whole, submit our lives to the ways of his kingdom, and prepare for his coming in glory?

Jesus' death and resurrection will make the world new. At the center of the new creation is the throne of God the Father, who gives authority over all things to his Son, "the Lamb" once slain, and all that is united to him is cleansed by the power of his blood.[1] From their presence, the Spirit goes rushing forth like waters of life to restore and replenish our world. All who will receive the Pursuing God are cleansed by the power of divine love, as the Spirit draws them through the Son to the Father, carrying all creation in their train.

"Then the end will come," we're told, when God has put everything under Jesus' feet, and Jesus in turn "hands over the kingdom to God the Father."[2] Jesus is not an egomaniac seeking his own glory, but a Son who delights to lift up and glorify his generous Father, rejoicing to bring creation to God. God is not a self-seeking tyrant, but a loving Father who delights to glorify his Son and restore the world through him. Together, in the joy of their Spirit, they give and receive glory and draw our world into their eternal communion of love.

Their holy love gives rise to their glory, its radiant splendor emanating from the beautiful perfection of who they are. And the outpouring of their glorious presence will flood the earth, "as the waters cover the sea,"[3] as the Father and Son pour out the life they've shared from eternity, from a reservoir of never-decreasing fullness that spills over in abundant overflow, showering their world in the power of their Spirit. And as the Spirit fills and draws all things through the Son, to the Father, their endgame is to fill all things with their very presence, "so that God may be all in all."[4]

God will baptize the world to cleanse it of the sin, death, and evil that deface and destroy his good creation, in order to raise it in the power of his Spirit, through the presence of his Son, into his embrace as the Father, in the eternal communion that marks their kingdom come without end.

God will flood the world.

APPENDIX I

Kill Your Son?

W hat are we to make of God's command to Abraham to sacrifice Isaac? This is one of the most difficult passages of Scripture, and brings together many of the themes we've observed in this book: a father and the sacrifice of his beloved son. Does God desire child sacrifice? Is Abraham's knife a foreshadowing of what God the Father will later accomplish at the cross with his beloved Son? What are we to make of this horrific command?

I love my children more than just about anything and tremble at the thought of being asked to consider such a thing. I'm not sure I could do it. Let's make a few observations to see how this passage arises from, rather than in contradiction to, the extravagant love of God.

GOD HATES CHILD SACRIFICE

A helpful recognition to start is this: when we zoom out to the broader biblical storyline, we find that God *hates* child sacrifice. When Israel sacrifices her children to foreign gods, God confronts her through the prophets, crying out, "I never commanded such a thing, nor did it even enter my mind!"[1] God rages against his people, saying, "You slaughtered My children and offered them up to idols by causing them to pass through the fire."[2] As I explored in my last book, the place where this happened, *Gehenna*, actually became Jesus' primary word translated as *hell* in our English Bibles, creating a powerful backdrop of idolatry and injustice for the location's imagery.[3]

The God of Israel stands against child sacrifice.

Yet child sacrifice was common in the ancient Middle East. The fact that Israel was still doing it centuries later in spite of God's commands against it is a sign of the cultural temptation it posed. Molech and Chemosh were ancient neighboring gods, mentioned in the Old Testament, who received child sacrifice. Archaeology has uncovered "ancient graveyards" of children's skulls and bones burned in sacrificial fires.[4] Other ancient gods, like Saturn, were believed to have devoured their own children, with the practice sometimes seen as an imitation of the pagan deities.[5]

The ancient gods could be brutal.

A second helpful observation is this: Abraham is *part of* this culture. He did not grow up in the modern West, but rather he was steeped in an idolatrous culture where sacrifice like this was common. As my friend Derek once pointed out, *Abraham didn't go to Sunday school.*[6] It's not like he had a leather-bound Bible with study guides like we have today. He doesn't have the Law and the Prophets that show up later in the biblical story, telling the people not to sacrifice their children. Abraham is a pioneer, who has left everything to follow God, and is learning more about this God as he goes in a gradual process throughout his life.

So when we first hear of Abraham's command to sacrifice

Isaac, our gut reaction is rightly, *Who would do such a thing!?* But this command would not have been shocking to the ancient world. There is a great cultural distance between Abraham's day and ours, and while we as twenty-first-century Westerners *should* feel shocked and repulsed by the command (we have a cultural conscience that has in many ways been shaped by a Judeo-Christian ethic that values life), it's helpful to recognize we are *not* the ones to whom the command was given—and it would not have been so preposterous and out of the question for Abraham.

In fact, the dominant Jewish tradition has held that God, in this encounter with Abraham, is actually *confronting* the ancient practice of child sacrifice and *replacing* it with animal sacrifice.[7] God breaks into the cultural context of Abraham's day, in other words, to meet him where he's at and set an alternative trajectory for his people with the goal that the cruel practice will eventually be abolished.

Let's take a closer look at how this shows up in the passage itself.

THE BELOVED SON

In Genesis, the story is depicted as a "test" for Abraham.[8] What exactly is God testing? God tells Abraham:

> Take your son, your only son, whom you love—Isaac—and go
> to the region of Moriah. Sacrifice him there as a burnt offering
> on a mountain I will show you.[9]

The order of words here is interesting. Jewish commentators have observed how God starts with saying just "your son," which is more generic, then moving to "your only son"—which ups the ante with a reminder that this is Abraham's *only child*.[10] Then God ups the ante even more, marking this unique child as the one "whom you love," reminding Abraham this is his beloved son. And finally, God speaks the name of the child in question, "Isaac"—which must hit like a hammer on the death knell of Abraham's heart.

There is nothing more valuable, no gift more precious, that Abraham has to give. In addition to Abraham's obvious fatherly love for his child, let's look at a few other reasons Isaac is so valuable.

Isaac is Abraham's firstborn.[11] In ancient culture, sacrificing the firstfruits from the land was a way of recognizing that the entire harvest was a gift from above. It was not so much a giving of something you created or produced on your own, as it was a *giving back* a portion of what you had received as a gift to begin with. Through this demonstration of gratitude, one hoped to secure favor for the rest of the gifts you'd received and the assurance of more gifts to come in the future.[12]

Beyond agriculture, this logic may have been at play with child sacrifice, too, at a time when large families were seen as a blessing. Your children were your farmhands to work the land, your retirement plan to help care for you in old age, your legacy to carry on your property, prosperity, and family name when you were dead and gone. What greater sign of devotion could be given to the gods? There was no greater sacrifice one could make.

So imagine Abraham being commanded to set his property on fire, dump his 401(k) in the ocean, and destroy all family records of his legacy for the next generation. That's a bit of the sense of what's going on here. In the modern West today, children are often looked at as a burden that cost a lot of money and restrict your social advancement opportunities, so small families are valued. But nothing could be farther from the ancient world, where children were seen as a blessing and large families were valued.

Your children were the future of your people.

This leads to a second reason Isaac was so valuable: he is not only the firstborn child, but the *only* child. Abraham and Sarah are already old, unable to have more children. So what is being threatened is not only Isaac, but the future of the nation. God promised Abraham to make him into "a great nation," and through his descendants to bless "all peoples on earth."[13] Abraham has left everything to follow God, trusting in this promise.

And it's hard to become a great nation when you don't have any kids.

So what is ultimately being threatened here is the promise itself. Isaac himself was a "miracle child," born only through the divine intervention of God. Isaac's name actually means *laughter*, because Sarah laughed when God said she'd have a child in her old age (she was an elderly, barren woman at the time), and because of the joy and laughter he brought them in their old age.[14] All of the promise they've given their lives for is bound up in this son Isaac.

So now, with this "test," the question arises: Does he trust the Giver more than he desires the gift? Does he just want the benefits of the promise, or does he trust the One from whom the promise was given? In the words of theologian and blogger Derek Rishmawy, "God was testing him according to his own standards of ultimate devotion even though he had no intention of accepting it."[15] God never intended to have Abraham follow through with the sacrifice, but to test Abraham according to the cultural standard of "ultimate devotion" in his day, to see if Abraham was as devoted to him as the idolaters of his neighborhood were to their gods.

God would then confront the great patriarch before the act could be completed, and replace the child with an animal—in an act that Israel would come to see as foundational for their sacrificial system.[16]

ISRAEL ON THE ALTAR

Israel was the original audience for this story. As they sat around the campfire and heard of their primeval ancestor Isaac on the altar, *they* were the children of Abraham, the "great nation" themselves, called to bear the blessing of God to the world. Isaac is their great-great-grandfather. So when Abraham raises the knife, it is not only Isaac who is bound on the altar, but they—the nation of Israel, their social body as a whole—in him.

If Isaac dies, they do not exist.

So this story had a very personal edge to it. Israel saw their identity and destiny as bound up with Isaac.

It's also helpful to remember Isaac was a young man, not a child, when this story took place. Commentators believe he was in his twenties, if not early thirties, given the chronology in Genesis.[17] And Isaac was strong enough to carry the firewood for the sacrifice up the mountain with the knife in hand, while Abraham, in contrast, is an old man by this time, more than a hundred years old.[18] So when ancient Israel heard this story, they naturally assumed Isaac could easily overpower Abraham if he wanted to.[19]

Genesis tells us nothing about Isaac's reaction when he finds out he is the sacrifice, but what is surprising is that there is no mention of a struggle, a resistance, a desire on Isaac's part to get out of the deal.[20] One is left with the impression that Isaac is a *willing* sacrifice, entrusting himself to his father, giving his life for his family and their God.

The children of Abraham are formed as a people who, like Isaac their forefather, entrust themselves to God even in the darkest and most confusing of circumstances.

Jewish tradition has taken the location of the story, Mount Moriah, as Jerusalem—the eventual location of the temple later in Israel's history. It is called "the mountain of the LORD" in the story, a place that God leads Abraham to, and a place where "God provides" for the sacrifice.[21] In Israel's history, this story becomes foundational for Passover and the sacrificial system: God provides a sacrifice to preserve the existence of his people from all that threatens the preservation of his promise and blessing to the world through them.[22]

Israel lives by grace.

So God in this passage, contrary to the caricature of a bloodthirsty deity, actually appears to be (1) testing Abraham's ultimate devotion; (2) confronting the ancient practice of child sacrifice and setting his people on an alternative, redemptive trajectory; and (3) establishing a foundation for the sacrificial system to preserve the existence of his people and bring his blessing to the world through them.

A PICTURE OF THE FATHER?

So is Abraham a picture of the Father? Does this story foreshadow the sacrifice of Christ on the cross? I think it's important to first recognize that nowhere in Scripture is this connection explicitly drawn. We have all sorts of other places where Jesus *is* depicted as the Passover lamb, the goats from the Day of Atonement, the high priest, the temple itself, and more. But nowhere is Abraham presented as a foreshadowing of the Father, or Isaac of Jesus. So we should take some caution before jumping too quickly to conclusions.

That said, one cannot get away from the story's resonance with themes from the cross like those we've explored in this book: the father's offering up of his beloved firstborn, the obedient son who goes willingly to his death, the threat to the promise that must be overcome, the hope of resurrection.

There are even subtle echoes in the details, like Isaac carrying the knife and firewood up Mount Moriah—the instruments he is about to be sacrificed with—an eerie foreshadowing of Christ carrying the wooden cross up Golgotha, on which he is about to be crucified. And if the Abraham story is to be read as a foundation to the Old Testament sacrificial system, then Jesus' fulfillment of that sacrificial system draws an inherent connection between his death and this story.

At the story of the cross, however, there are some important differences. The human agents wielding the knife, so to speak, are God's *enemies*—Israel, the Roman Empire, and us—whereas Abraham is his friend. Unlike Abraham, we are acting in rebellion against God rather than obedience to God. The death of the beloved Son at the cross is an act not of our faithfulness and trust in the heavenly Father, but rather the climax of our unfaithfulness and rejection of the heavenly Father, who encounters us in the person of his Son.

So when it comes to human agency, the cross is the antithesis, or opposite, of Mount Moriah.

And yet, if we look at Abraham as a type not of us, but of the Father, there is some symmetry. Like Abraham, the Father willingly offers up his Son—in this case for us to be reconciled, the promise to be fulfilled, and the Abrahamic blessing to come to all the peoples of the earth.

And Abraham points not only to the cross but to the resurrection: he believes God will raise his Son. The author of Hebrews looks to Abraham as a model of faith, observing how:

> By faith Abraham, when God tested him, offered Isaac as a sacrifice . . . even though God had said to him, "It is through Isaac that your offspring will be reckoned." Abraham reasoned that God could even raise the dead, and so in a manner of speaking he did receive Isaac back from death.[23]

This is crazy. Abraham trusts that God's faithfulness is even stronger than death. His trust in the heavenly Father's goodness and power, even when that which he most loves and cherishes is threatened, points to the hope of resurrection. Abraham's receiving of his beloved son "back from death," even if metaphorically, becomes here a foreshadowing of the Father's receiving his beloved Son back from the grave.

I've often thought there's no character in the Old Testament who can empathize with the sufferings of Christ so much as Job, the righteous sufferer. And similarly, there's perhaps no character like Abraham who can so empathize with the Father's sacrifice of his beloved Son. However, whereas Mount Moriah displays Abraham's ultimate devotion to his heavenly Father, Golgotha moves in the opposite direction, displaying our heavenly Father's even greater devotion to us.

WE ARE ISAAC

Moving to look at the story from the angle of Jesus, things take on one more light. Jesus is not Isaac at the cross—he is the ram. We are Isaac, whose existence is threatened under the divine judgment that hangs over us. It is we who are held under the power of sin and the grave; death comes to all. Similar to Israel hearing the story of Isaac and seeing their own body on that altar, we hear the story of Jesus and should see our own existence threatened on the chopping block—he is the head of humanity, the blessing to the nations, and the promise of the Father, in whom our fate is bound.

But Jesus is bound to the cross as the substitute in our place, like that ram in the story of old. In the redemptive humanity of Christ, God takes our wickedness, exclusion, and forsakenness upon himself in order to extinguish it in the power of divine love and set us free to live within his ultimate devotion for us.

The cross is that place where God the Father, through the Son and in the Spirit, raises the knife through Israel, through the Roman Empire, through us as wicked, rebellious, fallen humanity, and plunges it into his own chest in the vicarious humanity of Christ, in order to bear our punishment, exhaust the destructive power of our sin, and bring us home to rest in the all-encompassing divine power of his sacrificial love.

APPENDIX II

Forsaken

If God and Jesus are in this together, then what are we to make of Jesus' famous cry, "My God, my God, why have you forsaken me?" To some, Jesus sounds caught off guard, like a child at the department store who turns around to discover his mother has disappeared. It's as if, in our fire rescue analogy from earlier, the second fireman picks up his walkie-talkie to call up to the helicopter, "Hey guys! What's going on? You were supposed to come get me by now. The flames are rising; I'm about to get roasted!"

Was Jesus expecting rescue and surprised to find himself forsaken?

A SONG OF TRUST

When Jesus cries out, he is singing the opening line to a famous song in Israel, Psalm 22. Back in Jesus' day, people knew their Hebrew Bible really well. Citing a verse was a way to draw the whole passage to mind, with all its surrounding meaning and context. Kind of like when you sing that lyric to a famous song, and suddenly everyone begins humming the rest of the tune with you.

Imagine Jesus, throat parched, body broken, and on the verge of death. To keep himself breathing on the cross, he would have to use all his faltering strength to heave himself upward by his impaled feet. So talking was no easy task. As he struggles to let out some of his final departing words, he chooses to sing this song for those who surround him—and his Father.

And it's a song of trust.

King David wrote Psalm 22 a thousand years before Jesus hung on that cross. It was a famous song, a "Top 40" hit in Israel, wherein David sings about his suffering. David's suffering song actually sounds eerily as if it's *Jesus* singing about his crucifixion. The king describes being surrounded by his enemies, a "pack of villains" who "encircle" him like "strong bulls," "roaring lions," and ravenous "dogs," and "open their mouths wide against" him.[1] Imagine Jesus singing these lyrics from Psalm 22 as he hangs on the cross:[2]

✓ They divide my clothes among them and cast lots for my garment.

✓ All who see me mock me; they hurl insults, shaking their heads.

✓ I am poured out like water, and all my bones are out of joint.

✓ All my bones are on display; people stare and gloat over me.

✓ "He trusts in the LORD," they say, "let the LORD rescue him."

✓ My tongue sticks to the roof of my mouth.

✓ My mouth is dried up like a potsherd.

✓ They pierce my hands and my feet.

✓ You lay me in the dust of death.

This is David singing, but it could just as well be Jesus. And the opening line to this song? "My God, my God, why have you forsaken me?" Jesus lifts himself with all his remaining strength and belts out the opening lyric to this famous tune . . . and the rest of the crowd starts humming along.

Jesus identifies with King David, his ancient ancestor, the archetypal king of Israel, whose line would give rise to the messianic King. Now that King is here. Jesus suffers in solidarity with King David, the most famous king of Israel's history. And David was more than just a solitary individual—as king, he was a representative for the people as a whole.

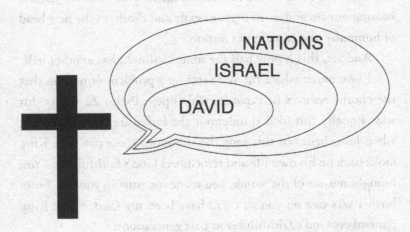

Jesus identifies not only with David here, but through him with Israel's suffering as the people of God. And Israel was not just another nation—they were a representative for the nations, a "kingdom of priests" before God. Jesus identifies not only with Israel here, but *through* Israel with the suffering of the world. As King Jesus is rejected, mocked, and forsaken in the grave, he identifies with King David, with Israel, with the nations—with us—in our suffering, forsakenness, and death.

At the cross, God is with us in our God-forsakenness. The Father enters our plight through the Son and in the Spirit to bring us home.

We are not alone.

BELTING OUT THE CHORUS

So let's return to our question: Was Jesus caught off guard? Expecting rescue only to find himself abandoned? No. Jesus is identifying with King David and Israel, with Adam and the nations—the King of the universe is identifying *with us*. Jesus is bearing our sin and suffering, our exile and death, as the new head of humanity and captain of creation.

And yet, this is only half the song. Psalm 22 has another half.

I love music where the verse sets up a problem or tension that the chorus resolves or explodes wide open. Psalm 22 works this way. Equally threaded throughout the lyrics are cries of trust— when Jesus belts out this song, he summons these too. The King looks back on his own life and remembers God's faithfulness: "You brought me out of the womb; you made me trust in you. . . . From birth I was cast on you . . . you have been my God."[3] The King remembers God's faithfulness to past generations:

> In you our ancestors put their trust; they trusted and you delivered them. To you they cried out and were saved; in you they

trusted and were not put to shame. . . . You are the one Israel praises.[4]

The King looks up and remembers, despite his circumstances, "Yet you are enthroned as the Holy One." Even when all seems lost, God will come through in the end. Even if the King is forsaken, he knows he's not forgotten. So he's able to cry out in hope: "You are my strength; come quickly to help me. . . . LORD, do not be far from me. . . . Deliver me. . . . Rescue me."[5]

And God shows up.

The climax of the song actually sounds a lot like resurrection. It goes on and on celebrating God's victory.[6] Now imagine hearing these lyrics, this time from the voice of Jesus as the Resurrected King:

I will declare your name to my people; in the assembly I will praise you. . . . For he has not despised or scorned the suffering of the afflicted one; he has not hidden his face from him but has listened to his cry for help. . . . All who go down to the dust [in death] will kneel before him. . . . They will proclaim his righteousness.[7]

This is the song Jesus quotes. And when God vindicates his suffering King, the endgame is this:

> All the ends of the earth
>   will remember and turn to the LORD,
> and all the families of the nations
>   will bow down before him,
> for dominion belongs to the LORD
>   and he rules over the nations.[8]

With his dying gasps, Jesus sings a song that looks up to his Father in trust and forward to his vindication on the other side of the grave. Though this song begins *forsaken*, it ends in *victory*. Jesus trusts the Father more than we do with an impenetrable love, and with his final breath declares, "Father, into your hands I commit my spirit."[9]

Grateful

I'm beyond grateful to:

Imago Dei Community: God has continually pursued me over the years in and through you, our amazing church family.

All those who read early versions of these chapters or interacted with the concepts and offered encouragement, critique, and insightful feedback: Paul Metzger, Scott McKnight, Derek Rishmawy, Adam Johnson, Tim Mackie, Nate Pyle, Dan Kimball, Jay Kim, Dave Lomas, Isaac Serrano, Paul Maxwell, Matthew Lee Anderson, Luke and Jillana Goble, Steve and Celestia Tracy, Ben Thomas, Paul Ramey, Jon Collins, Zech Bard, Steve and Beth Plymale, John Heintzman, Ben Wachsmuth, and Sebastian Rogers. The stellar crew at DCJA, particularly Don Jacobson, Blair Jacobson, Laurel Boruck, and Martin Raz: inspired to know you as more than just agents but friends.

The phenomenal team at Thomas Nelson, particularly Matt Baugher, Adria Haley, and Lori Cloud: it's truly a privilege getting to work with the best in the field.

Scott Erickson (scottericksonart.com): for the amazing images, exhilarating conversations, and ongoing creative inspiration.

Roman Candle, Heart, and Little T, where much of this book was written: for the hospitality, humor, and best hot coffee in town.

And above all, to my wife, Holly Beth; daughter, Aiden Ivey; and sons, Torin James and Jacob Valdez—I delight in you all, have found the greatest joy in doing life together, and have discovered through you how deep a husband and father's love can go (I'd pursue you guys to the end of the world).

And above that: Father, Son, and Spirit, *Soli Deo Gloria*.

Notes

Introduction

1. A. W. Tozer, *The Knowledge of the Holy* (New York: HarperCollins, 1961), 1.

Chapter 1: Into the Canvas

1. John 1:3; Colossians 1:15–16; Hebrews 1:2.
2. 1 Peter 1:20 ESV.
3. 1 Corinthians 8:6.
4. Athanasius, *The Incarnation of the Word of God (De Incarnatione Verbi Dei),* translated by A Religious of C.S.M.V. S.TH. with an introduction by C. S. Lewis, available online at: www.worldinvisible .com/library/athanasius/incarnation/incarnation.1.htm (the quote appears in chapter 1, section 1).
5. 1 Corinthians 5:3–4; Revelation 22:1–5.
6. Genesis 2:7–8; 3:8.
7. Genesis 1:4, 10, 12, 18, 21, 25, 31.

Chapter 2: Pulling Back the Rib Cage

1. Matthew 4:1.
2. Deuteronomy 8:2.
3. Matthew 4:2.

4. Matthew 4:4, quoting Deuteronomy 8:3.
5. Exodus 16:3.
6. Matthew 4:6, paraphrased.
7. Matthew 4:7, quoting Deuteronomy 6:16.
8. Exodus 17:3.
9. Exodus 17:7.
10. Matthew 27:40.
11. Matthew 4:8–9, paraphrased.

Chapter 3: The New Captain

1. Hebrews 4:15 NASB.
2. Every person bears the image of God, and all are worthy of dignity and respect before the God whose image we bear. While sin can never eliminate that image, it can do its darnedest to try. Part of sin's very agenda is to attack that dignity, to tarnish that respect, by severing us from the Creator who bestows such worth upon us.
3. Matthew 9:35.
4. John 21:25.
5. "The Love of God" by Frederick M. Lehman, 1917, with this particular verse supposedly written by Meir Ben Isaac Nehorai, 1050. Lehman reported that this verse "had been found penciled on the wall of a patient's room in an insane asylum after he had been carried to his grave." See http://library.timelesstruths.org /music/The_Love_of_God/.
6. Mark 5:28.
7. Mark 5:30.
8. The woman suffered from menstrual bleeding that occurred irregularly throughout the month, likely the condition known today as *menometrorrhagia*. This would have placed her under the purity regulations of Leviticus 15, though in a constant state of uncleanness, given the frequency of her condition. L. Lewis Wall has an interesting article on the topic, "Jesus and the Unclean Woman," in *Christianity Today* (January 13, 2010), available online at www.christianitytoday.com/ct/2010/january/17.48.html.

9. Mark 5:34.

10. 2 Corinthians 5:21.

Chapter 4: God on the Prowl

1. Genesis 3:9.

2. Genesis 3:10.

3. Genesis 3:5, paraphrased.

4. Thomas K. Johnson, *The First Step in Missions Training: How Our Neighbors Are Wrestling with God's General Revelation* (Bonn, DEU: Verlag für Kultur und Wissenschaft, 2014), 23.

5. Genesis 3:22 NKJV.

Chapter 5: Coming Down the Mountain

1. Exodus 19:8 NKJV.

2. Exodus 19:10–13.

3. Exodus 19:16–18.

4. Exodus 20:18.

5. Exodus 20:19–20.

6. Exodus 20:21. John Sailhamer gives a more detailed exegetical treatment of this in *The Meaning of the Pentateuch: Revelation, Composition and Interpretation* (Downers Grove, IL: InterVarsity Press, 2009), 44–46, 355–415.

7. That word *together* is important. Many today tend to think of the Law in the Bible as an individual thing, just between me and God, a ladder I can climb to make God happy. But the Law is inherently *social*. Just before Israel gets to Sinai, in the scene right before the mountain, Moses is tired and worn-out from dealing with all the disputes and conflicts among the people. He takes his father-in-law's wise advice to delegate, delegate, delegate, and selects capable leaders as judges to resolve conflict and promote the peace of the people. But these judges need guidelines for how to do this. Enter the Ten Commandments in Exodus 20. God is giving his vision for *life together*. This is what it looks like for them to love each other, rather

than tear each other apart, to live together with him as his people. Amid their propensities for division and death, these commandments are boundary markers oriented toward their life as a community. And God stands at the center of this vision as their King.

8. Exodus 19:6.
9. Exodus 24:3 ESV.
10. Exodus 32:1.
11. Exodus 32:25.
12. Sailhamer, *The Meaning of the Pentateuch,* 29.
13. Exodus 34:29.
14. Exodus 35–Leviticus 16.
15. Leviticus 17–26.
16. Sailhamer, *The Meaning of the Pentateuch,* 42, 46.
17. Galatians 3:19.
18. Augustine, Homily 7 on the First Epistle of John. This is a paraphrase of his words in paragraph 8: "Love, and do what you will." Available online at the website of New Advent, www.newadvent.org/fathers/170 207.htm.

Chapter 6: Romance in the War Zone

1. John 3:17.
2. John 3:19 NKJV.
3. John 3:19 THE MESSAGE.
4. Hans Boersma, *Violence, Hospitality, and the Cross: Reappropriating the Atonement Tradition* (Grand Rapids, MI: Baker Academic, 2004), 49.

Chapter 7: Reckless Love

1. Luke 15:5–6.

Chapter 8: Olympic Father

1. Luke 15:13.
2. See, for example, Deuteronomy 21:18–21. For those who might find this overly harsh, blogger Derek Rishmawy, a former college pastor

and current doctoral student, has a helpful post, "Understanding the Execution of the Rebellious Son," available online at http://derekzrishmawy.com/2015/07/08/understanding-the-execution-of-the-rebellious-son/.

3. Luke 15:15–16.

4. Leviticus 11. For a helpful video on Leviticus that places the food laws within the broader logic of the book, see the Bible Project's "Leviticus," posted on YouTube on May 6, 2015, and available at www.youtube.com/watch?v=WmvyrLXoQio.

5. My paraphrase of Luke 15:17.

6. See endnote 2, above.

7. Luke 15:18–19.

8. Luke 15:20.

9. Luke 15:22–24.

Chapter 9: Welcome Home

1. Luke 15:1–3 THE MESSAGE.

2. Luke 19:10 NKJV.

Chapter 10: Dumb Farmer

1. Matthew 13:3.

2. Isaac Watts, "Joy to the World" (1719).

3. Matthew 13:4, 15, 19. When Jesus says here that the person "does not understand" the message of the kingdom, we should not interpret this in a mere intellectual sense, like a child who does not understand a quantum physics lesson. In context, Jesus is quoting Isaiah 6, where the backdrop for people not seeing or understanding is that "their heart has become calloused." In their rebellion against God, they have shut their eyes and closed their ears; in their pursuit of idols they've become distracted from the pursuit of their Creator.

4. Matthew 13:19.

5. Matthew 13:21.

6. Matthew 13:22.

7. Matthew 13:23.

Chapter 11: A Mighty Oak

1. Bien is one of my friends; the details of her story and quotes used here come from my conversations with her over the last few years.

2. 1 Samuel 16:11–13.

3. 1 Corinthians 1:26–31.

4. Matthew 13:32.

Chapter 12: Selling the Farm

1. Matthew 13:44.

2. Matthew 13:46.

Chapter 13: Lion and Prey

1. John 10:18, paraphrased.

2. Luke 9:51 ESV.

3. Mark 8:31. See also Mark 9:12; Luke 9:22.

4. Mark 8–10 is regularly recognized by commentators as a crucial turning point in Mark, when Jesus begins predicting his death and setting his eyes toward Jerusalem and the cross. The disciples continually struggle to see or understand it, are confused, and reject this future for Jesus. The passage is bookended by two accounts of Jesus healing blind men, with the first story having the strange occurrence where Jesus has to touch the man's eyes "twice" for the healing to take—a great setup for the disciples whom Jesus will have to repeatedly confront in this bookended section with his coming death before they finally see and "get it."

5. This is not to deny the sorrow and distress Christ feels in Gethsemane (Matthew 26:36–46), but to place it within his context of mission and personal agency in relation to the cross.

6. Galatians 2:20 NASB.

7. Mark 10:45.

8. Matthew 16:24.

9. Genesis 2:17; cf. Genesis 3:3–4.
10. Ezekiel 37.
11. Romans 5:12.
12. Romans 5:21.
13. Ibid.
14. This is the famous maxim of Gregory of Nazianzus, which appears in his "Letter to Cledonius."
15. Hebrews 2:14; Hebrews 2:17 TNIV.
16. Hebrews 2:18.
17. Hebrews 4:15.
18. Colossians 1:15.
19. See John 14:9.
20. 2 Corinthians 5:21.

Chapter 14: Jesus Is a Wall Street CEO

1. On Bank of America's role in the housing crisis, see the *New York Times'* timeline: "Bank of America and the Financial Crisis," available online at www.nytimes.com/interactive/2014/06/10 /business/dealbook/11bank-timelime.html?_r=0#/#time333_8794. Accessed June 30, 2015.
2. I'm grateful for this analogy to Timothy Keller, who uses a similar example in *The Reason for God: Belief in an Age of Skepticism* (New York: Dutton, 2008), 187.
3. The New Testament implicates Israel, Rome, and all humanity in the death of Jesus. See, for example, the declaration that Jesus came to "his own, but his own did not receive him" in John 1:11 (Israel); the attention paid to Pilate during the trial in John 18:28–40 (Rome); and Paul's declaration that "all have sinned and fall short of the glory of God" in his expounding of the significance of the death of Christ in Romans 3:23 (humanity).

Chapter 15: Muggers and Physicians

1. Jeremiah 25:9, 29; 43:10; Ezekiel 21; cf. Ezekiel 30:24–25. Jesus also alludes to Babylon's armies as *God's* armies in Matthew 22:7.

2. Jeremiah 25:15 and 28:14; 29:4, 7, 20; Ezekiel 39:28.
3. Habakkuk 1:6, 12.
4. 2 Chronicles 36:15–17, emphasis added.
5. Cf. Jeremiah 20:4; 23:3; 29:4, 7, 20; 31:10.
6. Matthew 27:46.
7. Also, Jesus is quoting Psalm 22:1 here, and as I show in Appendix II: Forsaken, there's a whole lot more going on when Jesus quotes Psalm 22 than might first meet the eye.
8. Luke 23:46; quoting Psalm 31:5.
9. 2 Corinthians 5:19 NKJV; emphasis added.
10. Colossians 1:19–20.
11. Genesis 50:20.
12. Ibid, paraphrased.

Chapter 16: For God So Loved . . .

1. John 3:16, emphasis added.
2. Romans 5:8.
3. 1 John 4:10.
4. Romans 5:10 NKJV.
5. After writing this chapter, but before this book went to press, Justus was showing great signs of progress in his recovery. His family has shared powerful, Christ-centered reflections on their journey with this illness that are well worth reading on Twitter under the hashtag #TeamJustus.
6. Professor and theologian Kevin Vanhoozer gives an excellent discussion on the differences between saying God actively endures versus passively suffers, and their significance, in *Remythologizing Theology* (Cambridge: Cambridge University Press, 2010), 400–4.
7. This doctrine is known as *impassibility* and has been normative for church teaching through most of history, but has been widely rejected in the twentieth century. My contention would be it is largely a caricature that has been rejected, as the historic shape of the doctrine has been widely misunderstood, and a healthy, robust version of *impassibility* is helpful to retrieve and reclaim.

For mature treatments, see Paul Gavrilyuk's *The Suffering of the Impassible God: The Dialectics of Patristic Thought* (Oxford: Oxford University Press, 2004) and Thomas G. Weinandy, *Does God Suffer?* (South Bend, IN: University of Notre Dame Press, 2000).

8. I put "emotionally unengaged" in quotes because the concept of *emotion* is recent and does have some problematic elements when applied to God. See the discussion in Kevin VanHoozer, *Remythologizing Theology*, 398–416.

9. J. Todd Billings, *Rejoicing in Lament: Wrestling with Incurable Cancer & Life in Christ* (Grand Rapids, MI: Brazos Press, 2015), 157.

10. It's important to remember this language is not univocal for God. As Billings puts it, "God's affections are never distorted through sinful, disordered passions. Thus, while we are to cherish and utilize these God-given ways of portraying how God relates to the world, we should also avoid thinking that 'love,' 'grief,' 'wrath,' or 'jealousy' mean exactly the same thing for God as they do for us. Unlike the love, grief, wrath, and jealousy that we see and experience with other humans, God's affections are perfect, self-derived expressions of his faithful covenant love." *Rejoicing in Lament*, 157.

Chapter 17: A Helicopter in the Forest

1. In the gospel of Luke, for example, it is in the power of the Holy Spirit that the Father sends the Son on his mission, a mission that climaxes at the cross (Luke 1:33–35; 3:16, 21–22; 4:1, 14, 18).

2. Romans 8:11.

3. 1 Peter 1:20; Revelation 13:8 NKJV; Ephesians 1:4; Romans 8:11.

4. Hebrews 12:2.

5. From "Miscellanies" in *The Works of Jonathan Edwards*, vol. 20, ed. Amy Plantinga Pauw (New Haven: Yale University Press, 2002), no. 993.

6. Amy Plantinga Pauw, *The Supreme Harmony of All: The Trinitarian Theology of Jonathan Edwards* (Grand Rapids, MI: Eerdmans, 2002), 107. On the quotation that appears in this passage, she is quoting Peter Bulkeley from *The Gospel-Covenant; or The Covenant*

of *Grace Opened* (London: M. Simmons, 1651), 31, in order to contrast Edwards's view against Bulkeley's.

7. Alexandre Dumas, *The Three Musketeers*, chap. 9 (1998), available from Project Gutenberg at www.gutenberg.org/files/1257/1257-h /1257-h.htm.

8. Karl Barth, *Church Dogmatics IV.1*, trans. G. W. Bromily (London: T&T Clark, 2010), 62.

Chapter 18: Destroy This Temple

1. John 2:19–21.
2. N. T. Wright, *The New Testament and the People of God* (Minneapolis, MN: Fortress Press, 1992), 225.
3. Isaiah 49:6 ESV; Exodus 19:6.
4. John 2:19.
5. Travelers to Jerusalem needed to make purchases for sacrifice. The phrase translated "den of robbers" in Matthew 21:13; Mark 11:17; and Luke 19:46 in the Synoptic Gospels' versions of this story draws on Jeremiah 7:11, with the Greek term used here for robbers (*lestes*) carrying more explicitly violent overtones than "economic exploitation," strongly associated with political revolutionaries. Jesus' primary immediate aim seems to have been an interruption of the ongoing daily sacrifices in the temple system, as an indictment on Israel's national rebellion and foreshadowing of God's coming judgment on the temple. See N. T. Wright's discussion in *Jesus and the Victory of God* (Minneapolis, MN: Fortress Press, 1996), 418–24.
6. Ezekiel 4–5.
7. Isaiah 20.
8. Jeremiah 19. See also Isaiah 8:1–4; Jeremiah 13:1–11; 27:1–15; 32:6–15; Ezekiel 12:1–25 for other examples of the prophets' dramas.
9. Wright, *Jesus and the Victory of God*, 413–18.
10. Matthew 21:18–21, which follows immediately after Jesus' actions in the temple. We're told the fig tree and mountain "into the sea" episode occurs "as Jesus was on his way back to the city" from nearby Bethany, setting the vicinity of Jerusalem as its context (vv. 17–18).

On this episode pointing towards the Temple's coming destruction, see N. T. Wright's discussion in *Jesus and the Victory of God*, 421–22, 494–95.

11. John 2:19, 21.
12. This can also be seen as a recapitulation of Babylon's destruction of the temple centuries earlier, in 586 BC, the signpost of the onset of exile.
13. Matthew 27:51.
14. John 2:19.
15. Revelation 21:22.
16. Revelation 21:3.

Chapter 19: Dead Meat

1. Check out The Bible Project, which uses this language in their excellent video introduction to the book of Leviticus at https://www .youtube.com/watch?v=WmvyrLXoQio (posted May 6, 2015).
2. Peter Leithart, *Defending Constantine: The Twilight of an Empire and the Dawn of Christendom* (Downers Grove, IL: IVP Academic, 2010), 328–29.
3. John 1:29 NASB.

Chapter 20: The God Who Walks Alone

1. Genesis 12:2–3.
2. Genesis 15:17.
3. Luke 22:20.
4. Luke 22:19.

Chapter 21: Soaking Up Death

1. Isaiah 6. Isaiah should not be in the Most Holy Place (as the high priest was only allowed to enter once a year on the Day of Atonement, and Isaiah is not a high priest), so this passage likely implies that the priesthood had become so corrupt that Isaiah now sees himself in this vision as a surrogate for the high priest. This backdrop also emphasizes the context of atonement, as God

cleanses Isaiah of his sin and Isaiah identifies with his sinful people and is sent to mediate God's message to them.

2. Isaiah 6:3.
3. Isaiah 6:5.
4. The Bible Project uses this imagery in their excellent video "Animated Explanation of God's Holiness," available online at https://www.youtube.com/watch?v=l9vn5UvsHvM (posted March 17, 2015).
5. Exodus 3:5 MSG.
6. Leviticus 11–15.
7. Isaiah 6:7.
8. See 1 Kings 6:29, 32, 35; 7:29, 36; 8:6.

Chapter 22: Fish on the Dock

1. "In Christ Alone" (2001), lyrics by Stuart Townend, music by Keith Getty.
2. John 10:10 NKJV.
3. Cf. Leviticus 26; Deuteronomy 11 and 28.
4. Romans 1:18, 24, 26, 28, emphasis added.
5. Matthew Levering, a leading Catholic scholar on Aquinas's thought, provided this summary during his talk "Atonement and Creation" at the Los Angeles Theology Conference at Biola University on January 15, 2015. A video of the talk, posted on YouTube on February 3, 2015, is available at https://www.youtube.com/watch?v=-eCcvd6kT_o&feature=youtu.be. (This quote is from that lecture and appears between 23:00 and 25:00, emphasis added.)
6. Ibid., emphasis added.
7. I'm grateful to Adam J. Johnson for pointing this out in a conversation on November 6, 2015.

Chapter 23: Furious Love

1. Miroslav Volf, *Free of Charge: Giving and Forgiving in a Culture Stripped of Grace* (Grand Rapids: Zondervan, 2005), 138–39. I've introduced the paragraph breaks into the quote to break up its length.

2. Volf's words are appropriate again here, too: "Once we accept the appropriateness of God's wrath, condemnation, and judgment, there is no way of keeping it out there, reserved for others. We have to bring it home as well. I originally resisted the notion of a wrathful God because I dreaded being that wrath's target; I still do. I knew I couldn't just direct God's wrath against others, as if it were a weapon I could aim at targets I particularly detested. It's God's wrath, not mine, the wrath of the one and impartial God, lover of all humanity. If I want it to fall on evildoers, I must let it fall on myself—when I deserve it." Ibid., 139.

3. D. E. H. Whiteley, *The Theology of St. Paul* (Oxford: Basil Blackwell, 1964), 63.

4. Joshua Ryan Butler, *The Skeletons in God's Closet: The Mercy of Hell, the Surprise of Judgment, the Hope of Holy War* (Nashville: Thomas Nelson, 2014). On Old Testament holy war, see especially pages 207–44; on New Testament governmental violence, pages 261–72; on God's judgment on Babylon, pages 273–91; on the king setting fire to his rebel city, pages 133–37; on the father booting wedding crashers, pages 141–46; on the landlord punishing the unruly tenants, page 232.

5. Anders Nygren, *Agape and Eros* (London: SPCK; New York: Macmillan, 1932–39), I: 75.

6. Leviticus 26:15–16. I'm grateful to the Mere Fidelity podcast (one of my favorites), whose "Atonement" episode (December 18, 2014) influenced some of the content in this section.

7. From Frederich Buechner, "Psychotherapy," from his blog, at http://www.frederickbuechner.com/content/psychotherapy-0 (accessed October 10, 2015).

8. 2 Kings 17:18.

9. Galatians 3:13.

10. See Mark 8:31; 10:33 NKJV; cf. 15:1. On "rejected" (*apodokimasthenai*): Jeremiah 6:30; 7:29; 8:9; 14:19. On "delivered over (*paradothesetai*) to the Gentiles": Leviticus 26:32–33, 38; cf. Psalm 106:41; Ezra 9:7; Hosea 8:10 LXX. In this section, I'm indebted to and grateful for

Jeremy Treat's discussion in his excellent book *The Crucified King: Atonement and Kingdom in Biblical and Systematic Theology* (Grand Rapids: Zondervan, 2014).

11. On *mocking:* Psalm 39; 79; 102. On *darkness:* Exodus 10:21; Amos 8:9–10; Mark 13:24. On *forsakenness:* see our earlier discussion of Psalm 22, in which many of these elements are combined.

12. Peter Bolt, *The Cross from a Distance: Atonement in Mark's Gospel* (Downers Grove, IL: Intervarsity Press, 2004), 133.

13. Deuteronomy 21:22–23; and Martin Hengel, *Crucifixion in the Ancient World and the Folly of the Message of the Cross* (Philadelphia: Fortress Press, 1977), 33–38; 84–85.

14. Galatians 3:13 NKJV; quoting Deuteronomy 21:23.

15. Galatians 3:13.

16. Mark 14:36; cf. Mark 10:38–39. On OT context: Psalm 11:6 NKJV; 75:8; Isaiah 51:17, 22; Ezekiel 23:31–34; Habakkuk 2:16.

17. Isaiah 51:22 ESV.

Chapter 24: Unraveling Creation

1. See Genesis 1:2.

2. John H. Walton, *The Lost World of Genesis One: Ancient Cosmology and the Origins Debate* (Downers Grove, IL: IVP Academic, 2009).

3. This is the thesis of John Walton's *The Lost World of Genesis One*, cited above (see particularly pages 71–91).

4. Genesis 2:15; Numbers 3:7–8; 8:26; 18:5–6. While we tend to read Genesis and Numbers as separate books, Israel read them as part of the same larger Pentateuch, or "five books" of Moses, with interconnected threads of Hebrew phrasing like these being much more obvious. The connection between Adam and the priesthood would be clear. And there are other strong threads connecting Eden and the temple. For example, the word for God "walking" back and forth (*mithalek*) in the garden (Genesis 3:8) is the same word later used to describe his presence in the tabernacle and temple (Leviticus 26:12; Deuteronomy 23:14; 2 Samuel 7:6–7). And "the cool of the day" when this happened (Genesis 3:8) was

the same time when Israel's morning and evening sacrifices at the temple were done, as the people came before the presence of the Lord (Exodus 29:38–43). Israel's worship practices were built upon the foundation of Eden's story.

5. John Walton gives a detailed description in *The Lost World of Genesis One*, pp. 80–82.

6. Genesis 6:3.

7. Genesis 6:13.

8. God has Moses and Aaron stretch out their hands toward the water (Exodus 7:19; 8:5), the land (8:16; cf. 9:8), and the sky (9:22; 10:12; 10:21).

9. This Old Testament backdrop helps make sense of the apocalyptic imagery of "beasts" and "the sea," which often appear together (cf. Daniel 7; Revelation 13). The sea represents *natural* forces of chaos (the *tohu va wohu*), and the beasts *political* forces of chaos (like Egypt): both are involved in attempting to drag creation back down into the abyss from which it came.

10. Psalm 78:49–50; combining the NIV and KJV.

Chapter 25: Communion of Love

1. For a great explanation of Rublev's "Holy Trinity" icon, which I've relied upon in this summary, see: http://www.sacredheartpullman .org/Icon%20explanation.htm (accessed July 20, 2015).

2. A helpful introduction to many questions Protestants sometimes have about icons, from an Orthodox perspective, can be found at: http://orthodoxinfo.com/general/icon_faq.aspx.

3. Church tradition has frequently taken Genesis 18 as an early appearance of the Trinity. See, for example, Augustine's *On the Trinity*, book 2, chapter 10.

4. Isaiah 9:6 NKJV.

5. John 8:54; 14:13; 16:14.

6. John 17.

7. John 14:11; cf. John 10:38.

8. John 14:9 paraphrased.

9. John 10:30.

10. Augustine of Hippo, *City of God*, trans. Henry Bettenson, repr. (London: Penguin Classics, 2004), 457.

11. C. S. Lewis, *The Four Loves*, 2nd printing repr. ed (n.p.: Mariner, 1971), 126.

Chapter 26: The Journey Home

1. http://www.sacredheartpullman.org/Icon%20explanation.htm (accessed July 20, 2015).

2. See Genesis 1:3, 6, 14.

3. Genesis 1:2.

4. See, for example, Genesis 15:1, 4; Numbers 24:2; 1 Samuel 15:10.

5. See John 1:14; 5:23; Luke 4:14; Acts 10:38.

6. John 5:19; 7:16; 12:49; cf. John 7:28; 8:28, 42.

7. Acts 10:38.

8. Genesis 18:7.

9. Revelation 5:12; cf. 5:6; 13:8.

10. 2 Peter 1:4 JUB.

Chapter 27: Life into Death

1. This may have implications for properly locating the doctrine of impassibility. God's affections in his *immanent* triune life are the impenetrable fountainhead from which God's affections in *economic* relation with the world arise. The Trinity has *more* love, not less, within their immanent divine life that comes prior to the world and grounds their active affection for the world. The world cannot act upon God so as to impede upon the Father, Son, and Spirit's prior love for one another. While they do not passively suffer the world in their divine life, they are in active love willing to sovereignly endure the cross to accomplish redemption.

2. Acts 10:38 NLT.

3. In the gospel of Luke, for example, it is in the power of the Holy Spirit that the Father sends the Son on his mission, a mission that climaxes at the cross (Luke 1:33–35; 3:16, 21–22; 4:1, 14, 18).

4. Romans 8:32 HCSB; Hebrews 7:27 NKJV; 9:14; cf. Ephesians 5:2.

5. Tim Keller, *The Reason for God: Belief in an Age of Skepticism* (New York: Dutton, 2008), 192.

6. Adam J. Johnson, *Atonement: A Guide for the Perplexed* (London: Bloomsbury T&T Clark, 2015), 77.

7. Benedict XVI, *Jesus of Nazareth: Holy Week* (San Francisco: Ignatius, 2011), 232.

Chapter 28: Bad Bridge

1. John 14:6.

2. John 14:8.

3. John 14:9–10.

4. John 14:10; 10:30.

5. John 14:23.

6. Union with Christ through the indwelling of the Spirit is a major theme of New Testament soteriology that, while distinct from the Trinity's immanent relations expressed strongly here in Jesus' high priestly prayer, is nonetheless inherently related.

Chapter 29: The True Myth

1. Bruce W. Young has a great paper on this theme in Lewis that I've relied upon here, "Lewis on the Gospels as True Myth," in *Inklings Forever* 4 (2004) available online at https://library.taylor.edu/dot Asset/5a009e17-201e-4206-89b4-52eadf3ecb9e.pdf, accessed September 8, 2015.

2. Joseph Pearce, "J.R.R. Tolkien: Truth and Myth," available online at: http://www.catholicauthors.com/tolkien.html (accessed November 12, 2015).

3. Ibid.

4. I'm grateful to my friend Jim Mullins for the image of janitorial work as microbiological warfare, along with many other stimulating discussions on the significance of vocation. Keep your eyes out for a book on the topic he's working on that will hopefully be out soon.

5. For a much more eloquent exploration of *Romeo and Juliet* as a signpost of the gospel, see Don Miller's chapter 14, subtitled "Why William Shakespeare Was a Prophet," in *Searching for God Knows What* (Nashville: Thomas Nelson, 2004, 2012), 215–32.

6. Acts 17:28.

Chapter 30: Upside-Down Kingdom

1. 1 Corinthians 1:27–31.

2. *Stanford Encyclopedia of Philosophy*, s.v. "Saint Anselm," 2.1, http://plato.stanford.edu/entries/anselm/#FaiSeeUndChaPurAnsThePro, accessed October 22, 2015.

3. Acts 9:2; 11:26.

4. Matthew 16:24 NLT.

5. Tullian Tchividjian, *Glorious Ruin: How Suffering Sets You Free*, repr. ed. (East Sussex: David C. Cook, 2012), 43.

6. See Genesis 11:4.

Chapter 31: Nazis and Whores

1. Jonah 1:2.

2. Matthias Schulz, "The Worst Ways to Die: Torture Practices of the Ancient World," in *Spiegel International* (May 15, 2009).

3. Nahum 3:1–4, 19.

4. Jonah 1:17; 2:10.

5. Daniel 7:3.

6. Jonah 1:4.

7. For some similarities with another minor prophet, see N. T. Wright's discussion of the relationship between Daniel's historical experience "in the lion's den" (Daniel 6) and his apocalyptic vision of the "Son of Man" surrounded by "four beasts" in the following chapter (Daniel 7), in which the historical experience of the minor prophet is dramatically intertwined with the national experience and eschatological hope of Israel; in N. T. Wright, *The New Testament and the People of God* (Minneapolis: Fortress Press, 1992), 291–97.

8. Jonah 2:3–4, 2, 7, 9.

9. Similar to Ezekiel's famous "Valley of Dry Bones" in Ezekiel 37, a picture of national hope for restoration from exile.

10. Jonah 3:5.

11. Jonah 3:8–9.

12. Jonah 3:10.

13. Jonah 4:2, paraphrased.

14. Jonah 4:3.

15. Jonah 4:9.

16. Jonah 4:10–11, paraphrased.

Chapter 32: Forgiveness Sets You Free

1. Célestin Musekura, the founder of African Leadership and Reconciliation Ministries (http://www.alarm-inc.org/), has written an excellent book with L. Gregory Jones on forgiveness that goes deeper into themes from this section, entitled *Forgiving as We've Been Forgiven: Community Practices for Making Peace* (Downer's Grove, IL: IVP Books, 2010).

2. From Ken Camp's interview of Célestin, "Give Up the Right to Be Right" in *Common Call* (Vol. 1, No. 5; May 2013). Available online at: http://alarm-inc.org/images/uploads/CommonCall-Magazine -Celestin.pdf. Accessed January 6, 2015.

3. Ibid.

4. Ibid.

5. Miroslav Volf, *Exclusion and Embrace: A Theological Exploration of Identity, Otherness, and Reconciliation* (Nashville: Abingdon Press, 1996), 113.

6. Ibid., 117.

7. Matthew 12:40.

8. N. T. Wright uses this analogy of a "perfect storm" to describe the crosscurrents between Rome, Israel, and God that collide in the event of Jesus death, in *Simply Jesus: A New Vision of Who He Was, What He Did, and Why He Matters* (New York: HarperOne, 2011), 27–56.

9. John 11:50.

10. Romans 5:8 KJV.

Chapter 33: Blind Date

1. Hosea 1:2 KJV.
2. Hosea 2:14–15.
3. Learn more about EPIK (*Everyman Protecting Innocent Kids*) at: http://www.epikproject.org/.
4. This quote is frequently attributed to Augustine, but appears to be a paraphrase of his statement about the Church: "Let us honour her, because she is the bride of so great a Lord. And what am I to say? Great and unheard of is the bridegroom's gracious generosity; he found her a whore, he made her a virgin. She mustn't deny that she was once a whore, or she may forget the kindness and mercy of her liberator." Augustine's Essential Sermons, sermon 213.
5. Cyprian of Carthage, *On the Unity of the Church*, 6 (available online at: http://www.newadvent.org/fathers/050701.htm).
6. "The Heidelberg Disputation: Theological Theses," thesis 28, on the website of *The Book of Concord: Confessions of the Lutheran Church*, accessed October 21, 2014, http://bookofconcord.org/heidelberg.php.

Chapter 34: Vampires

1. John 6:53, 56–57.
2. This was true of the early church as well. As J. N. D. Kelly, a renowned Protestant historian of the early church, observes, "Eucharistic teaching, it should be understood at the outset, was in general unquestioningly realist, i.e., the consecrated bread and wine were taken to be, and were treated and designated as, the Savior's body and blood." *Early Christian Doctrines*, 5th ed. (London: Continuum, 1977), 440.
3. Augustine, *The Confessions*, trans. Henry Chadwick (Oxford: Oxford University Press, 1991), 124.
4. Alexander Schmemann, *For the Life of the World* (Crestwood, NY: St. Vladimir's Seminary Press, 1988), 25.
5. William Cavanaugh, *Theopolitical Imagination: Discovering the*

Liturgy as a Political Act in an Age of Global Consumerism (London: T&T Clark, 2002), 47–49.

6. Lesslie Newbigin, *The Gospel in a Pluralist Society* (Grand Rapids: Eerdmans, 1989), 82–83.

7. Romans 10:15; Isaiah 52:7.

Chapter 35: Kingdom in the Wilderness

1. First Corinthians 10:2 refers to the Red Sea as Israel's baptism.

2. John 6:33–35, 48–51.

3. 2 Corinthians 3:6.

4. cf. Romans 9–11; Galatians 6:15–16.

5. On other Passover references to Jesus' death, see John 6:4; 1 Corinthians 5:7. Also, Jesus' identity as a lamb (John 1:29, 36; 1 Peter 1:19; Revelation 5–7; 12:11; 13:8) is significant itself, since lambs were primarily associated with the Passover, other animals being central for other sacrificial events, like the Day of Atonement.

6. Joachim Jeremias, *Jerusalem at the Time of Jesus* (Minneapolis: Fortress Press, 1975), 57.

7. Luke 22:7.

8. Luke 22:15–16.

Chapter 36: Bigfoot Jesus

1. 1 Corinthians 15:27; Ephesians 1:22; cf. Hebrews 2:8–9.

2. Psalm 8:4–6, emphasis added. I've modified the second line of the NIV's translation to "son of Adam," with the ensuing singular pronoun, to reflect the resonances in the Hebrew of *ben-Adam* ["son of Adam"] with its echoes of the Eden story.

3. Psalm 8:9 NKJV.

4. Romans 8:21.

5. 1 Kings 5:3.

6. 1 Corinthians 15:25–26.

7. Abraham Kuyper, *Kuyper: A Centennial Reader*, ed. James D Bratt (Grand Rapids: Eerdmans, 1998), 461.

8. Ephesians 1:23.

Finish

1. Revelation 22:1.
2. 1 Corinthians 15:24.
3. Habakkuk 2:14; Isaiah 11:9.
4. 1 Corinthians 15:28.

Appendix I: Kill Your Son?

1. Paraphrase of Jeremiah 7:31; 19:5; 32:35
2. Ezekiel 16:21 NASB; cf. Ezekiel 20:31.
3. Joshua Ryan Butler, *The Skeletons in God's Closet* (Nashville: Thomas Nelson, 2014), 35–52.
4. Jon D. Levenson provides an account of this ancient practice and some of the archaeological finds in *The Death and Resurrection of the Beloved Son: The Transformation of Child Sacrifice in Judaism and Christianity* (New Haven: Yale University Press, 1993), 18–24.
5. As the early church father Tertullian observed, "Saturn did not spare his own children; so, where other people's were concerned, he naturally persisted in not sparing them; and their own parents offered them to him, were glad to respond, and fondled their children that they might not be sacrificed in tears." *Apology,* ed. T. R. Glover and W. C. A. Kerr (Cambridge: Harvard University Press, 1977), 47.
6. Derek Rishmawy, one of my favorite bloggers, has an excellent post on this passage that I've drawn upon in this appendix; check it out here: http://derekzrishmawy.com/2014/10/20/abraham-cultural -distance-and-offering-up-our-moral-conscience/ (accessed November 16, 2015).
7. See the variety of nuanced perspectives that show up throughout Jon D. Levenson's *The Death and Resurrection of the Beloved Son.* As Levenson observes, one possible reading of the aqedah (the story of "the binding" of Isaac), is that it does not *forbid* the sacrifice of the child but *permits* the substitution of an animal for the firstborn (what Levenson calls the "restrictive" interpretation). However, he observes, "exponents of the notion that the aqedah is an etiology

of a particular sacrificial practice rarely, if ever, subscribe to this restrictive interpretation . . . Instead, they subscribe to the second type of etiology and see the story as *opposing* animal to human sacrifice, endorsing the former and anathematizing the latter. Shalom Spiegel, for example, writes, 'Quite possibly the primary purpose of the Akedah story may have been only this: to attach to a real pillar of the folk and a revered reputation the new norm—abolish human sacrifice, substitute animals instead." *The Death and Resurrection of the Beloved Son,* 112. Though Levenson raises critiques as to whether child sacrifice can so easily be dismissed in some of Israel's early texts. Levenson also observes how for both Judaism and Christianity, the primary significance for Abraham is *not* interpreted in the dominant traditions as centering on his willingness to slay his son, but rather his radical *trust* in the promises of God in the face of such overwhelming obstacle (cf. pp. 125ff).

As Jon D. Levenson observes, this passage is a "treasured text" for both Judaism and Christianity, in which "the normative teachings of both those traditions condemn [child sacrifice] categorically," in *The Death and Resurrection of the Beloved Son,* 109.

8. Genesis 22:1.

9. Genesis 22:2.

10. For example, one midrash on Abraham's conversation with God brings this dynamic out as follows: "'Your son.' He said to him, 'I have two sons. *Which* son?' he answered him, 'your favored one.' He said to him, 'Each is the favored one of his own mother.' He replied, 'the one whom you love.' He said, 'Is there a limit to the affections?' He answered, 'Isaac.' And why did He not reveal it to him immediately? In order to make him more beloved to him and to give him a reward for each utterance." *Genesis Rabbah. 55:7* quoted in Levenson, *The Death and Resurrection of the Beloved Son,* 127.

Though it's true that Ishmael is also "the seed of Abraham" through Hagar, the preceding passage in Genesis 21 recounts the process by which Ishmael is removed from being reckoned in the line of Abraham's descendants. For a fuller discussion of some of the issues involved here, see Levenson, *The Death and Resurrection of the Beloved Son,* 82–110.

11. On Ishmael not being reckoned the firstborn, see the previous endnote.

12. Moshe Halbertal explores this theme of sacrifice within the cycle of gift-giving in his excellent little book, *On Sacrifice* (Princeton: Princeton University Press, 2012).

13. Genesis 12:2–3.

14. Genesis 18:10–15; 21:1–7.

15. http://derekzrishmawy.com/2014/10/20/abraham-cultural-distance -and-offering-up-our-moral-conscience/.

16. The Abraham story has a strong affinity with the first Passover, in which the Israelite firstborn is saved from the Destroyer through the blood of a sacrificial lamb (Exodus 12:1–28). Many Jewish interpreters have seen the aqedah (the story of "the binding" of Isaac) as an etiological foundation story for the Passover (see Levenson, *The Death and Resurrection of the Beloved Son,* 111, 173ff.

17. See, for example, Dave Miller's "How Old Was Isaac When Abraham Was Told to Offer Him," available online at: http://www .apologeticspress.org/apcontent.aspx?category=11&article=1272 (accessed November 16, 2015).

18. Genesis 22:6; 21:5.

19. Examples of this show up in rabbinic literature. For example, in one midrash, Rabbi Isaac reflects on Isaac as a willing offering, saying, "At the moment that Abraham sought to bind his son Isaac, he said to him, 'Father, I am a young man and I am fearful that my body will tremble out of fear of the knife and I cause you sorrow, so that the slaughter will be rendered unfit and this will not be accredited to you as a sacrifice. Therefore, bind me very tightly.' Immediately 'he bound his son Isaac' [Gen 22:9]. Can one bind a man thirty-seven years old (another version: twenty-six years old) without his consent?" *Genesis Rabbah* 56:8.

20. Genesis does tell us that Abraham hides from Isaac that he is the sacrifice when they make the journey up the mountain, in verse

8, in a way that subtly foreshadows the hopeful conclusion to the story, but we are told nothing of Isaac's actual reaction when they reach the top of the mountain and he discovers he is to be placed on the altar.

21. Genesis 22:2, 9, 14.
22. On the Jewish tradition of interpreting Mount Moriah's location as Jerusalem, and thus the aqedah as an etiological foundation story for the temple's sacrificial system, see Levenson, *The Death and Resurrection of the Beloved Son,* 114–24. On the Passover connections, see pp. 111, 173ff.
23. Hebrews 11:17–19.

Appendix II: Forsaken

1. Psalm 22:12–13, 16.
2. Psalm 22:18, 7, 14, 17, 8, 15b, 15a, 16, 15c.
3. Psalm 22:9–10.
4. Psalm 22:4–5, 3.
5. Psalm 22:19–21.
6. And this progression toward victory continues in the following Psalms 23–24, climaxing as the "king of glory" arrives on Mount Zion for an "enthronement" scene to receive his kingdom. When Jesus' audience heard him quote Psalm 22:1, this whole climactic sequence would have been drawn to mind.
7. Psalm 22:22, 24, 29, 31.
8. Psalm 22:27–28.
9. Luke 23:46, quoting Psalm 31:5. This is also a psalm of David, with similar themes of looking to God in trust while being attacked and experiencing God's faithfulness in the end.

About the Author

Joshua Ryan Butler serves as pastor of local and global outreach at Imago Dei Community, a church in the heart of Portland, Oregon. Joshua oversees the church's city ministries in areas like foster care, human trafficking, and homelessness; and develops international partnerships in areas like clean water, HIV-support, and church planting. Joshua is also a worship leader who enjoys writing music for the life of the church. Joshua's wife, Holly, daughter, Aiden, and sons, Torin and Jacob, enjoy spending time with their friends over great meals and exploring their beautiful little patch of the world in the Pacific Northwest.

Also Available from
Joshua Ryan Butler

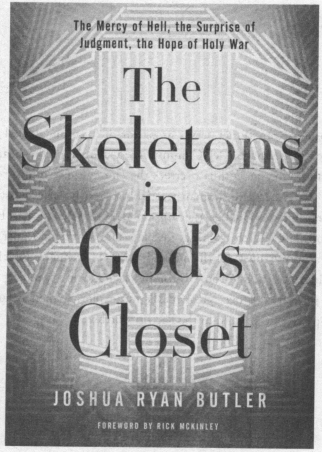

The Mercy of Hell, the Surprise of
Judgment, the Hope of Holy War

The
Skeletons
in
God's
Closet

JOSHUA RYAN BUTLER

FOREWORD BY RICK MCKINLEY

ISBN 978-0-529-10081-8

W PUBLISHING GROUP

AN IMPRINT OF THOMAS NELSON